DIRECTORS IN PERSPECTIVE

General editor: Christopher Innes

Bertolt Brecht

DIRECTORS IN PERSPECTIVE

What characterizes modern theatre above all is continual stylistic innovation, in which theory and presentation have combined to create a wealth of new forms – naturalism, expressionism, epic theatre, etc. – in a way that has made directors the leading figures rather than dramatists. To a greater extent than is perhaps generally realized, it has been directors who have provided dramatic models for playwrights, though of course there are many different variations in this relationship. In some cases a dramatist's themes challenge a director to create new performance conditions (Stanislavski and Chekhov), or a dramatist turns director to formulate an appropriate style for his work (Brecht); alternatively a director writes plays to correspond with his theory (Artaud), or creates communal scripts out of exploratory work with actors (Chaikin, Grotowski). Some directors are identified with a single theory (Craig), others gave definitive shape to a range of styles (Reinhardt); the work of some has an ideological basis (Stein), while others work more pragmatically (Bergman).

Generally speaking, those directors who have contributed to what is distinctly "modern" in today's theatre stand in much the same relationship to the dramatic texts they work with, as composers do to librettists in opera. However, since theatrical performance is the most ephemeral of the arts and the only easily reproducible element is the text, critical attention has tended to focus on the playwright. This series is designed to redress the balance by providing an overview of selected directors' stage work: those who helped to formulate modern theories of drama. Their key productions have been reconstructed from promptbooks, reviews, scene-designs, photographs, diaries, correspondence and – where these productions are contemporary – documented by first-hand description, interviews with the director, etc. Apart from its intrinsic interest, this record allows a critical perspective, testing ideas against practical problems and achievements. In each case, too, the director's work is set in context by indicating the source of his ideas and their influence, the organization of his acting company and his relationship to the theatrical or political establishment, so as to bring out wider issues: the way theatre both reflects and influences assumptions about the nature of man and his social role.

Christopher Innes

The boxing ring used in the 1927 Baden-Baden production of *The Little
Mahagonny*. Neher's stark and grotesque sketches dominate the
background. Brecht stands to the right of the boxing ring.

Bertolt Brecht

Chaos, According to Plan

JOHN FUEGI
University of Maryland

CAMBRIDGE
UNIVERSITY PRESS

Published by the Press Syndicate of the University of Cambridge
The Pitt Building, Trumpington Street, Cambridge CB2 1RP
40 West 20th Street, New York, NY 10011–4211, USA
10 Stamford Road, Oakleigh, Melbourne 3166, Australia

First published 1987
Reprinted 1988, 1991, 1994

Printed in Great Britain at
the University Press, Cambridge

British Library cataloguing in publication data

Fuegi, John
Bertolt Brecht: chaos according to plan.
– (Directors in perspective)
1. Brecht, Bertolt
I. Title   II. Series
792′.0233′0924   PN2658.B7/

Library of Congress cataloguing in publication data
Fuegi, John.
Bertolt Brecht: chaos, according to plan.
(Directors in perspective)
Bibliography: p.
Includes index.
1. Brecht, Bertolt, 1898–1956 – Dramatic production.
2. Brecht, Bertolt, 1898–1956 – Stage history.   3. Brecht,
Bertolt, 1898–1956 – Knowledge – Performing arts.
4. Authors, German – 20th century – Biography.   5. Theatri-
cal producers and directors – Germany – Biography.
I. Title.   II. Series.
PT2603.R397Z61927   1987   832′.912   86–12979

ISBN 0 521 23828 5 hardback
ISBN 0 521 28245 4 paperback

SE

Contents

Illustrations

Preface

Brecht is the Key figure of our time, and all theatre work today at some point starts or returns to his statements and achievement.

Peter Brook, *The Empty Space* (New York: Avon Books, 1969), p. 65

Though it is now generally acknowledged on all five continents, in socialist and non-socialist countries alike, that Bertolt Brecht (1898–1956) profoundly changed our whole conception of playwriting, acting and directing, it is a curious fact that very little has been published to tell us either how Brecht really worked with actors, or how his epoch-making productions were put together in rehearsal. Overwhelmingly, studies of Brecht have been largely theoretical in nature. For the hapless actor or director or student of drama who wishes to know what Brecht did in real theatrical situations, there has been precious little available in published form in any language including Brecht's own. Beyond Brecht's own theatre company, the Berlin Ensemble's own rather haphazard book *Theaterarbeit* (*Theatre Work*), Carl Weber's essay, Eric Bentley's recent memoir, Angelika Hurwicz and Gerda Goedhart's *Brecht Inszeniert: 'Der kaukasische Kreidekreis'* (*Brecht Stages "The Caucasian Chalk Circle"*), Hans Curjel's and Erwin Leiser's *Gespräch auf der Probe* (*Rehearsal Conversations*), and the so-called 'model books', containing scores of photographs designed to give a sense of how the production looked on stage, that Brecht himself prepared of his own productions of *Mother Courage*, *Galileo*, and *Antigone* (all in German), one must comb countless memoirs in a wide variety of languages, interview large numbers of people on several continents and gain access to the actual recordings of Brecht in rehearsal which are not yet available in published form, in order to have a sense of how Brecht dealt with real problems in real theatres and how these problems were solved.

Treating theory in much the way Brecht treated it (for him it had a valuable place outside the theatre but almost none in actual day-by-day staging practice), let us enter Brecht's world of practical problem-solving. Let us look at the theatre as he found it first in his home town of Augsburg, then later in the southern theatre capital, Munich, and later still on the stages of Berlin, Paris, London and New York. Then let us examine how he worked on these various stages.

Acknowledgments

This book is dedicated to Stefan Brecht, Hans Bunge, Eric Bentley, Marieluise Fleisser, Jo Francis, Elisabeth Hauptmann, Angelika Hurwicz, Isot Kilian, James K. Lyon, Käthe Rülicke, Ekkehard Schall, Helene Weigel, John Willett, and Manfred Wekwerth whose professional and personal support made this book possible. The index was prepared by Aaron Douglass Fuegi.

Thanks are also due to the following for permission to reproduce their illustrations:
The Berlin Ensemble: jacket, frontispiece, and 21, 23–4, 27–35, 43, 48–52; The Brecht Archive: 9, 18; Ernst Becker, Berlin: 1; Darstellende Kunst-Fotoarchiv, Berlin: 16; K. Fassmann: 15; Gerda Goedhart: 36–42, 44–7; Carl Koch: 13, 19; Märkisches Museum, Berlin: 14; Erwin Piscator: 8; Querschnitt: 17; Ernst and Renate Schumacher: 3, 11; Dr Steinfeld: 5, 10, 20; Theatre Museum, Munich: 2; Dr Tornquist: 22; Kurt Weill: 12; John Willett: 4, 6–7; Zurich Schauspielhaus: 25–6

1 Setting the scene

In order to understand the position of the European theatre in 1898 at the time of Brecht's birth in the small south German town of Augsburg, then part of the kingdom of Bavaria, let us hypothesize a scene in which we join all the major people then working in innovative theatre as they gather in Augsburg for Brecht's christening.

Georg Büchner, Brecht's real theatrical godfather who, had he lived, would have been eighty-five at the time of Brecht's birth, had died many decades before. But among those who were active and could have come to the christening are the aging Norwegian Ibsen with his friend, the Danish critic Georg Brandes, and his fellow Norwegian playwright Björnson; Chekhov, discreetly on the edge of the crowd, coughing blood into a handkerchief; standing close by are Chekhov's theatrical patrons Stanislavski and Nemirovich-Danchenko who are thoroughly enjoying the company of their mentor, the founder of ensemble playing, George, Duke of Saxe-Meiningen; Strindberg — Angst-ridden — is there, as is the lanky George Bernard Shaw whom the infant Brecht will praise in print in future years. Shaw is closely attended by the founder of London's independent theatre, Jack Grein; Wedekind slouches in, showing his contempt for the middle-class values of Brecht's all too middle-class parents; Meyerhold, who has not yet turned from Stanislavski to "biomechanics," is using the occasion to talk about theatre and revolution with the great Munich theorist Georg Fuchs, who was heavily to influence Meyerhold's work on "the theatre theatrical"; Emile Zola, the exponent of "Naturalism", is there, close to Henry Becque and Eugène Brieux. Between Zola and Gerhart Hauptmann stands Count Tolstoy conversing alternately in flawless French or German with his fellow playwrights about the work of the Freie Bühne in Berlin and asking André Antoine, founder of the Théâtre Libre and the newly established Théâtre Antoine, about the newest work in Paris; a cliquish group of Young Turks, Edward Gordon Craig, Max Reinhardt and Leopold Jessner stand apart, torn between reverence and contempt for their "elders"; two young playwrights, Arthur Schnitzler and Carl Sternheim, feel a little out of place among these luminaries for they are closer in age to the noisy five-year-old Erwin Piscator and Ernst Toller at the edge of the crowd than to the greybeards Ibsen and Tolstoy.

Although this gathering never did take place, the point is that though

Brecht in later years would extravagantly declare himself to the American stage designer, Gorelik, to be the "Einstein of the new stage form," in point of fact much of the groundwork for Brecht's own theatrical practice was already in place. Already, although Naturalism and Realism were establishing themselves on various European stages from Europe to Moscow, there were counter-currents of Symbolism and even the beginnings of Expressionism which would be in full flood before the emergence of Brecht the playwright. From the welter of brilliant experimentation at the close of the nineteenth century, the incipient playwright could pick and choose elements that would go to form his own unique theatrical style, a style far more than the sum of its constituent parts, of course, but dependent on those parts and on those people who had created them. At the imaginary christening party the alert listener would have heard talk of experimentation covering the whole spectrum from Stanislavski's "the art that hides itself" to Jarry's or Meyerhold's or Shaw's art that brazenly draws attention to itself. And the bitter commentators on the mores of the bourgeoisie – the heirs of Büchner – would have been so numerous as to almost drown out all the other voices at such a christening party. Anyone listening carefully would have clearly heard that all of European society and the theatre reflecting that society was, like the century itself, at a decisive turning point.

By the time Brecht turned twenty, the Habsburgs, Romanovs and Hohenzollerns would be driven from their thrones, the Bavarian monarchy would have given way to an (albeit shortlived) Soviet, and many but not all of the plush and kitsch values of the old imperial theatres would be similarly driven out. Dead in the trenches of "The Great War" were most of the words Europe had lived by, such as "Honor," "Courage" and "Glory." Gone were the bright colors of the old military as the new technology of war demanded dark, unpolished steel and the drab khaki. Militant Marxism rode roughshod over complacent Catholicism and Russian Orthodoxy. In physics, as a result of the work of Einstein in Zurich and Berlin, other scientists (to Einstein's own dismay) began to wonder seriously if the dice rather than some more lofty force might rule the world of the atom and of sub-atomic particles. Not only were the earthly institutions themselves crumbling, but it began to seem as if the great chain of being itself was not a bright and shining symbol of closely linked hierarchical order, with kings and queens as the earthly counterparts of a divine and benevolent heavenly majesty. That chain now seemed like a rusty flail that humankind must forcibly remove from its raw and bloody back. Disorder beckoned on every side. Economic stability was a thing of the past. So, too, was the primacy of Western Europe, as the newcomers, the USSR on the one side, and the USA on the other grew in strength and importance. New ideologies would be responsible for the spilling of rivers of blood from the Yangtze to the Rhine. As the century turned, these developments were not clearly visible to even the keenest observers, but as the new century entered its teens even the most casual and withdrawn spectator could not fail to see that an old world was being shattered and would be replaced. But with what? Where would Europe's dance of death lead? Was there somewhere in this maelstrom of blood a voice of reason, some new path to a stable peace in a just world? Those who returned from the trenches wondered of the "eternal values" if "Art," like everything else, "was shit." It is against this backdrop with all its horror and many unanswered questions that we should imagine the development of a person who would reshape the modern stage.

Into the stable world of Brecht's comfortably middle-class home in Augsburg would come a tide of change sweeping all before it. His Gymnasium class would be decimated by the First World War. Revolutionary and reactionary forces would fight it out in the very streets of Augsburg. But it is difficult to sense all this in the early years. At the turn of the century the Brecht family album is a monument to middle-class stability. The earliest picture of Brecht taken in 1899 in the studio of Martin Brothers, Augsburg, has him posed in a gorgeous ruffled knee-length white dress with a huge straw hat on at a rakish angle. A rather dour, dark-skinned child clutches a small trumpet and stares fixedly at something off camera. No hint here of the Brecht who would become the scourge of the bourgeoisie. Nor can we really find much of a hint in Brecht's highly conventional schooling. He attended the standard schools and more or less diligently studied the standard subjects. In his early years he was walked from school by one of the family servants. The first premonition of Brecht the director came when he was nine years old. At that time he ordered (and they literally obeyed) the neighborhood children and his brother Walter to bring their toy soldiers to a field near the Brecht house. There, under Brecht's direction earthworks were set up and soldiers disposed according to battle plans Brecht derived from both Napoleon and Frederick the Great. His style, like that of his martial models, was lordly and domineering. He knew what he wanted and did what was necessary to get it.

In 1914 Brecht got his first opportunity to be a stage director. Heinrich Scheuffelhut recalls the group that formed around the sixteen-year-old Brecht buying a used puppet theatre and taking it on a handcart to Rudolf Hartmann's (another school friend's) house. Brecht, recalls Scheuffelhut, "was really in his element as a stage director and theatre manager." The details of the actual production, as recalled by Scheuffelhut, anticipate in an uncanny way many of the characteristics of the Berlin Ensemble:

we set up the theatre in Rudolf's room. To the left and the right of the theatre we hung up wash lines and hung pieces of cloth over the lines so that the actors could not be seen by the spectators. We had gotten some paper maché puppets at the time we bought the theatre. The puppets were about 5" high and had wooden handles. Through long slits in the stage, the figures could be moved back and forth and could bow towards the front. The girls sewed the clothes for the puppets. For footlights and for lighting effects we used a simple battery and used flash powder for lighting. During performances the puppets were worked by Brecht, his brother Walter, Rudolf Hartmann, Rudolf's cousin Ernestine Müller and myself [Heinrich Scheuffelhut]. In our repertoire we had scenes from Weber's *Freischütz* and *Oberon*, Büchner's *Leonce und Lena*, Goethe's *Faust*, Shakespeare's *Hamlet* and scenes from Wedekind. The audience was made up of parents and neighbors. The customers we thought of as being well to do got reserved seats for which they had to pay two marks. The money we earned we used to buy better puppets and props. Once Ernestine did not give her lines correctly and one of the other actors called her a cow. Eugen jumped in at once and said that one does not say such things, certainly not to girls.

We soon moved the theatre from the apartment to a warehouse where old furniture from our parents' houses was stored. Here Brecht, together with us, staged Gerhart Hauptmann's *Biberpelz*.[1]

The choice of repertoire is particularly interesting here because if we add the name of Bertolt Brecht to the list of playwrights produced by the school children in 1914, we have the basic outlines of the repertoire of the Berlin Ensemble. As we shall see, "big city Brecht" very frequently drew inspiration from elements that were present in the small town environment of the precocious teenager.

By the time the Brecht group bought the puppet theatre his artistic interests were becoming apparent in a number of ways. He began to write and was published in the local Augsburg newspaper. He took up the guitar and composed songs which he sang to his own accompaniment, mesmerizing his audiences. One friend from the Augsburg days notes: "He did not sing in a polished way, but with a passion that swept others along, drunk from his own verses, ideas, and creations as other people would be drunk from wine and his singing made those who heard him drunk also."[2] This view of the effect of Brecht's singing is shared by someone who heard him perform at the Augsburg brothel, "Seven Bunnies," where he sang to wild applause Goethe's "Bajadere," a song about a god and an Indian temple prostitute.[3] At this time Brecht also began to attend the theatre and the opera in Augsburg. He read voraciously and indiscriminately, classics, detective stories, and the avant-garde. He became interested in the visual arts and offered commentaries on the brilliant drawings of his friend, the future set designer, Caspar Neher. He went to every new film and fell in love with Chaplin and the Keystone Kops.

Another major lowbrow "artistic" interest of Brecht's at this time was the kind of singing done at the fairs which were held regularly in Augsburg. There was a singer from Hamburg who had a wooden leg and who returned every year to Augsburg to present "penny-dreadful" songs (*Moritaten*). He brought with him a wooden stand on which were hung garish horror pictures (fig. 1), and would flip from one picture to another, pointing with his cane at

Fig. 1. In this picture, taken at the Augsburg fairgrounds at the time of
Brecht's youth, a helpless victim is "saved by mother love" from a large
and vicious bird of prey. The hand organ on which the musical
accompaniment was cranked out is prominent in the foreground of the
picture.

each nightmare scene. Each "history" was introduced in a way that clearly anticipates Brecht's later stage work. Accompanying himself on a barrel organ while his little daughter passed the hat, the singer would begin:

> People, hear this story.
> It happened recently.
> I'll report it true/
> Let's draw a moral from it.

There would then follow "histories" with names such as "The Robber's Bride," "Madness and Mother Love," "The Gruesome, Murderous Deed of Heinrich Thiele and his subsequent Execution," and the tale of "The Forester's Beautiful Daughter." At times he would offer pure folk songs that contained magical reversals of fortune in exotic lands. One such song began:

> My greatest dream, my single wish
> Was, to sail the high seas to Africa.
> There came a prince from foreign and strange parts,
> He bought me and six Germans besides.

An eyewitness reports that each time the singer reached the words "foreign parts" he would dramatically mark the end of the line with a stream of brown tobacco juice.[4]

All the constituent parts of Brecht's theory of theatre are present in this scene: the singer narrates rather than attempting to impersonate (in a Stanislavskian sense) either Heinrich Thiele or the Forester's Beautiful Daughter; the history has an overt moral purpose that is underscored by clear gestures and clear pictures of the scenes described; music is an important and highly visible part of the performance; the performance takes place in daylight with no lighting tricks to baffle the audience; the audience is free to smoke and to come and go at will as each small tale is separated from the one before and the one after. The subjects chosen for the songs are a panorama of many of Brecht's own chosen subjects with their emphasis on engaging thieves, on violent actions, exotic locales, erotic encounters and wildly improbable geography. But we rush too far ahead if we conclude that any of this was clear to Brecht in 1914. All we know is that he was strongly drawn to these performances and that echoes of the one-legged Hamburg organ grinder will be heard throughout Brecht's theatrical career.

At such fairs the teenage Brecht would usually have at least one female admirer in tow. They would compete with each other on the swings and would adjourn "to piss in the bushes" or "make love like horses," like Baal (one of Brecht's earliest dramatic creations), in the open air to the horror of staid old Augsburg society. It was becoming ever clearer as the war wore on that Bertolt Brecht (unlike his brother Walter) had no intention of following in his rather conservative father's footsteps. At all hours of the day and night young men and women came to his Bohemian attic apartment in his parents' house. Neher's drawing of Baal had a place of honor on the slanting ceiling above Brecht's bed so that the Syrian fertility god got a clear view of everything going on below. But as the war went on and more and more of his classmates enlisted and died in Flanders, it became clear to Brecht that he needed to find a way to avoid that fate. He learned that medical students could get draft deferments so he promptly enrolled at the nearby University of Munich, ostensibly as a student of medicine. But medicine was really a front for his ever more intensive involvement in drama, in cabaret life, and in Munich's fledgeling "film industry." He frequently traveled back to Augsburg (a short train ride from Munich) to spend time at his family home. One visitor, his childhood friend Friedrich Mayer, recalls a scene from 1918 which shows Brecht's continuing interest in the theatre and gives some details of his manner of working as a coach or director:

In the summer of 1918, Pzanzelt [another of Brecht's childhood friends] took me along to Brecht's attic flat. We found there were already other guests present. Neher, on leave from the front, was there as well as a young girl with long black hair. As I learned, she was attending the local St. Anna School. She wanted to become an actress and that was why she was visiting Brecht. He worked hard with the girl. As we listened, she had to declaim the same passage over and over again. Brecht tried to make something of this. But she was unable to express herself in the way that he wanted to hear. Suddenly she lost her nerve, stormed out of the door, ran down the stairs and out into the street. Brecht picked up her script which she had left on the table and quietly went to the window, called to the girl and threw her script down to her from the second floor. Hastily she picked up one sheet after another from the street as Brecht observed her from the window and laughed with delight.[5]

The insensitivity to the discomfiture of others (often women) that this scene reveals is as true of the later Brecht as it was of the medical student who commuted back and forth between Munich and Augsburg.

At the very end of the war, despite his "medical student" talisman, Brecht was finally drafted. He was sent not to Flanders and to death, but back to Augsburg and the comfort of his family home. It is important to look very closely at Brecht's return to Augsburg and his so-called military service, because in most accounts of Brecht his own fictional version of his life has tended to displace the facts. This is a pity, since his real life was at least as interesting as the widely accepted fictionalized versions of it.

Despite published accounts that Brecht's military service inflicted great psychic wounds upon him, the facts are as follows: according to his brother, Walter, Brecht served at the military VD clinic in Augsburg from October 1, 1918 until January 9, 1919. Of this period, only half was actual war service in any sense as the Armistice was signed on November 11, 1918. There is not a shred of evidence that Brecht did amputations or performed brain surgery during his time at the clinic. The cagey Brecht himself later said (in an interview with a Russian who apparently did not completely understand Brecht's German), "had I been asked to do surgery, I would have done it." The fact is he was never asked, but it is virtually certain that he was trying to get the interviewer to think that he had been. Throughout his life Brecht would seek to control his own public image. He preferred to present the facts of his life as he thought they should have been; thus his life became a dramatization of facts. During this time, Brecht mostly stayed at home and worked on drafts of *Baal* and *Drums in the Night*, and these "dirty" texts were then cleanly typed by one of his father's secretaries. When he emerged from his attic at all he walked around in public – not in his military uniform but with his hands in his trouser pockets, wearing a pullover (no jacket), usually with no hat, yellow shoes and carrying a riding crop as he declared (quoting Nietzsche) "when you deal with women, don't forget the whip." In order not to interrupt work on *Baal* or liaisons with various young women, on a number of occasions, when he was supposed to report personally to the VD clinic, he sent his maid in mob cap and apron to deliver the duty roster.

Another legend that Brecht himself created from this period is how deeply involved he supposedly was in revolutionary politics. Though the period at the VD clinic coincides with the Bavarian revolution which broke out on November 7, 1918, and was bloodily put down in the late spring of 1919, Brecht's sole confirmed role in the revolutions in Augsburg, Munich and Berlin seems to have been that of an observer, taking notes as raw material for his play about a returning veteran's attitude towards revolution. Like his veteran, who turns his back on the revolution and goes home to bed with his sullied bride, Brecht did much the same, but with the additional outcome of a brilliant study of postwar disillusionment, *Drums in the Night*. As grenades exploded in the streets, Brecht stayed at home. Later, after his January release from military service, he went back and forth from Augsburg to Munich, where he had returned ostensibly to continue his medical studies. Others might fight for or against revolution, but fighting was not for Brecht. He made love, not war, and wrote plays rather than political manifestos. Like Kragler he stayed at home "to increase himself," and as his love affairs began to bear fruit declared: "let them grow these little Brechts!" As the socialist government in Munich was overthrown by right-wing radicals (Brecht's brother Walter among them) some of whom (though not Walter) would later become the core of Hitler's private army, Brecht swung on the swings at the Augsburg fair. In Neher's diary we find an entry for May 4, 1919: "Evenings at the fair. Lights. Beautiful."[6] For Brecht and Neher and their friends there were tales of kidnapping in Africa and of the "Forester's Beautiful Daughter" as the smoke of counter-revolution still drifted over Munich. In a few weeks Bie Banholzer, growing big with a little Brecht, would be off to the country to have the child in order to disturb as little as possible the middle-class proprieties of her family in Augsburg. Brecht himself made no attempt whatsoever to hide his unmarried paternity, but organized a highly public christening party for the baby and at the same time began public liaisons with various other women, while lecturing each that she must have a wholly monogamous relationship with him and insisting on written contracts specifying these terms.

The highly public quality of Brecht's affairs reflects a deliberate determination by him to shock the bourgeoisie. He moved in an atmosphere of radical bohemianism while retaining as his home base the comfortable attic apartment with maid service at his bourgeois parents' home and secretarial service at his father's office. He was intent on not being ignored. He did anything and everything to attract public attention. His poetry, his plays and his earliest published theatre criticism threw all middle-class decorum to the winds. Confronted simultaneously by two women who both became pregnant, and asked to declare which one he would marry, he shrugged and smiled and said laconically: "Both." Asked to write theatre reviews he declared the local theatre to be bankrupt. Asked in a drama seminar at the University in Munich to comment on the then popular dramatist Hanns Johst's play *The Lonely One*, Brecht denounced the play and the playwright (later in a private and rather oily letter Brecht sought to ingratiate himself with Johst, who was to become a personal friend of Hitler's) and declared he could write a better one in four days. He did. The name of the play was *Baal*. From a life of middle-class rectitude in Augsburg the twenty-year-old Brecht had become Baal, just as he began to lead the life of his theoretical models, Wedekind, Villon and Rimbaud. A couple of years later he would note in his diary: "What an extraordinary creature the human being is . . . The way he takes things into his body, goes around in wind and rain, makes little young humans out of other humans, by glueing himself to them and filling them with fluids, to the accompaniment of groans of pleasure." "O God," he prayed in his diary, "O God, please let my sight always cut through the crust, pierce it."[7] He was to have his far from pious wish. Before his death, as playwright/poet/director he would cut through the crust of dull and orthodox routine and would help create a new stage, a new drama, a new poetry, a new literary language: extraordinary achievements for a person who would spend a third of his life exiled from his homeland, his theatre and his mother tongue, living out of suitcases and, as we now know, always just a half step ahead of the Gestapo, the KGB, and later the FBI and the CIA. Suspected everywhere, he would earn the signal distinction of being *persona non grata* to all the major and minor intelligence agencies of both the East and the West. Even in death he would remain a scandal, an enigma and a person "on whom one cannot rely."

2   A monarch stripped of grandeur

In future I shall produce nothing but flaming mudpies made of shit.

Bertolt Brecht, 1920[1]

From 1913, as Brecht first became involved in the world of theatre, the long forgotten work of Georg Büchner began to be staged for the first time in Germany. Suddenly, texts that had lain largely unread and totally unstaged since Büchner's death in 1837 seemed absolutely relevant to the European experience. Apart from the performances of *Moritaten* by the one-legged organ grinder from Hamburg, there is probably no single text or a performance of a text that is more important to our understanding of Brecht as a nascent director and playwright than the 1919 Frankfurt production of *Woyzeck* with his future wife Helene Weigel playing her first professional role and Albert Steinrück playing Woyzeck.[2] The shabby Woyzeck's philosophy of life anticipates the most famous line Brecht ever wrote: "First comes eating then morality." The world Büchner depicts is one of fairs similar to the Augsburg fairs of Brecht's youth, a world of sexual license and of murderous passion. In *Woyzeck* it is one stripped completely bare of traditional notions of heroism, morality, propriety and decorum. Though any one of a number of the short scenes that make up the play could be cited to show Büchner's[3] affinity to Brecht, there is one scene that sums up a world view shared by both writers. In this scene a grandmother tells the following story to some little girls:

Once upon a time there was a poor little girl who had no father and no mother. Everyone was dead, and there was no one left in the whole wide world. And the little girl went out and looked for someone night and day. And because there was no one left on earth she wanted to go to heaven. And the moon looked down at her in a friendly way. And when she finally got to the moon, it was a piece of rotten wood. And so she went to the sun. And when she got to the sun, it was a faded sunflower. And when she got to the stars they were little golden flies, stuck up there as though they were caught in a spider's web. And when she wanted to go back to the earth, she found that the earth was a tipped over chamber pot. And she was all alone. And she sat down there and she wept. And she sits there to this day, all alone.[4]

The world, we learn, is literally a pile of shit, and if this is not bad enough we are also told that it is pointless to look to the heavens for aid for we, like the child, will find none there. For those who returned from the blood and pus and latrines of the First World War to the chaos of the postwar world it is not surprising that Büchner's excremental view seemed extraordinarily apposite.

The mood in *Woyzeck* is precisely the one we need if we are to understand Brecht's early plays and what Brecht sought to achieve in the staging of these plays. If the theatrical world was ready to recognize and stage Büchner, then it was also ready for Brecht.

It was a propitious moment therefore when Brecht went to see one of the leading figures of the Munich theatre, Lion Feuchtwanger. In 1928 Feuchtwanger recalled this first meeting: "At the end of 1918 or the beginning of 1919, soon after the outbreak of the so-called German Revolution, a very young man came to my Munich apartment. He was small, badly shaved, neglectful of his clothes . . . He kept close to the walls, spoke in the Swabian dialect, had written a play, was named Bertolt Brecht. The play was called *Spartacus*."[5] It was appropriate for Brecht to seek out Feuchtwanger. Feuchtwanger was in a position to open doors and he was also young enough and experimental enough to be open to new talent regardless of its outward appearance. Brecht, in order to stress how different he was, declared to Feuchtwanger at this first meeting that he had written *Spartacus* (later at Feuchtwanger's suggestion to be renamed *Drums in the Night*) solely for pecuniary reasons. Feuchtwanger read the play, liked it and then telephoned Brecht to ask why he had lied to him in saying that he had written the play merely for money. Brecht then reiterated the claim, bellowing over the phone in his almost incomprehensible Swabian dialect. The "conversation" ended with Brecht announcing that he would bring over another play which, unlike *Spartacus*, was good. The "good play" was *Baal* and Feuchtwanger liked it too.

This was the beginning of what was to become a lifelong friendship. Lion and Marta Feuchtwanger became involved in Brecht's affairs. Using his theatrical contacts and with his knowledge of the world of publishing, Feuchtwanger began to help Brecht get established as a playwright and poet. Many otherwise closed doors would now begin to open.

In exactly this same period (1918–19) Lion Feuchtwanger was similarly approached by another young man. Marta Feuchtwanger remembers an occasion in a café in Munich's fashionable park, the English Garden, when she and Lion noticed a "silly looking young man" at an adjacent table. When the Feuchtwangers got up to leave, "the silly looking young man" rushed over to help Lion into his coat.[6] He was a war veteran, an unemployed aspiring artist from Vienna with an interest in establishing himself in set design in the Munich theatre. Feuchtwanger did not open doors for him and the "silly looking young man" embarked on a different career. His name was Adolf Hitler. In the best biography of Hitler, Joachim Fest asks the following disturbing question: "But was he [Hitler after he became *Der Führer*] any the less an unsociable, easily depressed artist personality whom the peculiar circumstances of the times, together with a monstrous special gift, had propelled into a realm for which he was never intended?"[7] We know from Fest that when the Feuchtwangers' path crossed that of Hitler in the English Garden, Hitler had not yet taken any steps on the political stage. The "silly looking young man" rejected by the Jewish playwright left the English Garden to pursue a career on a different stage which would violently interrupt the worlds of Brecht, Feuchtwanger and millions of others.[8]

In contrast to Hitler and with remarkable rapidity, Brecht, helped by Feuchtwanger and other influential friends, established himself in Munich and began to make forays into Berlin where, often as a direct result of performing his own songs at private parties and at Trude Hesterberg's political cabaret, "The Untamed Stage," he speedily got to know everyone who was anyone in the world of theatre and publishing in Berlin. During one visit to Berlin in early 1922, Moritz Seeler, a vigorous promoter of "new talent" in Berlin, impressed by Brecht's verbal brilliance, agreed to have

Fig. 2. Otto Reigbert's set for the Munich 1922 *Drums in the Night*. Directed by Falckenberg.

Brecht direct *Parricide*, written by Brecht's friend Arnolt Bronnen. This was to be a showcase production of this avant-garde piece in which three of Berlin's leading actors, Agnes Straub, Heinrich von Twardowsky and Heinrich George, agreed to work without pay. Brecht, with no directing experience, exuded confidence and determination as though he had been in the theatre for decades. The rehearsals became a nightmare for the actors. Here they were, working without pay, but having to put up with what the horrified Bronnen saw as "the sadistic lashes of the young director."[9] In his thick Augsburg accent, but in "dry, clearly articulated syllables" Brecht stated that in his view "all their work was so much crap." Rows increased daily. Finally George shouted down the director and threw his script into the fifteenth row, before all 250 angry pounds of him thundered out of the theatre altogether. Agnes Straub collapsed in hysterics while the calm Brecht, with his German "r" rolling more sharply than usual ordered: "The rehearsal will continue." Twardowsky simply sat with his head in his hands. At this Brecht, according to Bronnen, "cleared his throat loudly, slammed shut his rehearsal book, loudly switched off the rehearsal light and said 'Good Day'." He then approached Bronnen who had been watching all this "his eyes gleaming in the dusk of the theatre with a sardonic glow," with: "Congratulations. With that bunch it would have never turned out right."[10] For anyone else, perhaps, this would have been a major setback, alienating three major actors and leaving a theatre manager in the lurch, but Brecht was to have an uncanny knack of turning what looked like failure into success.

In 1922 *Baal* and *Drums in the Night* were published. In a letter inviting the Berlin critic, Herbert Ihering, to Munich for the September 1922 premiere of *Drums in the Night*, Brecht declares: "I know exactly how much I am asking, but very much indeed depends on it for me. Since Berlin has ceased to make experiments, it has become extremely difficult to obtain decent criticism at a time when one needs it most."[11] This dismissal of Berlin, with all the experiments by Piscator, Jessner and Reinhart, did not seem to bother Ihering, for he was there in Munich on the opening night. Directed by Otto Falckenberg in the Munich Chamber Theatre, the production was, in Ihering's critical judgement, quite extraordinary. Otto Reigbert's set (fig. 2) clearly owed more to Expressionist distortion than to Realist verisimilitude. How much Brecht contributed either to the set design, or to the streamers that hung in the auditorium instructing the audience "not to stare so romantic-ally," or the Chinese paper lantern "moon" used in the production, cannot now be determined. But whether these "Brechtian" elements actually were suggested by the playwright himself or not they were to become part of "the Brecht style." Ihering's review of *Drums* in the *Berliner Börsen–Courier*, could hardly have been more enthusiastic. It began by acknowledging Brecht as a

Fig. 3. Otto Wernicke, Erwin Faber, Maria Koppenhöfer in *In the Jungle of the Cities*. Erich Engel's production. Set by Caspar Neher. Production of this play: Munich, the Residence Theatre, May 9, 1923.

genius and went on to state that "overnight the twenty-four year old writer *Bert Brecht* has changed the literary shape of Germany." "Brecht," he went on, "in his nervous system and in his blood is drenched with the horror of our time. This horror surrounds men and things in half-light and an ashen atmosphere. It increases in intensity during the act and scene breaks. It both sets the figures free and swallows them up again. The figures give off a phosphorescent glow." Ihering concentrated more on Brecht generally than on the specific production of *Drums*: "Brecht himself feels the chaos and putrefaction in his own body. That is why his images convey an unparalleled force." Basing his views on a reading of *Baal* and *In the Jungle of the Cities* (which he had taken the trouble to read in manuscript) as well as the *Drums* performance, Ihering went on to characterize Brecht's use of language: "One feels this language on one's tongue, on the palate, in the ear and up one's spine. Lacking conjunctions it rips open perspectives. It is brutally sensual, melancholically tender. There is coarseness in it and abysmal sadness. Grim humor and the lyricism of pity." In Ihering's view though much of this was captured by Otto Falckenberg's production of the play, its real power was best felt when Brecht sang and accompanied himself on the guitar. It was then that one really felt "the whip driven rhythms of his sentences." For with Brecht's plays "one knows from the first word that a tragedy has begun."[12] These are remarkable words from one of the two leading critics of Germany's theatre metropolis Berlin. Herbert Ihering was in fact so impressed that, after contemplating dividing the 1922 Kleist Prize for drama between Brecht and Arnolt Bronnen, he decided to give it to Brecht alone. With the receipt of this prize Brecht became a national figure and each premiere of a new play became a critical event.

The same year saw the publication and premiere of another play, *In the Jungle of the Cities* (fig. 3) in Munich, the premiere of *Baal* in Leipzig, and Brecht's appointment as a dramaturg at the Chamber Theatre in Munich. Each publication, each premiere called forth violent debate in the German press. Some critics called him the Messiah come to save the theatre, while others, speaking for the self-appointed "moral majority" of that period, saw him as a wrecker seeking to throw the German theatre into a cesspool of his own creation. Either way he was not ignored. When *Baal* opened in Leipzig in late 1923, for instance, there was a chaotic scandal unprecedented in Leipzig theatre history. In a piece that helped both to draw audiences and to increase pressure to close the show, one reviewer (Berlin's Alfred Kerr) summed up the production: "Liquor, liquor, liquor, naked, naked, naked women." Brecht slouched around Leipzig unshaved, shabby, in a worn leather jacket, abused corduroy trousers out of which poked "November grey" underwear, a cheap sporting cap, with a blue signet ring on one hand, and wearing round wire frame glasses of the sort that charities used to issue to the unemployed. But this standing affront to the bourgeoisie, theatrically and very deliberately, highlighted his down-at-heel appearance by staying at a hotel of almost feudal elegance: The Fürstenhof (The Prince's Court Hotel).

Although Alwin Kronacher was the director on record for the 1923 *Baal*, Brecht actually was the de facto director of the play in the weeks of rehearsal. Possibly the Leipzig management, knowing that he had recently caused a theatrical scandal in Berlin by insulting the whole cast of *Parricide*, were wary of contracting Brecht as a director but wanted the Kleist Prize recipient available *if* he would behave himself. From records of that period we can reconstruct how Brecht behaved as a director starting out. The best account of his work in Leipzig is provided by the actor Rudolf Fernau (Johannes in the 1923 Leipzig *Baal*) who published his memoirs in 1971.[13] Looking back on the production (though perhaps reading into the events of 1923 theories of "epic acting" that were not articulated until years later), Fernau gives us a fascinating glimpse of Brecht at work.

At the invitation of Dr Kronacher, Brecht turned up at the City Theatre. Without further ado, he took over the direction of the play with what Fernau describes as "modest sovereignty." With the first words the actors spoke, Brecht, in his strong Swabian accent, interrupted to say that he had written *Baal* not to support Expressionism but as a blow against this highly emotional tendency in the arts. He then began to act out each role in order to demonstrate how it should be played. He stressed that each sentence was as important as the play as a whole and should be worked on with great care.

Though the cast greeted Brecht with polite scepticism (they had surely heard of the *Parricide* debacle) they were, according to Fernau, quickly won over. The actresses who objected to Brecht's ostentatiously unwashed state were told by Kronacher that this was simply part of his "Villon and Rimbaud phase." This "phase" would last the rest of Brecht's life, but Kronacher's assurances, though wrong, had the desired effect on the cast. Soon they were all wound around Brecht's little finger. At times he would pedantically insist on a theoretical approach to problems, then suddenly throw all theory out. The general impression he made was one of "a many-layered, sympathetic and extraordinarily iridescent chameleon who had us fascinated and bewitched."[14]

Typical of Brecht's working method in Leipzig, and indeed of what was to become a lifetime practice, were his individual sessions with actors outside the formal rehearsal period and his disregard for the original text of the play. Each day the text would be viewed afresh as Brecht the director denounced (half in jest but half seriously) Brecht the playwright. "How could anybody write such shit?" he would ask rhetorically, and would scribble new lines, new scenes, new acts and insist that these be learned immediately. So changing would the chameleon be, that Brecht the theorist would openly fight with Brecht the director, Brecht the poet, Brecht the playwright and Brecht the blatant womanizer. No one could predict which Brecht would predominate at any given moment. But somehow, out of the cacophony of the Brechts arguing with one another would come a production that worked as a unified artistic whole as each contributed a valuable piece to the final mosaic.

At the first run through of *Baal* (and this would be the case in virtually all subsequent Brecht productions) chaos reigned. Totally swept up by the brutal Bohemian atmosphere of the play, the cast behaved as if they all were drunk. Many in fact were drunk and liquor bottles piled up in every corner backstage. Fights began and ended. Lothar Körner, totally caught up in the vicious, amoral title role of *Baal*, stormed at Brecht before throwing his script at him and stalking off to lock himself in the men's room where he continued to bellow at the director. The leading actress, Margarete Anton, fainted and was carried off. Brecht remained unmoved by all these carryings-on, but after Anton recovered from her faint he did publicly enquire about the color of her underwear saying that he had been thinking about the question for three days, wondering whether she was wearing a pink rather than a sky blue slip. She lifted her skirt coquettishly and said, "grey," to which Brecht is supposed to have replied, "Grey, friend, is all theory."[15] With the recovery of Anton and Körner, rehearsals resumed. Complaining that Körner's delivery of the Baal ballad "by speaking as though he were a head taller than his actual height actually made it come out as though he were a head shorter," Brecht grabbed the guitar, leapt on a chair and electrified the cast with his own mesmeric rendition of the ballad.

On the day of the premier, Körner claimed that his throat could not stand Baal's bellowing any more and that he would not be able to go on. Anton looked like Ophelia after the drowning. Kronacher was a nervous wreck. Brecht remained calm and was writing new text for that evening's opening. When the curtain rose, Körner and Anton were ready. In the theatre sat not only the local Leipzig critics, but also all major German critics including Berlin's best known, the rivals Herbert Ihering and Alfred Kerr. Describing the opening night, Brecht's critical supporter Herbert Ihering noted something that would turn out later to be true of almost all Brecht first nights until he went into exile in 1933: the audience was divided between those who liked what Brecht was doing and those who came to shout him down. In Ihering's description, parts of the audience initially booed the play but then the positive forces won the upper hand "threatening, endless applause." Then, in the words of another critic present at the first night, "Amidst the fighting sound of whistles, boos, and applause, there appeared [on stage] a shy, pale, slender youth, the poet Bertolt Brecht, who then retreated immediately to the wings and then fearfully came back to the protecting hand of the theatre manager. The look on his [Brecht's] face: My god, what have I done here . . ."[16] Later, when the city authorities looked into the production they found it much too scandalous for Leipzig and *Baal* was removed from the repertoire. The day after the Leipzig premiere all Germany would hear about Brecht's genius and the scandal being committed in Leipzig, as Brecht had again managed to get the Berlin critics to attend his production. Before midnight the director himself had left Leipzig, off to commit new, publicized indiscretions in other German cities. One thing that Brecht would never allow: that he be ignored and forgotten.

His next scandal, following close on the heels of the Leipzig affair, took place in Munich and with the active cooperation of Brecht's theatrical mentor, Lion Feuchtwanger. At Feuchtwanger's urging, Brecht and the set designer Caspar Neher had been taken on at the famous but financially troubled Chamber Theatre in Munich. Perhaps because the theatre was so behind with the bills that no theatrical agency wanted to give the theatre any more scripts, the management felt that Brecht should stage a play for which no royalties had to be paid. As is so often the case, even today in German theatre, the Chamber Theatre management proposed staging a Shakespearean play. Though this did not appeal to Brecht at the time,[17] perhaps because people would not have tolerated major textual changes in one of the well-known plays, he and Feuchtwanger began to consider the work of Shakespeare's contemporary, Christopher Marlowe. Rather than selecting one of Marlowe's best-known and more epic plays such as *The Jew of Malta*, *Tamburlaine*, or *The Tragical History of Dr Faustus*, they turned instead to the less well-known *Edward the Second*, then being revived in London by the Phoenix Society. According to various contemporary accounts, what won Brecht over to *Edward the Second* was Feuchtwanger's description of a supposed scene in the play in which the king's head is dunked in a latrine. It is also likely, if we consider that several of Brecht's other plays of the same period have similar subject matter, that the fact that Edward would give up his family and throne in order to maintain his homosexual friendships would also have appealed to the Brecht of 1923,[18] who was himself flaunting highly public and highly ambiguous relationships with Arnolt Bronnen and Caspar Neher.

In the Elizabethan *Edward the Second* Brecht had found something that was virtually guaranteed to stir up the bourgeoisie. This would be the kind of production seen by the Nazi "moral majority" – then making its first big push in Munich – as precisely the kind of "decadent filth" that would be swept away if ever the Nazis were to come to power. But threatened as artists were in Munich in 1923–4, they were also supported by an artistic community that was in the forefront of the European avant-garde. Yes, you would run into Hitler and Göring at the cafés in the English Garden, but you were just as likely to run into members of the experimental "Blue Rider" school of painting, or one of the Mann brothers, or Bruno Walter or Rudolf Bing. In a concentrated way, the Munich of 1923 was simultaneously a hotbed for great creativity in the arts, was home to an extremely strong left-wing element in politics, and yet also contained the nascent National Socialist Party in its most rabid right-wing form. Out of these elements would be formed the audience that would be simultaneously repelled by and attracted to the work of the young Bertolt Brecht.

Once the selection of *Edward II* had been announced, Feuchtwanger and Brecht began the preparation of a script. They worked without acknowledgement (a quite typical Brecht practice throughout his life) from a pre-existent text, Walter Heymel's German translation. As the "junior partner" in the enterprise, despite his almost complete lack of English at this time and probably mainly working from Heymel's German version, Brecht would prepare a first draft of the text, to be corrected by Lion Feuchtwanger whose English was good. According to Feuchtwanger's account, Brecht had usually rendered Marlowe's verses in what Feuchtwanger saw as too polished a German form. Feuchtwanger proceeded to "rough up" the text to give the play a form better fitted to its increasingly shabby content.[19]

Given the shaky financial situation of the Munich Chamber Theatre in 1923–4, Brecht was accorded an amazingly free hand with the *Edward II* production. Not only was he allowed to use key actors who were already under contract to the Chamber Theatre, but he was also in a position to hire freelance actors and even to raid the Munich Residenztheater for its principal male star, Erich Faber, to play the role of Edward. In the role of the young king Edward III who, at the play's close, must pass judgement on his own mother and her lover, the usurper Mortimer, Brecht insisted on casting one of his personal friends, the Latvian actress Asja Lacis who spoke virtually unintelligible, heavily accented German. As would so often be the case in Brecht's later career, set and costume design was assigned to Brecht's immensely gifted childhood friend, Caspar Neher. Brecht himself handled the music for the piece. If we note the shaky financial situation of the Munich Chamber Theatre and the fact that in these troubled economic times even as famous a director as Max Reinhardt could only very rarely insist on his own exclusive casting of a play and his own unlimited rehearsal schedule, Brecht's contract for the *Edward II* production is nothing short of astonishing. Brecht was not only given a free hand in casting, but full-scale, main-stage rehearsals with lighting, props, set, etc. available for the full run of the rehearsals. In addition, the contract stated that no one could interfere with his rehearsals and that no premiere could even be scheduled until Brecht deemed the production ripe for public presentation. All of these contractual conditions anticipated the last and highest stage in his career when Brecht, with Helene Weigel, ran the Berlin Ensemble. In Munich, in 1923, the only way this comparative luxury could be paid for at the Chamber Theatre was for the theatre to resort to the unusual expedient of bringing in the popular entertainers, Karl Valentin and Liesl Karlstadt, to do their brilliant stand-up comic routines in the theatre each evening. The evening receipts directly subsidized Brecht's daily rehearsals. As Brecht was a great admirer of the comedy team and had in fact put in a guest appearance with their comic orchestra (fig. 4) the solution of the theatre's main financial problems through this expedient was an apt one. Instead of a radical gap of what is sometimes called "high" and "low" culture, the "high" Chamber Theatre freely borrowed from the "low" music hall cabaret. As Brecht was consistently to seek to bridge this gap in his own stage productions, his literal dependency here on Valentin and Karlstadt is significant. As the theatre was being shared, there was ample time for Brecht to study the Valentin/Karlstadt comic routines and for Karlstadt and Valentin to comment on the way the *Edward II* production was shaping up in rehearsal.

It is now possible, even some sixty years after the events themselves, to reconstruct not only a picture of the 1924 premiere of *Edward II* in Munich but also a fairly detailed picture of the rehearsal process itself. With this production Brecht instituted a procedure that would become a hallmark of his directing style: he encouraged people to attend his rehearsals and welcomed suggestions from his "audience". As several members of this Munich "audience" have either published their memoirs or have consented to be interviewed, we have a remarkably clear picture of how Brecht worked as a director. By careful examination and cross-referencing of the recollections of his co-workers and observers we can answer a number of basic questions about his directing style, questions concerning such things as pre-production planning, casting, attitude towards the text of the play, use of lighting, style of sets, methods of working with actors, and his use or abuse of ideas volunteered by others. Sifting through all these materials we can see how much Brecht's late directorial style is fully anticipated in the *Edward II* production.

Before rehearsals began Brecht did not have a final text of the play but he did have a clear notion of the style he wished to impose. He knew rather clearly what he wanted to have on stage but he also knew even more clearly those elements he wanted, at all costs, to avoid. There was to be none of the reverence or "plaster monument grandeur" that had once characterized the German treatment of the classics from at least Goethe on. But neither was there to be any attempt to present detailed Naturalism in the style of Stanislavski. A bourgeois living room with its fourth wall removed was not Brecht's idea of what the theatre should be about. Nor was he committed to the stylization of frenzied emotion of the then rampant Expressionists, though the political concerns of that group were not wholly alien to him even in 1923–4. The religious orientation of many of the Symbolists was, however, alien to Brecht. But though there was much to reject in German provincial theatre of this period, Brecht also had a large number of positive impulses available to him in Munich in late 1923. The Büchner revival had opened the way for a frank and revolutionary treatment of the human body

Fig. 4. Brecht puts in a guest appearance with the "orchestra" of the famous Munich comedians, Liesl Karlstadt (to Brecht's left) and Karl Valentin (to Brecht's right). Performances of this group kept the Chamber Theatre afloat in Munich during the period in which Brecht was rehearsing his first official production, *Edward II*, there in 1924.

on stage. Wedekind's own stage appearances had prepared Munich audiences for Brecht's treatment of risqué themes. The Munich critic Georg Fuch's two books *The Stage of the Future* (Berlin, 1903) and *The Theatrical Revolution* (Munich, 1906) had been read throughout Germany and had indeed by 1914 already exerted a powerful influence on the Russian avant-garde, particularly on Meyerhold.[20] In the arts generally, Futurism, the Blue Rider group (based in Munich) and the Dadaists had already undermined the pillars of the classical temple of arts. Theatrical art specifically, through the media of Büchner, Jarry's experiments, the writings of Fuchs, the stage work of Wedekind, Brahm, Reinhardt and Jessner, the revival of interest in the sprawling work of the Elizabethans, the translations of Far Eastern drama by Feuchtwanger and Klabund, and the news reaching Munich from Moscow through Brecht's friend Asja Lacis about the work of Tairov, Mayakovski, Meyerhold and the "Factory of Eccentric Actors," prepared the way. The more we know of Munich in this period the more we can see that the constituent parts of Brecht's theatrical vision were not unique to him, but what was new was the manner in which these elements were then blended together.

Of the various eyewitnesses of the pre-rehearsal preparations and the rehearsals themselves, the single most detailed, sensitive and sensible account is provided by Bernhard Reich who was at the time a fellow dramaturg at the Munich Chamber Theatre and the husband of Asja Lacis, a Latvian revolutionary and stage director. Reich describes the following scene in Munich in late 1923: "My wife, Anna (sic) Lazis (sic) and I were sitting in the English Garden when Brecht and his wife, the lovely Marianne [Zoff] went by. They stopped. Mutual introductions. Anna Lazis had studied in Moscow at Kommisashevski's theatre and knew the new Russian theatre. Brecht interrogated her. He was visibly interested in information about Soviet Russia and its cultural politics. This conversation was followed by many others."[21] This illustrates several important things about Brecht and his manner of working. Yes, Brecht was really interested – as Reich notes – in the information that Lacis could provide on Russian experimental theatre, but he was also interested in Lacis herself. Within minutes of meeting he had engaged her as his "assistant" on the *Edward II* production and shortly after became convinced that she should play the role of Edward II's young son. When Brecht insisted on casting her as the young Edward, there were howls of outrage on the part of the Chamber Theatre management. Rudolf Frank, then second in command at the Theatre, states in his memoirs:

It's true that Brecht would later sniff out a lot of talent and would properly use this talent, but at that time, in 1923, he got it into his head that the role of the young prince (Edward III) had to be played by a non-actress, Asja Lacis, who was an impossibility: overweight, totally without talent and unable to speak proper German. I advised him against this. To no avail. I asked Mrs Lacis herself to give up the role but she was just as stubborn as he was. I barged in on Falckenberg and asked that he as director [of the Theatre] use his power. He remained silent. Adolf Kaufmann, regrettably, was out of town. I tried the most extreme measures and so insulted the lady that anyone else would have thrown the tiny role at our feet. But on her elephant hide all insults were shrugged off as I called her "cow," "catastrophe," and "the ruin of the Chamber Theatre." Finally I said to Brecht, "Dear Brecht, this ugly woman is going to cost you more than the loveliest woman would cost."[22]

But Brecht was not to be swayed. If he wanted somebody in a role he simply insisted on his absolute rights as a director. So the rehearsals began with Lacis functioning both as assistant and as a member of the cast.

Typically, Brecht's rehearsals were open. As far as I have been able to reconstruct, it appears that he kept the whole cast and whole stage crew present at all times. Spectators could come and go at will. Often Brecht would ask such casual observers for their suggestions and if they were good ones he would adopt them. By most theatre directors' standards the rehearsals were quite noisy and seemingly chaotic. Brecht himself would be totally unrestrained in his responses. He would laugh heartily when pleased and would bellow mightily when displeased. Years later he would say that he allowed himself two major temper tantrums during any given production. If the actors and the spectators got at all out of hand he would firmly bring things back under his own control. If the audience got too noisy he simply declared "I'll have the room cleared if you're not quiet."[23] Though this was technically his first production as an independent director, observers agree that he behaved as if he were a veteran of many successful productions.

His usual practice during rehearsals was to sit or stand in the middle of the third row or so of the seats. From this position he would then run up the small flight of stairs to the stage and would demonstrate how he wanted something done. By all accounts, at every stage of his career (and the recordings made of his Berlin Ensemble productions certainly support this point of view), Brecht could and did brilliantly demonstrate any nuance of any role, male or female, young or old. This did not mean that an actor had to follow Brecht's demonstration but it did mean that he established a very high acting standard and an actor would have to come up with something even better in order to have it considered. But each new day of the two months of rehearsal brought a new version of the text. Brecht always came into a rehearsal and acted as though everything he had said the day before was provisional. He would passionately argue against solutions he had previously supported. He exhibited the same behavior here as he had during the rehearsals of *Baal* in Leipzig: Brecht the director would take to task Brecht the playwright. Reich describes this unusual situation as follows:

The rehearsals were the most curious that ever happened on a German stage. Brecht the director would become smitten by a particular performer. The director Brecht would then complain bitterly about the playwright Brecht who dared to denigrate such a great acting talent with such an inadequate part. After the rehearsal Brecht the dramatist wrote additional lines for the performer. A certain scene would not work during rehearsals. The nervous director Brecht so berated the incompetent dramatist that finally, after a lot of pushing and shoving, the dramatist would scribble a sensible version. The closer it came to the time of the dress rehearsal the more intensive became the cooperative work between the dramatist and the director. During the final rehearsals great stacks of new text were handed up to the actors on stage as they rehearsed.[24]

As his/her part could change overnight, obviously the Brechtian actor had to be very flexible. Equal flexibility was required of the set designer, light technicians, stage carpenters etc. Brecht was not inhibited by the knowledge that money had been spent on constructing something a certain way. He would cheerfully and apparently with complete disregard of expense, start all over again if he thought something no longer worked.[25] Each day, therefore, the text was in a state of change, and as it changed everything else had to shift so that it stood in proper relationship to the new text. For somebody such as Rudolf Frank who had to pay attention to costs and schedules these seemingly chaotic rehearsals must have required an extraordinary amount of faith that somehow this new director would finally pull things together in a meaningful way.

For the actors, everything that Brecht did was new and often bewildering. An example of such confusion was the scene when the king's favorite, Gaveston, is to be hanged on stage. Reich reports of the rehearsal:

Those playing the soldiers who were to hang the king's favorite, made, initially, a few gestures that might have represented a hanging for those with a willing imagination. Every other German director would have simply gone on. Brecht interrupted the scene and demanded that the actors do it properly: tie the hangman's knot and fasten the rope to the beam above. Shrugging their shoulders the actors tried to follow the unexpected instructions of the director. Brecht stopped again and demanded grimly and unswervingly that they repeat the hanging. He then set them the task of hanging Gaveston as though they were virtuosos of the gallows. The public should enjoy (he said) watching how they actually hanged the young man. Brecht then repeated the scene patiently and seriously.[26]

Years later Brecht did a 1950 production at the Chamber Theatre and Eric Bentley, who was present, notes:

Naturalism was a bad word in Brecht's vocabulary yet I think it must be applied to his voice work with actors. Many of the German actors made all plays sound grandly declamatory like Schiller, Brecht wanted, on the contrary, to sound down to earth like Büchner. So when they made his lines sound like Schiller, he would send them out with Egon Monk and me for coaching in the desired kind of speech. We had to completely change their speech melody. If an actor had a long speech we would break it down into short units that could be treated as quick remarks in a present day conversation. "How could you say that, talking with me now, or to your wife at breakfast?" With some difficulty the actor would find what ought to have been the easier – the most natural – way of phrasing and intonation. This was Brecht's answer to *Wallenstein*.[27]

I cite Eric Bentley's observation here because I believe that, though it refers to work done in 1950, it reflects Brecht's work of 1923–4. He would insist that the hanging scene in *Edward II* look and sound as though these actors quite naturally conducted hangings as an everyday, professional obligation. The scene must look natural rather than bombastic, phony, or "staged."

Another scene that well illustrates Brecht's working method and his objectives as a director is where Baldock plays the role of traitor to the king and, by a prearranged signal, hands him over to his enemies. In a fine piece of sustained analysis, Bernhard Reich sees in Brecht's rehearsal of this particular scene some absolutely key elements of what would be called later "epic theatre." Reich writes:

It was striking that in *Edward* Brecht concentrated so much on the betrayal scene. This scene required a different way of setting the scene than was usual at that time. The guiding directorial principle was not the tension inducing one of asking: 'will the hidden king be found?' or 'when will he be found?' but rather the objective of the director was to set forth the "how" of the king's being found. The spectator is "anxious" to discover the way in which a traitor behaves. Not so much where the action is going but rather how one gets there.[28]

Reich goes on to support this view of the important *Edward II* rehearsals by citing Brecht's famous 1930 set of principles of the "epic theatre," where he notes that in his theatre the emphasis is more on the path to a goal than on the goal itself. Trying to establish a source for Brecht's arrangement of the betrayal scene and to anticipate his later practice with the Berlin Ensemble, Reich goes back to the one-legged singer at the Augsburg fairs:

He [Brecht] picked from the deep impressions left by the barrel organ singer one major element – one may call this the naivete of representation . . . The composers of fairground *Moritaten* neither allow themselves to be led astray by reflections on the material, nor do they let themselves be overly specific through the use of minute nuances in the material. This fairground theatre strives to present things in an unmistakable and coarse way (they represent only the basics) . . . Handing over the handkerchief to Edward (the pre-arranged signal of betrayal in the play) – the gesture imitates the devotion and gentle submissiveness mimed by Judas in his relationship with his Lord – this arrangement is precisely like the fairground "histories."[29]

Crucial to all these observations is Brecht's extraordinary emphasis on the visual elements of a production. In a sense, one can see his theatre as a silent theatre in the way that we speak of silent film where Chaplin or Keaton act out complex actions without any need for words. One of Brecht's main objectives seems to be that the play would be intelligible to an audience sitting on the other side of sound-proof glass. But, going beyond the silent film, the aural line of the play is not neglected but is also to be so finely tuned that the play should be wholly intelligible to a blind listener. The precise attention to both the visual and the auditory portions of the production then produces an extraordinarily rich audio-visual text for the spectator/listener, as both eye and ear are fully engaged at every moment of the production. There are no dead spaces in such a production. Each instant is packed with layers of aural and visual meaning that can be read or experienced from the combined assault on the senses that is built into the production. The net effect is, as Ihering had observed, richly sensuous theatre in which the force of Brecht's seductive personality is fully turned upon the audience. The usual result is, as Herbert Ihering had noted, that spectators emerge from such a spectacle shaken to the very core of their beings. Wherever one turns to impressions of Brecht's contemporaries of the 1920s, it is always the same: his sensual, seductive, mesmeric quality is commented on by men, women, young and old. The playwright Zuckmayer, for instance, noted of Brecht the performer: "When he picked up the guitar, the hum of conversation ceased," while all around Brecht people sat "as though caught up in a magic spell." Zuckmayer, himself a professional singer at the time was, by his own admission, "completely captivated, moved, charmed."[30]

There is no ground for imagining that this Brecht, the Brecht of the fairgrounds, the Brecht who performed in brothels, beer halls, truck stops, and the outdoor cafés of Munich, did not carry over into the *Edward II* production. With this in mind, let us look at some of the descriptions of the performance itself. The dramatist Marieluise Fleisser years later set down her recollections of the production. "This was," she recalls, "street-singer-like theatre," in which Brecht used "disconcertingly simple and at the same time easily perceptible means that quietly sawed on one's nerves." Particularly unnerving, she recalls, was the "Song of the Ballad Seller." The seemingly innocuous refrain "Intercede for us, Intercede for us" is charged with extraordinary power through a sustained piece of stage business. Fleisser writes:

Ghostlike before my eyes stand the tall stage flats of the London houses with (their) many small window shutters; suddenly all the shutters fly open, and out of every window pops the head of someone speaking, and all of these heads together recite some kind of a prayer that is more an indictment than a complaint, interrupted, as in a litany, by the oft-repeated "Intercede for us." This "Intercede for us," however, is not a request for mercy, but much more a hasty, hostile whisper that gets on one's nerves with its ice-cold threat, and everyone recognizes that this is nothing less than revolution. And after the last ghostly "Intercede for us," the shutters fly closed again with one dry crash.[31]

In Fleisser's recollection the dungeon scene had an almost electric charge. Edward, standing in a pool of castle sewage scrapes out his empty mess tin with a lead spoon, a sound rather like scraping chalk on a blackboard. This unnerving sound was then accentuated by the king's half-demented shaking of a metal net that was hanging between him and the audience. Each time the crazed Edward, looking for the murderers who lurked just outside the dungeon, barged into this metal net he sprang back "as though the net were electrified" ("mit Strom geladen") (fig. 5), a device used again by Brecht in 1936 in his Copenhagen production of *The Roundheads and the Pointed Heads* (fig. 6). Meanwhile, the charged atmosphere of the play could hardly have been reduced by scenes in which Brecht had the soldiers of the competing armies goosestep across the stage at breakneck speed on rickety planks strung high above the stage, a device anticipating Grusche's crossing of "the two thousand foot chasm" in *The Caucasian Chalk Circle*. Commenting on the

Fig. 5. The 1924 Munich production of *Edward II*. The dungeon scene where the half-crazed Edward (played by Erwin Faber) shakes the metal net that separates the stage space from the audience.

supernumeraries who made up the armies of the *Edward II* production, Rudolf Frank notes:

There marched the ranks of the army, slowly, silent as machines, terribly tired, through grey mud out of darkness. Orders echoed randomly, coldly, and at the last announcement, "truce," the ranks slumped down, to sleep on the bare earth. In this English army with their filth-encrusted helmets was personified not only the terrible 1550s but also all the armies of the European World War.[32]

Fig. 6. *The Roundheads and the Pointed Heads*. Premiere (in Danish) at the Riddersalen Theatre, Copenhagen, November 4, 1936. Director of record was Per Knutzon as Brecht was having work-permit difficulties in Denmark. Brecht's influence on the production can be clearly seen by comparing this photograph with fig. 5. Once Brecht finds a particularly striking visual image (in this case the metal net) he tends to use it over and over again for various other plays.

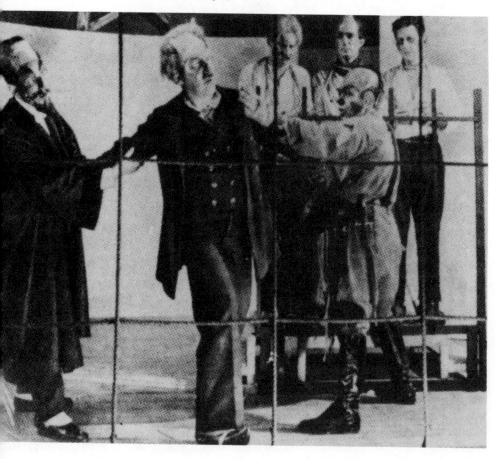

Though Frank does not note this fact, we learn from Reich that it is also probable that these armies had an even more local and contemporary model, Hitler's ragtag stormtroopers whose brief seizure of power in Munich in November 1923 had been seen first hand by Brecht and had briefly interrupted his rehearsal schedule. Joachim Fest confirms the existence at that time of military bands who transformed the Munich area "into a bivouac of brutish soldiery."[33]

But for all the meticulousness of the months of rehearsal, opening night of the play was, by all accounts, a rather mixed success. Scene changes were made with such torturous slowness that the final curtain did not come down until almost midnight. Rudolf Frank recalls the evening:

The major role of Mortimer was played by the highly talented [Oskar] Homolka. Because he drank, I ordered that no alcohol was to be taken into the dressing rooms. But there came Brecht right in the middle of the show with a litre of cognac which Mortimer downed right away, and a quarter of an hour later staggered onto the stage, and stammered and tottered through the rest of his role, until fat Mrs Lazis appeared in her trouser-role and, as Brecht had demonstrated to her, pointed her finger at Mortimer and spoke the one word of which her role consisted: "Murderer." But her grasp of German was so bad that it sounded not at all like "*Mörder*" but rather exactly like "*Merde!*" The laughter was like that which greeted Valentin's performances until finally the audience began to hiss. Even Brecht's admirers could not convince themselves at the end to come up with the kind of applause appropriate to a premiere. Leopold Jessner, who had come from Berlin for the premiere, blustered angrily, but his rage was directed only against Homolka: "An actor like that ought to be disqualified from the profession." And yet the failure injured neither Brecht nor Homolka. Only the Chamber Theatre was damaged by it; for Brecht, the endless rehearsals, the wrong casting, the drunkenness of Homolka, and the failure of the premiere were only "experiments," a series of "attempts" [*Versuche*] as he was to call all his written works later.[34]

Bernhard Reich's summary of the importance of the production to Brecht himself as a director is remarkably similar to Frank's. Reich writes:

What did the *Edward II* production achieve for Brecht? Hardly that which he'd hoped for. The production was greeted in Munich and beyond as an unusually talented piece of work by its director, nothing more. That the production contained the seeds of a new way of writing plays, and that a new technique of acting was revealed, all that was not recognized at that time. I don't want to charge his contemporaries with shortsightedness, but I do want to make the observation that in the normal way of things we only recognize the newness of many things when we see the results of them later in their more developed stage. One needs more than normal vision to see a developed picture of something that is only in an embryonic stage.[35]

Beyond the elements noted by Reich, Fleisser and Frank as being present in an embryonic state in the *Edward II* production, it is also important to note that all the seeds of confusion about Brecht's theatrical style are also present in 1924. The catchwords of later Brechtian theatrical theory have been retroactively applied to the *Edward II* production even though, so far, no evidence has turned up to show that these catchwords existed at that time. Yes, Ihering tells us about distance, but he also tells us that Brecht's texts lashed audiences to fury and that Brecht's plays were tragedies from the first word. We know that Brecht avoided the sustained cry of horror of the Expressionists but we also know that he deliberately electrified audiences. We know he rejected "method" Realism but we also know that he paid unusually close attention to Naturalism in dialogue and to the realistic appropriateness of all stage props and many stage actions – the hanging scene is a good example of this. In order to fully comprehend the complexity of the stage event *Edward II* in Munich in 1924, we should not try to answer the rhetorical question: was it *either* cool/rational/distant *or* hot/passionate/ engaged? It was neither. It was both and it was much more. Instead of asking the usual very simple questions, let us try something rather different: let us try to see why dichotomy has so little place in helping us to account for the raw power of Brecht productions when seen by audiences familiar or unfamiliar with his tangled and radically contradictory theatrical theories. Wrong questions are usually asked, and wrong answers are given because much of the debate around Brecht is based on wrong notions of "audience response." Most critics seem to assume (as Brecht himself so frequently did) that "cool" acting triggers "cool" audience responses. There is no verifiable evidence in support of this connection. Though we can go back to the "cool" acting theory of Plato's *Ion*, or to Diderot's eighteenth-century observations on the paradox of the "cool" actor and "hot" audience response, or can look at Meyerhold's 1904 insistence on using "cold" acting to get "hot" responses, I suggest that we turn to the modern aesthetician E. H. Gombrich and his seminal essay "Meditations on a Hobby Horse"[36] to try to explain the apparent paradox of "cold" acting's power to generate "hot" audience responses. Though Gombrich, to the best of my knowledge, has never examined Brecht, and I know of no evidence that Brecht was familiar with Gombrich, I nevertheless feel that Gombrich's aesthetics can contribute to a deepened understanding of the playwright. In moving away from the detailed *trompe-l'oeil* style of Realism that we associate with the names of David Belasco and the early work of Stanislavski, and in moving towards a theatre which resolutely stressed its own theatricality (the theatre of the Elizabethans and several strands of the theatre of the Far East come immediately to mind as predecessors for this), Brecht created a practical stage aesthetic with striking parallels to Gombrich's deceptively simple "hobby horse" theory of mimesis.

Those familiar with Gombrich will recall that he presents a modern and empirically founded aesthetic theory at odds not only with classical Greek mimetic theory but also with the major tenets of nineteenth-century theory, and the politico-aesthetic twentieth-century mode known as Socialist Realism. Keenly aware of modern advances in the psychology of visual perception, Gombrich applies modern scientific discoveries to the too long unchallenged classical theories of mimesis. Gombrich observes:

Pliny, and innumerable writers after him, have regarded it as the greatest triumph of naturalistic art for a painter to have deceived sparrows or horses. The implication of these anecdotes is that a human beholder easily recognizes a bunch of grapes in a painting because for him recognition is an intellectual act. But for the birds to fly at the painting is a sign of complete "objective" illusion. It is a plausible idea, but a wrong one. The merest outline of a cow seems sufficient for a tsetse trap, for somehow it sets the apparatus of attraction in motion and "deceives" the fly. To the fly, we might say, the crude trap had the "significant" form – biologically significant, that is. It appears that visual stimuli of this kind play an important part in the animal world. By varying the shapes of "dummies" to which animals were seen to respond, "the minimum" image that still sufficed to release a specific reaction has been ascertained. Thus little birds will open their beaks when they see the feeding parent approaching the nest, but they will also do so when they are shown two darkish roundels of different size, the silhouette of the head and body of the bird "represented" in its most "generalized" form.

An "image" in this biological sense is not an imitation of an object's external form but an imitation of certain privileged or relevant aspects. It is here that a wide field of investigation would seem to open. For man is not exempt from this type of reaction.[37]

This generic theory of "audience response" to "certain privileged or relevant aspects" of an object rather than to the object itself or to a full mimetic representation of that object is then given human specificity in Gombrich's application of his theory to a child's "hobby horse." In another crucial passage Gombrich writes:

The "first" hobby horse (to use eighteenth-century language) was probably no image at all. Just a stick which qualified as a horse because one could ride on it. The *tertium comparationis*, the common factor, was function rather than form. Or, more precisely, that formal aspect which fulfilled the minimum requirement for the performance of the function – for any "ridable" object could serve as a horse. If that is true we may be enabled to cross a boundary which is usually regarded as closed and sealed. For in this sense "substitutes" reach deep into biological functions that are common to man and animal. The cat runs after the ball as if it were a mouse. The baby sucks its thumb as if it were the breast. In a sense the ball "represents" a mouse to the cat, the thumb a breast to the baby. But here too "representation" does not depend on formal similarities, beyond *the minimum requirements of function* [italics added]. The ball has nothing in common with the mouse except that it is chasable. The thumb nothing with the breast except that it is suckable. As "substitutes" they fulfil certain demands of the organism. They are keys which happen to fit into biological or psychological locks, or counterfeit coins which make the machine work when dropped into the slot.

In the language of the nursery the psychological function of "representation" is still recognized. The child will reject a perfectly naturalistic doll in favour of some monstrously "abstract" dummy which is "cuddly". It may even dispose of the element of "form" altogether and take to a blanket or an eiderdown as its favourite "comforter" – a substitute on which to bestow its love.[38]

If we can accept Gombrich's hypothesis that it is function rather than form that guides our responses to sensual stimuli both in "the real world" and in the world of art objects or "representations" of a real world, then we can apply this hypothesis to the long and distinguished history of the non-realist or non-Naturalist theatre. We can postulate that in terms of psychological function it has mattered but little to the theatre spectator whether he or she viewed either a full mimetic stage representation, the Realism of a Stanislavski or a Belasco, or the highly stylized representations of the classical Greek theatre, the medieval European theatre, the Elizabethan theatre, the Punch and Judy show, the theatre of the Far East, or the singers at the Augsburg fair of Brecht's youth. However stylized the language, the setting, the costuming, and the acting of a play, nevertheless it would appear that such mimetic "substitutes" satisfy some basic biological and psychological needs. In Gombrich's terms, the "hobby horse" of the Elizabethan theatre, the Augsburg fairground, the Punch and Judy show or the tale told by Büchner's grandmother, or the Javanese shadow play can be satisfactorily "ridden," though the staging is at a very considerable remove from detailed mimesis. It is abundantly clear, for instance, that emotional audience response was an everyday occurrence in the highly stylized Greek theatre. It seems to have mattered not one whit to classical audiences that a male actor played the female roles of Clytemnestra, Medea, or Antigone and that this actor played in a setting devoid of realistic detail. It would seem that this presentational style of acting[39] satisfied, at a deep level, "the minimum requirement of function." The counterfeit, though by no means exact, was enough to "make the machine work when dropped into the slot." Likewise, to name but one other example from the long history of "presentational theatre" it is very clear that Shakespeare was fully aware of the fact that he was not working in a fully mimetic or representational mode when in the prologue to *Henry V* he writes:

> But pardon, gentles all,
> The flat unraised spirits that have dared
> On this unworthy scaffold to bring forth
> So great an object: can this cockpit hold
> The vasty fields of France? or may we cram
> Within this wooden O the very casques
> That did afright the air at Agincourt?[40]

Fully aware that mimesis in any full and direct representational sense is quite impossible under such conditions, in his presentational theatre Shakespeare has the chorus tell the audience that it will have "to piece out our imperfections with your thoughts." And, speaking specifically of the lack of real horses on his stage he recommends:

> Think, when we talk of horses, that you
>   see them
> Printing their proud hoofs i' th' receiving earth.[41]

Reduced to the linguistic echo of "the horse itself," may we imagine that these mere shades of horses yet "served the minimum requirement of function" and triggered an audience's response and caused the audience "to piece out these imperfections," in a psychologically satisfying way? In fact may we go so far as to postulate that the human response (as distinct from the response of flies or of birds as in Gombrich's examples) is more complex and potentially more satisfying? May we not suppose that, for an adult member of Shakespeare's audience (then and now), there is the psychological pleasure of responding to Shakespeare's linguistic shades of horses and thus the pleasure of the conscious participation in such deception? This pleasure in deception as deception is not, we may assume, accessible to other members of the animal kingdom, but is directly relevant to a "theatre theatrical," a theatre pleasurably self-conscious in the presence of the interplay of "reality" and of the "depiction of reality."

Once we have freed ourselves from the tyranny of the ill-founded assumption that only full mimetic representation can generate profound emotional responses in theatre audiences, we are ready to look closely at Brecht's theory and practice of stage mimesis with its complex mixture of "Realism" in the Stanislavskian sense and its self-conscious, non-realistic "theatre theatrical" elements reminiscent of the chorus's initial speech in *Henry V*. With this in mind, let us briefly go back to the "hanging scene" in *Edward II*. The reader will recall that Brecht wanted the actors to have a realistic grasp of the "craft of hanging." He provided a working gallows and a realistically appropriate rope. At the same time, however, the realistic gallows was set against a backdrop that made no pretense at deception: the set was ostentatiously askew and drew attention to itself as painted canvas. Further, the soldiers doing the "realistic" hanging do it in "whiteface" so stark as to suggest the makeup worn by clowns in the circus. It is this simultaneous use of the ostentatiously non-realistic "whiteface" and the carefully detailed "Realism" of the preparations for the hanging that constitute a typically complex and deliberately contradictory Brechtian stage statement. We are at one and the same time "inside" and "outside" a "real" event. As we analyze this complex stage construct, we might ask ourselves whether, from the point of view of the 1924 German spectator, Brecht created an event meeting Gombrich's criterion: "the minimum requirement of function." To return to the "hobby horse," has Brecht not created here an eminently "rideable" object? Is the scene sufficient to "transport" a spectator? What are the minimum requirements of "transport" and do they have very much to do with literal mimesis? From eye-witness accounts of the production, it is clear that the introduction of ostentatiously theatrical elements such as "whiteface" did not undercut the emotional impact of the play in any way whatsoever.[42]

Were we to jump ahead to a later stage of Brecht's career and look closely at the 1929 production of his play, *Didactic Play of Baden-Baden*, we would find an even more striking example of what constitutes sufficient "minimum image" in terms of spectator responsiveness. There was built into this production an extraordinary example of what we can surely now call "hobby-horseness." In order to demonstrate how inhuman people are to one another, Brecht constructed a clown figure with monstrously extended wooden legs and arms and a very large and very obviously false head (fig. 7). The patently false extremities of the clown were then sawn off by two other clowns in a way which exaggerated the act of sawing. Yet despite the "hobby-horse" character of the clown figure, it is reported by Hanns Eisler, the composer, who was present at the premiere, that the grotesque sawing of the clown's wooden limbs caused members of the audience to faint because of the gruesomeness of the scene. The way Hanns Eisler recalls the scene, two clowns, after a discussion concerning man's inhumanity to man cut off the wooden feet of a third clown. "These feet," says Eisler, "were obviously made of chunks of wood. This crude byplay disturbed a number of spectators. Several fainted even though it was clear that only wood was being sawed and that this was certainly not a naturalistic production." A "famous music critic," sitting next to Eisler was so affected that Eisler "helped him out of the auditorium and got him a glass of water."[43] If we may assume that the stick figure of the clown in the *Baden-Baden* play had more in common with Gombrich's hobby-horse than with Stanislavski's meticulous stage Natural-ism, and if we believe that audience members did in fact find the scene to be deeply moving then we can surely see in the scene an exemplary illustration of Gombrich's thesis that we can be moved by art objects whose representational level only fills 'the minimum requirements of function'. In the *Didactic Play of Baden-Baden*, the stick figure or image of a person was apparently quite sufficient as a "minimum image" to "release a specific reaction" akin to that which we might assume would have been released had a "maximum image" with a high degree of representational verisimilitude been employed in the *Baden-Baden* play.

If the logic we have applied thus far is sound and if Gombrich's theory of functional substitutes or "dummies" can be applied correctly to stage "representation," one will trigger an emotional response whether or not one fleshes out the "minimum image" with a greater level of naturalistic detail. Applied directly to each step of Brecht's career as a playwright/director, as he continuously engaged in informal experiments which carried him away in some particulars from the literal mimesis of Stanislavski, we can see that we should *not* expect that audiences must have remained cool and distant just because Brecht deliberately departed from literal Realism. Though Brecht himself fairly consistently expressed discomfiture[44] when audiences responded in an emotional way to his plays, we may suggest that it would have

Fig. 7. The large wooden clown that was sawn apart in Brecht's July 28, 1929, Baden-Baden musical festival production of the *Baden-Baden Cantata of Acquiescence*. Music by Hindemith and Eisler. Conducted by Alfons Dressel and Ernst Wolff.

been very surprising had audiences *not* responded to stage images that seem to have more than met the Gombrich standard of "minimum image."

Whether we turn to early play productions or to ones from the thirties or the famous Berlin Ensemble productions of the fifties, we consistently find in Brecht that, though he avoided the use of detailed mimesis as a guiding principle for a whole production, he nevertheless always maintained a substantial portion of "literal presentation" in each production. I know of no Brecht production from any period of his life where he did not use the mixed or contradictory mimetic style[45] exemplified by that "whiteface" hanging scene. As with *Edward II*, he would simultaneously draw attention to the theatricality of a production while providing a substantial portion of "realistic detail." If we assume that only literal presentation/mimesis will trigger strong audience responses, we will be led to try to believe that Brecht's audiences were left largely unmoved. If we grant, however, that Brecht consistently provided a highly representational "minimum image," then we can better understand the apparent incongruity that audiences were in fact deeply moved by his "cool" productions.[46] With Gombrich's theses of the "minimum image" as a guide, we can avoid the oversimplification of attempting to classify Brecht's work as being *either* "realistic" *or* "formalistic," or *either* emotional *or* non-emotional (intellectual) in its impact. We need to keep these deliberately unresolved dialectical contradictions in order to understand Brecht.

For people seriously concerned with the theatre today, it continues to be fruitful to look both at Brecht's theoretical statements and his actual stage productions. What we will find there, I think, is a highly modern and sophisticated "self-reflexive" mimetic mode well suited to twentieth-century experimentation both in the arts and in the sciences. I hope that we can live comfortably with the paradox that such a modern stance is wholly consistent with several main strands of the classical theatre. It is clear that Brecht was never more modern than when he was borrowing formal, structural and stylistic elements by returning to the richly stylized theatre of the Elizabethans or of the Far East. The "hobby horse" which served Aeschylus and Shakespeare so well has galloped into the modern theatre with Brecht astride and shows no sign of being ready to be put out to pasture. Though Gombrich's beast is but a crude creature of the nursery, perhaps we can never be too sophisticated not to be transported by it. Whatever it may lack in "formal mimetic completeness" is surely of less importance than its demonstrable functionality. Is it possible that this ungainly wooden creation of the nursery can outrun the "real" horses of Stanislavski and Belasco? Contemporary stage practice would suggest such an unlikely conclusion. The "horses" who draw the stagecoach in *Nicholas Nickleby* or the horses of

Equus, "printing their proud hoofs i' th' receiving earth" seem to satisfy audiences at the deepest levels. But I would suggest that the modern theatre owes the acceptance of the reintroduction of the presentational mode and the consequent emancipation of the modern stage to the example first set by Brecht in the 1924 Munich production of *Edward II*. In going back in a very fresh way to an Elizabethan model, Brecht tried to bring back the fast pace and rich flexibility of the Elizabethan stage as an alternative model for those dissatisfied with the sheer slowness and expense of the Stanislavskian model of *trompe-l'oeil* staging. That was Brecht's historical contribution as a director even though he had a horde of forerunners. By going backwards Brecht showed the way for the modern theatre to move forward. He was the one who gained the widest acceptance for the mixed mimetic style in the modern theatre.

3   Berlin dances with death

Berlin   Berlin
Halt ein!   Stop!
Besinne Dich. Come to your senses.
Dein Tänzer ist You're dancing with
Der Tod.   Death.

Paul Zech[1]

Fig. 8. Piscator's use of film to provide a suitable revolutionary background for his stage play, *Sturmflut*, at Berlin's Volksbühne in 1926. The film was used by Piscator to provide his stage with a so-called "fourth dimension." The production was highly praised by Herbert Ihering.

The blood spilled on the streets of Munich by "the silly looking young man" in his 1923 comic opera Putsch was scarcely dry and Hitler had only just begun his sentence at the Landsberg Fortress (where he would write *Mein Kampf*), when the artistic intelligentsia of Munich, all too aware of the rampant anti-semitism at the root of Hitler's politics, moved *en masse* to Berlin.

Whether Brecht went there because of Hitler or because Berlin offered greater theatrical opportunities is an open question, but there are reasons to think that Brecht (unlike many of his friends such as Feuchtwanger) did not at first see Hitler as a real threat. According to Arnolt Bronnen's memoirs, he went with Brecht in June 1923 to a Hitler rally in Munich, where "young Brecht, with the typical Bavarian love of pageantry, delighted in the spectacle, and the mass direction and mass performances of the Hitler-clique."[2] Perhaps those who left Munich thought that suave, avant-garde, cosmopolitan Berlin would be more hospitable to artists and Jews than provincial Munich, breeding ground of Nazism and centre even then of what was referred to grandiosely as "The Movement" (*Die Bewegung*). But Berlin had its own homebred Nazis. Otto Strasser was then even more powerful in Berlin than the pathetic Hitler was in Munich. Berlin had had its full share of right-wing political assassinations with the deaths of Rosa Luxemburg and Karl Liebknecht, and to shouts of "Shoot down the goddam Jewish sow/Murder Walther Rathenau" the Freikorps fanatics had indeed shot down the moderate leader Rathenau in June 1922. But these shots, presaging the widespread horror and violence of the Third Reich, perhaps sound louder to us now than they did at the time. Then they blended with many other noises in Berlin, at that time (with Moscow and Paris) one of the three major artistic capitals of Europe and the battleground where major artistic and political impulses from the East and the West were fought over. Here 100,000 White Russians rubbed shoulders with the visiting "Reds" such as Lunacharski (Soviet Minister for "Enlightenment" and a frequent visitor to Berlin), Karl Radek, Bukharin, and Borodin (specialists in exporting revolution for the Comintern), novelists, filmmakers and playwrights such as Ilya Ehrenburg, Mayakovskii, Eisenstein, Asja Lacis, and the "Peasant Poet," Esenin, husband of Isadora Duncan. The visitors told tales of brilliant artistic experimentation in a "Moscow decorated with Futurist and Suprematist canvases" and where "demented squares battled with rhomboids on the peeling façade of colonnaded Empire villas,"[3] the Moscow of the "Factory of Eccentric Actors," and of the poet Mayakovskii – in his bright yellow jacket with one rounded and one pointed lapel – urging the ambush not only of White Guards but of the museums as well. And when the Russians came to Berlin they found a wide-open city, a veritable Mahagonny where every

pleasure was for open sale. When Asja Lacis arrived in 1922 she lived in a
house in Berlin with Alexei Tolstoy, Boris Pilniak, Andrei Beli, Remizov and
other visiting Russian writers. She remembers Tolstoy organizing a "Night
Life" expedition in Berlin. They drove through innumerable confusing
backstreets to an alley where they went up some pitch dark stairs. "After a
signal was given, a door was opened. We entered a magic room with trees,
with flowers and with naked women. The room was very warm and smelled
of hyacinths."[4] Drugs were freely sold in this Berlin and every possible taste
was catered for.

When Brecht made his first wide-eyed visit to Berlin in 1920 he was
impressed with both the level and the abundance of bad taste, which he took
to with relish. While conducting, as usual, a number of love affairs, he began
at once to establish contacts in various branches of the arts. Though he did
not actually move to Berlin until 1924, after the *Edward II* production in
Munich, he made a number of forays into the northern city from 1920 to
1924. And though he had some setbacks in this "Jungle of Cities," he
established himself with remarkable speed. Clearly, Brecht was as ready for
Berlin as Berlin was for Brecht. It seemed that no sooner had he arrived than
suddenly Brecht was everywhere. Arnolt Bronnen, who first met him in
Berlin in the winter of 1921–22, notes in his memoirs (written in the third
person):

He [Brecht] got to know in weeks more friends than the other would get to know in years.
Brecht had already long since spoken with actors known to Bronnen as stars and only
through newspapers. Though he did not yet have any contracts for staging his plays he
was already negotiating with Klöpfer, Kraus, Wegener, George [all stars in the Berlin
theatre] for them to take roles in his plays. He knew all the dramaturgs, Reinhardt's Felix
Holländer, as well as Jessner's Dr Lipmann, and he knew the most important literary
business people such as Ludwig Berger and Heinrich Eduard Jacob; and at at least three
presses, The Three Masks Press, Propyläen, and Kiepenheuer he had a group of engaged
supporters who stretched from the head of the press to the youngest secretary.[5]

How was this achieved? It is clear that Brecht's adeptness at physical and
intellectual seduction enabled him to take over any social occasion he
attended. Bronnen describes one such event:

An evening at Dr Hermann Kasack's, the young head editor of the Kiepenheuer Press. A
small house in Potsdam, narrow, a small hallway, narrow steps; the steps used in lieu of at
least twenty chairs. One saw only heads, there wasn't enough room to see anything
below these heads. It was a publishing party, Fasching, imported from Munich, hectic,
intellectual, Kasack directing things with his pointed, sharp sentences, until Brecht sang.
Did he sing? He created magic. He sang "The Ballad of the Dead Soldier." It was uncanny
how he conjured out of people's bones Fasching, inflation . . . They became lemurs; he
alone was human.[6]

Everywhere he went he sang of sex and death. Augsburg, Leipzig, Munich,
Berlin, salon, truck stop, brothel, the location did not matter, the result was

always the same: Brecht exercised the magnetic force we now associate with major rock music stars. Those who heard Brecht sing were swept off their feet. Bronnen's response is simply typical. After meeting Brecht for the first time he says to himself: "Love, great love in the world, give him to me for a friend."[7] Confined briefly in the Charité hospital in Berlin, Brecht was not alone even there: he was besieged by groupies. He rejoiced at the stream of visitors–lovers and continued to write, write, write, totally undisturbed by interruptions. The "interruptions" themselves became the subjects of the poems and plays he wrote at this time. And when he left hospital he would sing the songs he had written there. Berlin was at his feet.

It is worth remembering that when I speak of Berlin being at his feet, I speak of the people who became the makers and the wreckers of the modern world. Voraciously interested in every aspect of high and low culture, Brecht moved not in one circle but in many. You would be as likely to find him captivating members of Einstein's family as mesmerizing a group of prize-fighters and six-day bicycle racers. His world included the German Crown Prince who was simultaneously having a love affair with one of Brecht's lovers. At the same parties he met key Comintern figures as well as members of the German aristocracy such as Count Kessler. At the parties where Brecht sang you could encounter dancers such as Mary Wigman, Isadora Duncan and Josephine Baker; composers such as Stravinski, Duke Ellington, Kurt Weill, Hindemith, Busoni, Stuckenschmidt, Krenek, and Schönberg; play-wrights such as Hauptmann, Zuckmayer, Hanns Johst, Arnolt Bronnen and Marieluise Fleisser; architects and designers such as Moholy-Nagy, Lissitzky, Walter Gropius and Marcel Breuer; actors and directors such as Fritz Lang, Erich Engel, Louise Brooks, Lotte Lenya, Max Reinhardt, Leopold Jessner, Josef von Sternberg, Sergei Eisenstein, Curt Bois, Peter Lorre, Ernst Lubitsch, Emil Jannings, Carola Neher, Werner Krauss, Leni Riefenstahl, Josef Pabst and Marlene Dietrich. The list can be extended almost indefinitely. What is important to note is that whatever the field of activity, in those heady days in Berlin, the people Brecht associated with were busy inventing key elements of a new world, a world brilliantly chronicled by George Grosz and Heinrich Zille, Christopher Isherwood, Käthe Kollwitz, Heinrich Mann and Count Kessler, and the fresh newcomer from Augsburg, Bert Brecht.

Brecht's seduction of Berlin was on the grandest scale. Nothing if not bold, he told anyone who would listen that he wanted to have all Berlin's theatres given over to him under the alliterative German slogan: "Brechts Bunte Bühne," "Brecht's Colorful Stage". He was willing to use every persuasive tool. He would write sycophantic letters to the person who would later become Hitler's favorite playwright, Hanns Johst, if Hanns Johst could open doors for him. He would so malign major actors at rehearsals that the newspapers were sure to pick up the story. Not content just to attack theatre people he also published a scatological broadside against the famous author of *Budddenbrooks*, Thomas Mann. Berlin might be loud, but Brecht's determination made him louder. He was Chutzpa personified. When the Berlin theatre critic, Herbert Ihering, had proposed to divide the 1922 Kleist Prize between the "terrible twins" Bronnen and Brecht, Brecht said he would have none of that and got his own way. In signing contracts with publishers and friends he was equally demanding and successful. His contract with Propyläen, with its handsome monthly stipend, was thought by the publisher to be exclusive but it turned out that often Propyläen could not collect a penny as the original contract excluded "plays written with others," and Brecht began to write almost all his plays "with others." Free of all prior conceptions of high and low culture, and grandly proclaiming "Nothing that's alive is immoral,"[8] Brecht wrote some advertising jingles for the Steyr automobile company and was given a car as recompense. Driving the new car with complete abandon he promptly smashed it up, and emerging unhurt, had himself photographed next to the wreck. He then exchanged this photo with the Steyr manufacturer for a brand new car. All of this activity absolutely ensured that Brecht was not ignored. He was ideal copy equally for the "yellow journals" and the leading intellectual journals and poetry magazines of his day; and was frequently interviewed on the new mass medium, radio.

But while he was successfully creating a carefully tailored mass media image of himself, Brecht was also working hard to improve his skills as a director and playwright. In 1924 he went to Berlin to take a job as dramaturg with Max Reinhardt's multiple theatre complex. At Reinhardt's theatres he had an opportunity to observe rehearsals of numerous plays which broke completely with "slice of life" Realism either in their dramaturgy or in Reinhardt's staging of them. The kind of plays favored by Reinhardt and other major Berlin directors in the 1924–5 season were virtually all "presentational" dramas. Among the productions John Willett notes in his *The Theatre of Bertolt Brecht* as being along "anti-illusionistic lines" in Reinhardt's theatres in 1924–5 were Shaw's *Saint Joan* with Elizabeth Bergner (a person who was to become a somewhat vacillating supporter of Bert Brecht); a production of Goldoni's *Servant of Two Masters* in which the actors draw attention to their roles as actors by discussing their parts with the prompter during the performance; a production of Molière's explicitly self-reflexive *Le Malade Imaginaire* with another of Brecht's friends, the great comedian Max Pallenberg; and lots of Pirandello, with particular emphasis on the highly self-reflexive *Six Characters in Search of an Author*. The following year, not only were there some six Pirandello productions in Berlin but Pirandello himself went there with three of his plays which were then produced in the original Italian. "In plays like these," writes Willett, "the actor stepped out of his role, just as in the Russian productions they had stepped off the stage and down into the audience; supposed spectators, as in Reinhardt's production of *Danton's Death*, might suddenly begin to take part in the play."[9] At a crossroads of international experiments in the theatre Berlin in the mid-twenties was an ideal place to observe "presentational" theatre of the pan-European avant-garde. If it was not the Italians then it was the Russians with Tairoff's and Meyerhold's productions and Eisenstein's highly experimental films. Though it was still possible to see rather old-fashioned representational theatre in Berlin in the mid-twenties, it is worth noting that such theatre was an exception rather than the rule. The "in" theatre was that of Tairoff and Pirandello and Piscator and Meyerhold. The contrasting status of the high priest of Naturalist theatre, Konstantin Stanislavski, is aptly summed up in Nicholas Nabokov's recollection of attending a visiting Moscow Art Theatre production of *The Three Sisters* in Berlin in either 1922 or 1923. Nabokov claims to have gone to see the play in the company of Brecht, Kurt Weill, Isadora Duncan and her husband, Esenin. The group "sniggered indecently" at the production.

Wherever one turns in the Berlin theatre of the twenties one sees that major assaults were being launched on the kind of theatre we associate with the early Stanislavski. All three of the major Berlin directors of the 1920s, Max Reinhardt, Erwin Piscator and Leopold Jessner, had all moved well away from the early style of Stanislavski by the time Brecht went to Berlin. However much Brecht may have liked to imagine himself later to be "the Einstein of the new stage form," in fact we can see Brecht as having been, in many ways, among the more conservative of the avant-garde directors of the 1920s. Yet, paradoxically, it is this very conservatism which is perhaps Brecht's greatest contribution to the modern theatre. He preserved the classical theatre but did so in a mode well suited to the modern age. He refused to be drawn into the trap of trying to represent "the real world" on the stage. He knew that this could not work, that it was massively expensive, and that it was pedagogically and artistically unsatisfying to try. Astonishingly, Brecht argued that the supposedly most revolutionary forms of theatre of the twenties – those of Eisenstein, Meyerhold and Piscator – were really not revolutionary at all. He stated flatly in 1928 (two years after he had first begun to study "the marxist classics"): "This theatre [that of Piscator] is in reality anti-revolutionary, because it is passive and reproductive. It has to rely on pure reproduction of existing – that is prevailing – types, *and will have to wait for the political revolution to get its own archetypes. It is the ultimate form of the bourgeois naturalistic theatre.*"[10]

Let us look very closely at the portion of Brecht's statement that I have italicized here. Brecht is supposedly only talking about Piscator in relation to a Germany which, unlike Russia, had not had a revolution. But everything Brecht says applies just as strongly to Piscator's explicit models, the Soviet directors, Meyerhold, Tairoff and Eisenstein, who lived and directed in a country that had by 1928 over ten years of successful revolutionary practice, but supposedly had not generated "its own archetypes." If we were correct in assuming basic similarities between the Russian avant-garde and the work of Erwin Piscator in 1928, then we can apply Brecht's conclusion to both groups. That is to say that Meyerhold and Piscator had created "the ultimate form of the bourgeois naturalistic theatre." At first glance this will strike many as a preposterous statement, but let me attempt to say why I am now convinced that it is a basically sound position and deserves the closest consideration as the cornerstone of Brecht's alternate and genuinely modern theatre practice.

It is now a commonplace of theatre history that, although Chekhov was delighted to have Stanislavski produce his plays at the Moscow Art Theatre, he felt that Stanislavski's "realist" style sometimes obscured rather than enhanced their poetic power. In a typical Stanislavski production, Chekhov's text was "enhanced" by a wealth of authentic "realistic" details of the set, of birds chirping, wood being chopped, and other "natural" noises. Trying to move beyond this, Meyerhold, as a member of the Moscow Art Theatre company, and Eisenstein, as part of the "Factory of Eccentric Actors" sought to go beyond the mere description of the pre-revolutionary bourgeois as presented in Chekhov and in Stanislavski's stagings of Chekhov, and to present instead their revolutionary material in a revolutionary form. They sought to present not small portraits of a dead or dying bourgeoisie but huge pictures of the world struggle for the revolution and the establishment of Soviet practices in Russia. In a memorable experiment Sergei Eisenstein took Sergei Tretiakov's play, *Gas*, and instead of trying to reproduce a real gasworks in a theatre, he decided to produce real theatre in a gasworks. Is it too far fetched, I wonder, to see in this experiment not so much a break with Stanislavski but rather a pushing of Stanislavski's methods to their outer and more absurd limits? Do not just have your actors absorb the atmosphere of a setting and bring it to the theatre but go to the setting and simply have the setting be itself. Instead of mere mimesis you can have "the real thing." This approach, so consistent with much nineteenth-century Russian Realist theory, was a fiasco in actual practice. The noise and heat of "the real gasworks" overwhelmed Tretiakov's text and upstaged the play. Faced with this fact, Eisenstein decided that the kind of work he wanted to do could not really be accommodated in the theatre at all and he promptly switched over to film. On film he knew he could record action in a real gasworks but could then show the film in a theatre without inconveniencing his audience with its smells and heat and din.

By abandoning the theatre for film Eisenstein enriched the film medium but did not contribute to a solution of the problem of how to deal with huge modern subjects such as technology or battles of international cartels using the limited resources of the stage. These were problems that Piscator in Germany, Hallie Flanagan in the United States and Meyerhold in Russia continued to wrestle with. Flanagan, Piscator and Meyerhold were determined to try to bring modern history in all its complexity onto the stage. With mammoth casts, lots of stage machinery and the use of projected slides or film strips, these directors attempted to do on stage the kind of thing that Eisenstein was now doing with relative ease in *The Battleship Potemkin* and *October*. But the economics of one filming of the storming of the Winter Palace which could then be shown to millions was (and is) totally different from having a convincingly large crowd of extras available in a theatre night after night. The cast on stage was as large as the paying audience in the auditorium. And the paying audiences in both Russia and Germany had precious little to pay with. Piscator's productions, for example, were an economic disaster. His four productions of the 1927–8 Berlin season brought his company close to bankruptcy. John Willett reports that each night just the dismantling of the massive set of *Cheers, We're Alive* alone cost more than had been projected for the entire cost of the whole production. It should not surprise us that Piscator eventually followed Eisenstein's lead and while he was in the Soviet Union temporarily abandoned the theatre for film.

In the face of this defection by many of his closest friends, Brecht's own persistence with the theatre is remarkable. We know that while still a teenager in Augsburg he was already smitten by the rather less than reputable cinema. When he got to Munich he worked intensively on film scripts and actually made a film with his friend, the comedian Valentin.[11] Further, when Brecht first visited Berlin he met two prominent film producers who urged him together with Arnolt Bronnen to enter a rigged film competition where Brecht and Bronnen were guaranteed the first prize of 100,000 marks. They did enter the competition and their prize-winning scenario was published in 1922. Despite the financial success of this early venture in film writing, Brecht nevertheless seemed to see better prospects for himself in the old medium of the theatre. Why? While continuing "on speculation" to churn out competent but not particularly good film scenarios (in much the way he went into writing advertisements in the same period) he nevertheless said flatly in a note written in 1922 that "the film industry thinks Kitsch tastes better than solid work."[12] And in 1926, in a note usually ignored by those seeking to tie Brecht closely and positively to the film medium,[13] Brecht wrote: "The film takes no responsibility, it doesn't need to extend itself. Dramaturgically it has remained so simple because all film is is a couple of kilometres of celluloid in a lead box. One does not expect fugues from a saw bent across someone's knee."[14] If we remember that when these words were written in 1926, film had already produced the principal works (supposedly much admired by Brecht) by Chaplin, Inge and Griffith in America, and that the "Golden Era" of the German Cinema (1919–25) was already largely over and had produced highly successful works by Murnau, Lang, Pabst, Wegener, and Wiene (most of whom were known personally to Brecht), we realize that his comment cannot have been based on ignorance of the medium. And if Brecht objected to the orientation of capitalist film (though he had not read any Marx until the end of October 1926) then he had the Soviet model to turn to with Lenin's extremely strong endorsement of the revolutionary power of the film medium, and concrete examples such as Eisenstein's *Strike* (1924) and *Potemkin* (1925), shown with shattering effect in Berlin to a score by Brecht's friend Edmund Meisel,[15] Pudovkin's *The Mechanics of the Brain* (a film on *Pavlov's Reflexology-1926*), Vertov's *A Sixth of the Earth* and Pudovkin's film version of Gorki's *Mother* (a work later adapted for the stage by Brecht in 1926). What Brecht seems to be articulating with the exaggeration, silliness, and stridency that marks so many of his critical pronouncements of the period is a rationalization of the fact that he felt drawn to the theatre rather than to film but that film was undercutting the very financial base of the theatre as many of the best directors and stars were drawn to the up-and-coming, highly popular medium. When he first visited Berlin in 1920 Brecht had made the following invidious comparison of film and theatre and had theatrically commited himself to the theatre using the royal "we":

The German drama is going right downhill, it seems, rapidly, willingly, obediently. The Berlin theatre capitalists are taking over its assets, forming the whole thing into a monopoly, the film all the time is pulling the mat from under it, has been pulling might and main for months now, disaster is sitting in the galleries, in the stalls, finally in the stage box and having a look as well. Now the rats are starting to leave the ship; Reinhardt's pulling out, Kerr [the Berlin theatre critic who generally opposed Brecht] has entrenched himself in Valhalla and reports that it's all "so beautiful." But we propose to take up our quarters in her and stand straddling the deck and see if we can't make her move ahead. Perhaps we'll drink up all the water that's leaked in through the hole in her side, perhaps we'll hang our last shirts from the yardarm to serve as a sail, and blow into it (that's your wind) and fart at it (there's your storm). And go to the bottom singing so that when the ship gets there she will have some content.[16]

Again, he wrote: "Money is being withdrawn from us [in theatre]. The film is advancing . . ."[17] The best Brecht seems to have hoped for in this phase of his work was that the blandishments of film could be resisted by theatre people and that certain elements of film could perhaps be incorporated as subsidiary elements (as Piscator and Meyerhold were doing) in theatre productions of an "epic" nature.

Significantly, on no occasion in his theoretical writings on the "epic theatre" did Brecht stop to consider seriously an idea that had long been obvious and that would even be obvious to Hitler and Leni Riefenstahl in Berlin and to Eisenstein in Moscow: that film constituted a more powerful and more cost effective medium for political education than the stage would ever be. Precisely because a film as a physical object was in fact "a few kilometres of celluloid in a lead case" it had particularly great revolutionary *and* conservative potential, as both Hitler and Lenin well understood. In its easily transportable form a silent film such as *Potemkin* or, later, a film with sound track such as Riefenstahl's *Triumph of the Will* (commissioned by Hitler) could be carried to every hamlet and could, of course, be taken around the globe and flung like a bomb into cities such as London, Paris, New York and Berlin. Feuchtwanger, in his novel *Success* (which features Brecht), notes that the film *Potemkin* had a revolutionary impact on tens of thousands of Berliners, far more than could be expected from any stage production of the same period. But stubbornly, consistently and emotionally Brecht defended the stage. The one major exception to this general practice in the pre-exile period is his film *Kuhle Wampe*, which had only limited success among its intended proletarian audience,[18] and which now seems curiously unaware of the approaching Nazi menace.

Brecht pressed on, looking for something that would enable him to bring the complex modern world into the theatre in an aesthetically, politically and economically viable form. Again and again we find him obsessed with form. Always the word "form" is linked to "the real world," the world of facts and figures and the problems of presenting them on stage. Always Brecht associates it with the word "epic". In 1929, during the economic crisis, he asked rhetorically: "What then must our great form be like? Epic. It must report. It must neither believe that one can identify (emotionally) with things in our world, nor must it even want to. The materials are enormous and terrifying and our dramaturgy must reflect this."[19] As the stock market collapsed, Brecht wrote: "The old form of drama does not permit us to present the world as we see it today. The typical fate of a person of our time cannot be presented within the framework of present day dramatic form."[20] He claimed: "The battles over wheat (the commodities exchange) etc. are not to be found on our stage."[21] What is important to note here is that though these battles were to be found on the stage (in the work of Piscator and Meyerhold) they were not to be found in a form that satisfied Brecht. So he continued his quest to bring complex modern subjects onto the stage. At one point he noted that "petroleum struggles against the five act form," and then went on: "Once we have to some extent orientated ourselves towards these materials, then we can go over to the inter-relationships of them, which today are horribly complicated and which can only be simplified through form."[22]

But what would this form be like? It is not clear that Brecht really had a positive answer. He was able to articulate that which he did not want but was far less clear about what he did want. This is reflected in his work of the mid- and even the late twenties. Project after project in this period is started and then dropped. There were no Brecht productions in 1925. He devoted more time to the study of economics than to play production as he attempted to understand how human relations are affected, indeed determined by economic forces. Gradually Brecht became convinced that the only way to really understand the complexities of the modern world and hence to provide the elusive organizational principle for his plays, was through the study of Marx. Already in December 1926 we find him "eight fathoms deep in *Das Kapital.*"[23] From then on it was the Marxist "classics" that would provide a structure for his work as a playwright/director. He now had an approach which he thought would help him find the *form* he needed to organize his dramatic raw materials. He would from now on consciously refer to Marxism as the ideology of reason and of order and capitalism as "the great disorder," the chaotic, the irrational.

But the adoption of Marxism as an organizational principle for under- standing the world did not solve the basic formal dramaturgical problem that Brecht had been wrestling with before he began intensively to study Marx and Engels in 1926. Both Meyerhold and Piscator had been deeply committed Marxists long before Brecht turned to Marx, but we know that Brecht had rejected their working method as being the ultimate form of "the bourgeois naturalist theatre." Not surprisingly then, he turned to the other main strand of revolutionary Marxist theatre, the so-called Agit-Prop Theatre, the theatre of *agit*ation and *prop*aganda. The time at which Brecht began to study Marx coincides with dramatic growth of the Agit-Prop movement in Germany. In 1927, the original "Blue Blouse" Agit-Prop group toured throughout Germany, and its basic organizational thesis (as originally published in Moscow in 1928) gives a sense of the aims and methods of such groups. The first four clauses ran as follows:

1   The "Blue Blouse" is a dramatic living newspaper that emerged from a period when newspapers were read aloud to the [largely illiterate] public.
2   The "Blue Blouse" is a form of agitation, a topical stage formed out of revolution, and is made up of a montage of political and general topics seen from the viewpoint of the class ideology of the proletariat.
3   The "Blue Blouse" is an active, lively, juicy, pointed and agile traveling theatre that can play in any place under any conditions.
4   The "Blue Blouse" is a form of club, a particular kind of amateur artistic work within a worker's club.[24]

Here, in contrast with the massive technological complexity and expense of Piscator's and Meyerhold's Marxist theatre, was an alternative form that was in many respects (but not all) more congenial to Brecht.

But the very flexibility of the "Blue Blouse" form and the totally bare simplicity of the group's playing style really swung too far away from Piscator to suit Brecht's emerging style (though he shows us such a company at work in his *Kuhle Wampe* film). Neither style was right. One was too massive and the other too spare. A further difficulty (and here the Piscator and the "Blue Blouse" styles were actually very similar) stemmed from the fact that the "author" as such had only a minor role in either style of production. As Piscator noted of his own phenomenally successful 1924 "Blue Blouse"-like production, the "Red Rumble Review," "much was raw and simply thrown together, a wholly unpretentious text."[25] For Brecht, who was simultaneously director, playwright and major poet, texts could be provisional only if *he* said they were provisional and only if *he* suggested major changes. When Brecht actually worked with Piscator in Piscator's theatre this difference emerged very clearly. Where Piscator assigned a relatively modest role to the text and hence to the role of the "author," Brecht stormed about in a rage declaring that his name was copyright and could not be taken lightly. He then left the Piscator collective when his authorial and directorial demands were not met. For all his later contemptuous declarations about bourgeois values and copyright and the heinousness of the sale of intellectual property, throughout his life Brecht maintained a double standard: he could steal from anyone but woe betide anyone who did not give him proper credit and did not pay him handsome royalties. To go a step further, it is clear that Brecht was not willing to give up his own privileged position as author and as director. All theory notwithstanding, his personality and practice inhibited collective work among equals. If he could not win others over to his point of view he usually left in a huff. His despotism was often "benevolent despotism" but there is no stage of his career where he did not insist on artistic control of the projects he was associated with.

A third strand of Marxist-oriented "theatrical" practice in Germany in the 1920s provided Brecht with a somewhat more congenial model. Throughout Germany, outside the fully professional musical world of the opera and the symphony, was a tremendous variety of musical clubs. Brecht's own father had belonged to one such club in Augsburg, but it was small compared to some of the massive amateur choirs of the major cities. Sometimes reactionary but sometimes progressive, these club choirs had considerable popular appeal. Their musical sophistication, combined with the fact that they were made up mostly of technically untrained voices, interested Brecht. As the twenties progressed he moved increasingly away from playwriting *per se* and became more and more a librettist, working with many of the major German composers of the decade. But where traditionally the librettist played a minor role compared to the composer, in Brecht's work there is always the sense that either the composer must follow the director's instructions, or Brecht would find himself another, more compliant partner.

The way Brecht worked with composers is consistent with the way he conducted all his relationships, both professional and private. To be involved with Brecht was to give up virtually all independence. By sheer force of personality and with a superb sense of theatre and of business Brecht drew people to him, used those people to the utmost and then felt free to reject them when they were no longer useful. And he did all that with such magnetic charm that scores of highly talented individuals were always ready to be a part of his circle. They knew they were being used but they stayed on anyway. His theatre is unimaginable without the sheer force of his personality. As Marieluise Fleisser, one of his lover/collaborators, said of him: "The man undermined and the man fascinated." Eventually rejected by Brecht and outraged by the horde of women around him at all times, this lover/collaborator would, like several of Brecht's friends, attempt suicide. Brecht's path would be strewn with people he fascinated and undermined and then drifted away from. Often these willing victims were women. Elisabeth Hauptmann's role as a collaborative writer in the twenties was absolutely indispensable, and long sections of Brecht plays were probably written by her.[26] Later, in exile, Margarete Steffin and Ruth Berlau made contributions to "Brecht's" major exile plays. After Brecht's return to Berlin, Hauptmann again became enormously important.[27] Each woman in each period was periodically required to adjust to Brecht's sexual and professional needs and to sometimes serve as lover as well as secretary and collaborator but to be ready to be displaced as lover (without rancor) and continue as co-worker as though nothing had changed.

Though Brecht attempted to argue theoretically for the desirability of a world of full equality, he himself never lived in such a world. The genius that had been recognized early on by Ihering was so extraordinary that he immediately dominated virtually any group no matter what his theoretical position on hierarchical structures and dominance might be. As Fleisser noted resignedly at one point in her brilliant and only slightly fictionalized memoir, "Avantgarde" (perhaps the single best piece of writing on Bertolt Brecht as a person): "His shoe size was larger than that of others, but he couldn't hack off a chunk of his own feet because of this."[28]

Innumerable other memoirs of this and later periods verify the accuracy of Fleisser's portrait of Brecht's personality. Always there is a bewildering and seemingly inconsistent mixture of reticence and arrogance, willingness to change and inability to do so, of tenderness shifting with blinding speed to brutality, of considerateness to others suddenly becoming vicious denunciation, of total sexual freedom for himself and none for his partners, of theoretical attacks on emotional dependence combined with the fact of crowds of people all being dependent upon him, a commitment to Marxism while living the life of the high bourgeoisie with a family maid, several secretaries, a large car and a country house as well as a place in the city. None of this fits together in any conventional way, and from a 1921 self-portrait we know that Brecht himself realized this. His diary entry for June 17, 1921 reads:

Eating cherries today in front of the mirror I saw my idiotic face. Those self-contained black bullets disappearing down my mouth made it look looser, more lascivious and contradictory than ever. It contains many elements of brutality, calm, slackness, boldness and cowardice, but as elements only, and it is more changeable and characterless than a landscape beneath scurrying clouds. That's why so many people find it impossible to retain.[29]

To accurately reflect Brecht's work as a director, we need to resist the temptation to choose between these various Brechts. To emphasize either coolness or intensity in his work is to wholly miss the point: he was both these things at all times. As Fleisser put it "the man is pure dynamite." So were his stage productions.

From 1924 to 1933 the techniques that have become fixed in public consciousness as "epic" or "Brechtian" were developed. The period was particularly complicated as Brecht, starting from an apolitical position very close to that of the Dadaists, moved to an explicitly pro-communist position. Brecht's stridency in support of communism grew steadily as the anti-communist forces of Hitler and of the old Prussian military caste increased in strength. It is worth remembering that many of the slogans that Brecht used in the heat of political battle in the late twenties and early thirties were responses to a specific set of extremely dire political circumstances, and not slogans that would work just as well in other very different political circumstances such as, to cite one example, the socialist section of Berlin in the very early 1950s. In Berlin in the earlier period the slogans needed to be starkly contrasted with Nazi propaganda. We must be wary of taking Brecht's statements out of their original historical context and at their apparent face value. For instance, let us look closely at his call for coolness and distance. If we take his intention to oppose Hitler's hysterical emotionalism with cool, distant, non-emotional argument too literally, we will miss the fact that Brecht was himself involved very deeply in the emotional fervor of opposition to Hitler. The fire of Hitler was being fought with the fire of deeply committed communism and Brecht very consciously fed the communist fire. In this connection it is important to note the enormous role played by music in the period 1924–33. Are we to believe that the Brecht who mesmerized Munich and Berlin with his singing would not use the power of music to help win adherents to his newly found political position?

Where Brecht in Munich had written his own music for his plays, after his move to Berlin the music of composers such as Kurt Weill, Paul Hindemith, and Hanns Eisler became a tremendously strong force. Beginning roughly with *A Man's a Man* in 1924–6, with original music by Edmund Meisel (who, as noted above, had written the score for Eisenstein's *Potemkin*) and a later score (since lost) by Kurt Weill, virtually everything had a strong musical component. And though productions of Brecht's earlier plays continued in Germany through the late twenties and early thirties, virtually all of Brecht's new plays are dependent on music. *The Little Mahagonny* (1927), *The Threepenny Opera* (1928), *Happy End* (1929), *Rise and Fall of the City of Mahagonny* (1930), *He Who Says Yes* and *He Who Says No* (1930), *The Measures Taken* (1930), and *Mother* (1930–1) were all produced as musical performances rather than simply as plays. And the theoretical writings of this period were overwhelmingly commentaries on practical work not so much with plays as with operas. Yet here again these commentaries were still often cited as though they applied as readily to plays as they do to operas (they do not) and to different sets of political circumstances (they do not). As Berlin danced with death in this period, much of the music for the dance was provided by Brecht's collaborators. Many of the songs to which Berliners tapped their feet were issued under Brecht's name (even if sometimes written by Elisabeth Hauptmann).

It is worth dwelling for a moment on the phenomenon of foot-tapping to "Brecht's" songs. In 1982 I attended a conference of the International Brecht Society and when I gave a talk on the mesmeric quality of Brecht's music, my talk was greeted with barely polite scepticism. Immediately afterwards a wonderful videotape production of *The Ocean Flight* (with Weill's music) was played for the scholarly audience. As I glanced around the auditorium I saw every foot, quite unconsciously, moving to the Brecht/Weill rhythm. If an audience of contemporary Brecht experts fully cognizant of the anti-emotional Brecht directives of the twenties, and at a comfortable distance from the political imperatives of Berlin at that time should react this way, what hope was there, might we wonder, for the politically engaged audiences of the 1920s to remain unmoved by the rhythms of the seductive Weill and Eisler, authors of innumerable marches and songs of exhortation? In fact, as the political struggle intensified, it is clear from examination of the scores written in close cooperation with Brecht in the pre-1933 years, that the most intense involvement by audiences was explicitly called for. To look at Brecht's theoretical pronouncements in isolation from the facts of performance is to misread him. Such misreadings are the rule rather than the exception in much contemporary Brecht criticism. But if we go back to the Brecht productions of the pre-exile period, we can see that a fully engaged and/or enraged audience rather than a "distanced" audience was a standard phenomenon. If there was one thing Brecht's audiences were not, it was cool and rational. They were raucous and passionately committed either for or against all that Brecht represented.

As we survey the developments in the Brechtian theatre and look at the historical context of these developments, it is necessary to take literally Brecht's own descriptive term for his work of the period 1924–33. He described all his work as *Versuche*, or as a series of highly provisional "experiments." After the meticulous preparation of *Edward II* in Munich, I know of virtually no other occasion until Brecht and Weigel established the Berlin Ensemble in postwar Berlin, that Brecht had an opportunity to produce a play slowly and carefully. In the period of 1924 to 1933 all of Brecht's productions (with the single exception of the long run of *The Threepenny Opera*) had extremely short runs, were produced in haste, and with Brecht often sharing directional responsibility with at least one other person. Overwhelmingly, whether Brecht directed one of his plays himself or whether they were directed by others, most of the productions had only very short, very noisy, very acrimonious runs. Either revivals of the early plays with their brutality of language and action, and extraordinary explicit sexuality so scandalized the authorities that the plays were taken off almost at once, or the later explicitly communist plays were such a provocation to the radical right that the conservative regimes in both large and small cities hastened to close the productions down in the interest of public safety. As early as May 1923, the world premiere of *In the Jungle of the Cities* with its brutal homo-erotic plot set in a mythical Chicago, directed by Erich Engel in Munich, had led to the firing of the theatre's dramaturg Jacob Geis, who had recommended the play, and to the closing of the show after only six performances. The Leipzig *Baal* had an even shorter run and the Munich *Edward II* also ran only briefly.[30] *In the Jungle of the Cities*, under the title *Jungle: The Downfall of a Family*, had had a brief Berlin run under Engel's direction in October 1924. This would be the dominant pattern throughout the twenties and early thirties. But although they ran only briefly, the staging techniques developed in these productions had an impact that is still felt, and even though Brecht did not always direct them himself, they established the characteristics of that which would become widely thought of as the Brechtian style.

The first of these brief but important productions that show the development of a Brechtian style of directing was a single matinée performance of *Baal*, co-directed by Brecht and the actor Oskar Homolka, that was staged on February 14 (a Sunday), 1926 (fig. 9). The impact of this production seems out of proportion to the brevity of its run. This experimental or "showcase" production could only be done at all if enough actors volunteered their services for a single Sunday performance. As the actors who volunteered were some of the leading lights of the Berlin theatre, it is important to note that after they had been exposed to the full force of Brecht's charismatic personality they were likely to carry his working methods back with them to their regular engagements in Berlin theatres. And Brecht's own genius for publicity was such that his premieres were guaranteed to produce uproar. The "moral majority" would be deliberately goaded to fury and this would trigger a counter-response from Brecht's ever-growing band of admirers who saw him as the apostle of a new and liberated theatre. The mixture was always explosive as it crammed into a small space all of the violent (fig. 10) counter-forces of the Weimar Republic itself. This particular Sunday afternoon performance in Berlin of *Baal* is described by the playwright Hanns Henny Jahn, who came to Berlin from the "province" of Hamburg at Brecht's personal invitation:

As I asked at the box office for my reserved ticket, I was verbally attacked in a very inappropriate way, by a man who stood there. It was the theatre manager. After I had timidly explained who I was, and where I had come from, he had a chair carried for me and placed in the already over-filled theatre. The performance began very late. The theatre

Fig. 9. Oskar Homolka as Baal and Gerda Müller as Sophie in *Baal*. Directed by Brecht and Homolka. Single matinée performance of "The Young Stage" at the German Theatre, Berlin 14 February 1926.

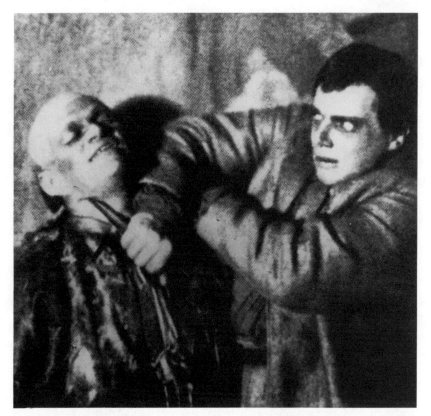

Fig 10. Here Franck as Garga starts to cut Shlink's (played by Kortner) throat. *Jungle*, Berlin 1924.

was charged with tension and impatience in a poisonous combination. It was hot. It was eerie. At some point, I believe it was after Orge's song: "The loveliest place on earth for him was not the grassy bank at his parents' grave [but the toilet]," an uproar erupted. Baal had left the stage, only the bar singer remained. People whistled, yelled, howled, and applauded. The actress playing the singer jumped onto the piano and sat on top playing the piano with her feet while singing "Allons, enfants de la patrie!" The noise became monstrous. I expected that the audience might panic. After all I was from the provinces, was not familiar with Berlin premieres and there I sat in the aisle on a movable chair. But it didn't get worse, just the same deafening noise which was kept up until the people who had started it were exhausted. Suddenly, there was complete silence, and in that silence one heard from one of the balconies: "You aren't really a supporter, you're just acting like one . . .". There followed the sound of a smack on the ear. Real applause began, got louder, and the play could go on.[31]

In this audience sat the critics Herbert Ihering and his conservative opponent, Alfred Kerr. According to Ihering, Kerr actually egged-on Brecht's opponents in the theatre. But in Kerr's review, though he felt that the play had really nothing to say, he noted one new development in the staging: Brecht's use of a compère or announcer in a dinner jacket who announced directly to the audience what would be presented in the following scene. In Ihering's review (after he denounced Kerr for unprofessional behavior at the premiere) he summed up the experimental production with its borrowed actors as follows: "In the main the production was excellent. In front of Caspar Neher's simple sets the actors played in a factual way. What was lacking was a pulling of things together, a tightening up through proper pacing and cuts in the text: Is this because of the difficulties inherent in such an experimental production, where a regular series of rehearsals were not possible?"[32] With critical opinion radically divided, discussion of the production was guaranteed even though it had only played for the one afternoon. Discussion was what Brecht was after. He wanted people to talk about him. He clearly understood that there was no such thing as bad publicity only good publicity. He had a gift of turning what many people would have seen as a failure (the fact that the production was not picked up by a major stage for a regular run) into success. As early as 1923 Bronnen had noted: "Brecht despite his defeats remained victorious; Bronnen, despite victories, failed."[33] For Brecht it was a badge of honor to be denounced by the conservative Kerr. Brecht would simply announce with utter conviction that he was the future and that Kerr and Kerr's kind of theatre was long since dead. The battle was for nothing less than the control of Berlin's theatres; and it would not be finally resolved until Hitler's power as German Chancellor was confirmed and he could use the forces of the German state legally to drive Brecht and all that he represented from the theatres of the expanding Reich.

In the same year as the Berlin *Baal* (1926), Jacob Geis, the same Geis who had been fired in Munich for promoting Brecht's *In the Jungle of the Cities*, staged *A Man's A Man* (a "Brecht" play written as was everything in this period, in close cooperation with Elisabeth Hauptmann) in Darmstadt. The production is notable in that this is the first known use of the nine-foot-high curtain (fig. 11) that has become a cliché of Brechtian theatre.

Early in 1927 began the active collaboration between the avant-garde composer, Kurt Weill and Bertolt Brecht. As Weill remembers the beginning of this working relationship, he had heard a production of Brecht's *A Man's a Man* over the radio and after writing a very favorable review of it he approached Brecht about using some poems for a work that he was preparing for a festival of modern music in July 1927. Brecht agreed to work with Weill and a number of poems were used from "Brecht's" (several of the items were actually written by Elizabeth Hauptmann) *Hauspostille* or *Domestic Breviary*, many of which were explicitly sexual and/or scatological, printed and bound like biblical homilies of the period. The collaborative work based on the *Domestic Breviary* was to be named *The Little Mahagonny*. The German title picks up the English word "song" as the existing German word *Lied* seemed too classical and in contrast the word "song" (always pronounced "zonk" in proper Brecht circles)[34] had an exotic and popular appeal in Germany in 1927, where American popular music forms were all the rage.

The fact that *The Little Mahagonny* was designed for performance at an avant-garde music festival had a great deal of influence on the form of the production.[35] As a curtain was not used for musical productions at the festival, the Brecht–Weill Songspiel was designed to be presented without one. Neher, whose name was now virtually synonymous with a Brecht production, prepared a series of sketches of violence and various kinds of greed (fig. 12) to be projected for the audience. A startling innovation, based on Brecht's fascination with boxing and metaphors of fighting, was the use of a small boxing ring as a platform for the singers of the "Zonks." One of the key singers was Lotte Lenya, whose hoarse inflections, limited vocal range, and barbarous English accent for the English-language "Alabama Song," were all pluses as far as Brecht was concerned. Brecht's idea of having the

Fig. 11. Ernst Legal as Galy Gay in *A Man's A Man*. Directed by Jacob Geis. Sets by Neher. Landestheater, Darmstadt, September 25, 1926. Note use of the famous half curtain here.

women do their songs naked did not appeal to Lenya's husband (Weill) or the festival authorities. Nevertheless, she did her solo from the middle of the boxing ring "in a hoarse voice with lascivious inflections".³⁶ The audience rose to its feet before the completion of the final number and booed and cheered and stomped and whistled. The singers, prepared for such reactions, pulled whistles out of their pockets and blew them at the audience. Brecht also had a whistle and blew it with authority. Lenya even waved a prepared placard saying she was all "für Weill." The audience reaction had been divided and the performers left the concert hall not really knowing whether the work had been a success. Later, in the hotel bar, the Berlin conductor Otto Klemperer slapped Lenya on the back and with a booming laugh quoted the pidgin English of the Benares song: "Is here no telephone?" At that, everyone in the bar sang the song. The new Weill–Brecht sound, with its mixture of popular with avant-garde form, had won over the toughest of audiences. The way was prepared for what would become Brecht and Weill's one popular success before 1933, the now legendary *The Threepenny Opera*. For Weill *Mahagonny* marked the beginning of compositions that would be whistled by popular audiences. For Brecht, on the surface, his working closely with an avant-garde composer like Weill looked like a most improbable way for him to reach out to the kind of proletarian audience that his increasingly Marxist theoretical pronouncements seemed to demand.

After the Baden-Baden festival, Brecht returned to Berlin to try to put into form some materials that he had promised to Piscator. This work, never to be completed, was *Joe Fleischhacker* (*Joe Meatchopper*), and was supposed to embody in play form much of Brecht's epic theatre theory with its now ever more Marxist orientation. While *Joe Meatchopper* occupied most of his serious attention, on the side, as it were, Brecht began to do some casual work with Elisabeth Hauptmann on her translation of John Gay's eighteenth-century parody of Italian opera, *The Beggar's Opera*. The Hauptmann work was called *Riff-Raff* (*Gesindel*). In the spring of 1928, having unsuccessfully scoured the usual theatrical agencies for a suitable play with which to open the Theater am Schiffbauerdamm, the producer Ernst Josef Aufricht went to an artist's café and casually asked Brecht if he might not have something suitable. Brecht mentioned his major project, *Joe Meatchopper*, but indicated it was nowhere near finished and anyway was promised for Piscator's theatre. Only when Aufricht got up to leave the café and asked for his check did Brecht mention that he did have a few scenes from *Riff-Raff* on the side. According to Aufricht, he could tell from Brecht's brief description of these scenes that the material "smelled of theatre."³⁷ Brecht promised to let him see the *Riff-Raff* material the next day. Only after Aufricht had accepted the play did he mention that the composer for the piece was Kurt Weill. For Aufricht,

Fig. 12. Neher's sketch of the whores for the 1927 Baden-Baden production of *The Little Mahagonny*.

who associated Weill with highly unpopular avant-garde music (apparently not knowing his semi-popular *Mahagonny Songspiel* score), Weill was a serious handicap. As insurance, therefore, Aufricht engaged a certain Theo Mackeben to work up the original *Beggar's Opera* music by Pepusch if, as expected, Weill's music was to be too high-brow to be used. Regardless of which score was chosen, Mackeben was put in charge of rehearsing the musical components of the production. Brecht, together with Erich Engel (a very responsible director and an old friend), were named to direct the production. Sets were to be designed by Caspar Neher. At the first run-through of parts of the Weill score, Aufricht finally became convinced that Weill's music was right for the production. Somewhere in this period, Brecht and Weill established the contractual terms for division of the royalties on the show that was now renamed (at Lion Feuchtwanger's suggestion) *The Threepenny Opera*. On the one hand, when *The Threepenny Opera* was first performed and Brecht's old enemy Alfred Kerr had attacked him for plagiarism (the unacknowleged use, supposedly, of a certain Klammer's translation of Villon), Brecht had defended himself by saying that the whole bourgeois notion "intellectual property" was an anathema to him, while on the other hand Brecht was making absolutely sure that his "rights to the intellectual property" (the phrase is actually used in the original contract as signed by Brecht) of *The Threepenny Opera* were secured in a way so secure that it ensured they could never be successfully challenged by Weill or anyone else. For Weill, at that time, the contract was one he felt he had to sign. According to Lotte Lenya, Brecht took Weill into a Berlin park, sat him down on a bench and made him an offer he could not refuse.[38] At that moment in 1928, Weill was the unknown and Brecht the at least semi-popular figure and so the royalty division was set to reflect that. The terms established in the park, and only slightly adjusted later when Kerr discovered that Brecht had plagiarized Klammer's German translation of Villon were: Brecht $62\frac{1}{2}$%, Weill 25% and Hauptmann $12\frac{1}{2}$%. Klammer was later given the odd $2\frac{1}{2}$% from Brecht's share.[39] These contractual figures, which remained the same during Weill's lifetime, would prove to be a source of extraordinary private bitterness for the composer and his wife,[40] and later when Brecht returned to Germany from exile, the fact that Brecht then single-handedly took over the personal management and distribution of *The Threepenny Opera* without bothering to consult Weill was an act of gross personal and business impropriety for which they never forgave him.[41]

But the hundreds of thousands of dollars involved for the Brecht and Weill heirs[42] as a result of the original "contract in the park" would surely have been very difficult to foresee in 1928. All Brecht was doing then was setting up his usual very "sharp" business contract that guaranteed, if there was money to be made, he and later his heirs would get most of it. But in the summer of 1928 the odds given in Berlin's theatre district were that the production would fail miserably. Rehearsals bordered on chaos. The text never seemed to get completely finished. The cast changed from day to day. Rosa Valetti, engaged to play Mrs Peachum, declared that what she had seen of the play was "lousy." So sure was she of its failure that she signed a new contract with "The Comic's Cabaret" to appear there the day after *The Threepenny Opera* opening as she felt the play would open and close on the same day. Carola Neher, originally engaged to play Polly, left for Switzerland to be at the bedside of her dying husband. When she finally returned from Switzerland to take up her role and found the part was now rather small, she threw her script on the ground at Aufricht's feet and walked out yelling "you play this thing alone!"[43] She was replaced, four days before the premiere, by the very competent Roma Bahn. Harald Paulsen, known in Berlin for his work in operettas, was dissatisfied with his part of Macheath and insisted on wearing a sky-blue cravat. Lenya was busy expanding her own part in cahoots with Weill. Weigel intended to play the madam of the Turnbridge brothel as a woman with no legs. When she came down with a threatened appendicitis, the show was rewritten and her part was cut. Meanwhile, the director on record, Engel, and his *de facto* co-director Brecht totally disagreed on the presentation of the music. Brecht "wanted to introduce a stage effect to distinguish between the action and the songs: when the songs started the author had the stage darkened, with old-fashioned oil lamps hanging from above, while a dummy organ, in front of which the musicians sat, was visible in the background."[44] Rather than agreeing to this, Engel wanted to give up the music altogether. After a shouting match Brecht and his supporters prevailed and the music was presented in the way he wanted. At the dress rehearsal, however, in the early hours of the morning, Brecht insisted on cutting out the Solomon "zonk" and shortening Peachum's and the Beggar King's part. The actor playing Peachum, Erich Ponto, threatened to walk out. Paulsen, in his sky-blue cravat, was now to be introduced by Kurt Gerron as the ballad singer singing the specially written ballad of "Mack the Knife" with its lugubrious but haunting echoes of the one-legged singer at the Augsburg fairs of Brecht's youth.[45] When the time came to work the machinery for the entrance of the messenger on the wooden horse who announces Macheath's reprieve from the gallows, nothing happened. "No horse, no play" said Brecht, but he was overruled by Aufricht. Aufricht wanted the final chorus to be scratched as he felt it sounded too much "like Bach." Caspar Neher told Weill that unless he overruled Aufricht and kept this final chorus it would be all over between him and Weill. The chorus was kept. Chaos reigned right up until curtain time. In later years, Brecht's associate Hans Bunge would say of Brecht's rehearsals: "he created chaos, according to plan."[46] I feel that this could already be said of the 1923 Leipzig *Baal*, the 1924 Munich *Edward II* and of the 1928 *The Threepenny Opera*. But in one way this production of *The Threepenny Opera* was useful as the one communally directed play in Brecht's career. Out of the loud, brilliant, and contradictory suggestions of a large number of highly talented individuals came a production now as famous as any in the history of the theatre.

When the curtain parted the Theater am Schiffbauerdamm (fig. 13), through a misunderstanding at the box office, the rivals Ihering and Kerr were seated side by side, an error guaranteed to torment both. On stage a number of actors stood around the hand organ player, the actor Kurt Gerron. When Gerron turned the handle of the organ and began to sing the *Moritat* of "Mack the Knife," not a sound came out of the instrument. Only with the second strophe did the alert orchestra jump in to accompany the singer. All the way up to the wedding scene the audience was frozen: no laughter, no applause. "Suddenly," writes Aufricht, "as the men on stage had finished singing the 'Cannon Song,' the breakthrough came. The audience did not slowly thaw but boiled over. Clapping, yelling, stomping, they demanded an

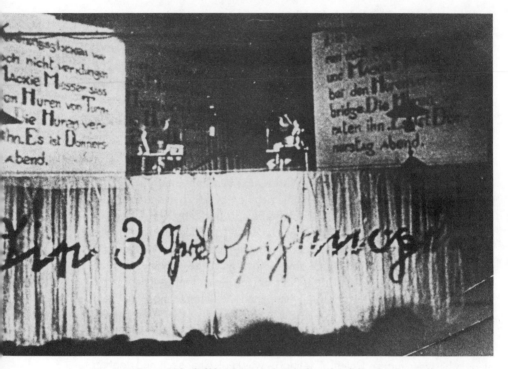

Fig. 13. The half-height curtain with the title of the play scrawled across it by Neher in the original production of *The Threepenny Opera* at the Am Schiffbauerdamm Theatre, Berlin, August 31, 1928. Director of record: Engel. Sets by Neher.

encore . . . From this moment on every sentence and every note was a success."[47] The audience left the theatre singing and whistling tunes such as the "Cannon Song" and, most famous of all, the *Moritat* of "Mack the Knife." The Berlin newspaper *BZ am Mittag* predicted an unprecedented run of five hundred performances. The prediction was accurate. Overnight, the contract signed by Brecht and Weill became worth a fortune. Count Kessler, the ever-alert and usually accurate observer of new social phenomena in Berlin noted in his diary: "A fascinating production, with rudimentary staging in the Piscator manner and proletarian emphasis (Apache style). Weill's music is catchy and expressive and the players (Harald Paulsen, Rosa Valetti, and so on) are excellent. It is the show of the season, always sold out: 'You must see it.'"[48] And everyone did see it. From the first tune, "Mack the Knife", to the finale that virtually begs an audience to join in, every tune was singable and danceable as the music moved from shimmy, to tango, to foxtrot, to music-box waltz, to jazz, and was heard in all the bars and dance halls first in

Germany and then abroad. The names of Weill and Brecht were spoken everywhere but that of Elisabeth Hauptmann hardly at all.

Though Brecht would later try very hard to rework *The Threepenny Opera* to bring out a clear social message in the text, the original (now classic) text is virtually as anarchistic as earlier plays like *Baal* and *Drums in the Night*. This anarchy, allied with the enthusiastic macho-racism of the "Cannon Song" (the song that thawed out the frozen Berlin audience at the first night), had enormous appeal in Germany in 1928. And of course, there was the villain-hero, Mack the Knife himself with his "accomplishments" as set forth in his opening *Moritat*: The deaths of those found along the Thames are not caused by plague or cholera but by Macheath, it is Mackie (of the endearing diminutive form) whose violence towards women (so characteristic of Brecht's early plays) is stated clearly (but engagingly) as "Jennie Towler is found with a knife in her breast," and then there are the "seven children and an old man" who die violently in a Soho fire set by Macheath, and in the last verse, a young widow who wakes only to be raped by Macheath. As the song ends the assembled whores laugh, Paulsen, in his elegant clothes, crosses the stage and Lenya speaks in her whisky stage whisper: "That was Mack the Knife." This was the song Berlin sang as it lurched towards the abyss. How alert, thinking, intellectual were those people who in the dance halls in 1928 sang and whistled cheery songs of genocide, rape, looting, burning, murder, robbery and of last minute reprieves from death for the perpetrator (figs. 14 and 15)? Might Berlin have rejoiced in fact to discover that the words for many of the proto-fascist songs in the play were supplied by Herrn Oberstleutnant a.D. (retired) Karl Klammer whose explicit anti-semitism was well known and deeply appreciated in his aristocratic Viennese circle of ex-army officers? How much ironic distance was there between the real Berlin and the extravagantly make-believe opera? It is one thing to create a theoretical construct called "epic theatre," with the deliberate separation of music, text and sets, but it is quite another thing to postulate that by separating things on the stage you thus ensure that these elements remain somehow separate in the mind of the spectator. What if then or now the feet still tap, and the lips still move, and where does the theory go? In my own view, *The Threepenny Opera* is indeed a dubious myth with proto-fascist and vaguely proto-socialist elements, and a large dose of very elementary and very effective fairy-tale elements promising escape when "the black ship" enters the harbor to save Jenny and her Berlin. The text with its music, despite Brecht's staging, is so engaging that it ensures identification and escape for its audience. The "minimal image," to use Gombrich's term, is so strongly there, in the music and in the text, that Brecht's staging is powerless to raise it above the identification threshold. *The Threepenny Opera* has such electricity that it arcs across the gaps of staging and fuses these "parts" in performance.[49] What Herbert Ihering wrote of the language of the earlier plays is just as true of *The Threepenny Opera*. When Brecht's words were accompanied by music, as noted by Ihering in 1922, Brecht's spectators were "lashed to fury" by "whipping rhythms." "In his nerves and in his blood," Ihering had said then, "Brecht is saturated with the horror of our time." Brecht himself, writing in 1922, describes his use of language in the early plays: "I mixed and put together words like strong drinks, whole scenes in words of specific texture and color such as would appeal to the senses. Cherrystone, revolver, trouser-pocket, paper-god — mixtures of that sort."[50]

The enormous financial success of *The Threepenny Opera* enabled Brecht thenceforth to only work on projects that really interested him. Until his exile in 1933, his main concern was for his "didactic" works. From 1929 as

Fig. 14. Ernst Busch plays the part of the *Moritat* singer in the 1931 film version of *The Threepenny Opera*. The singer tells the tale of Macheath's gruesome deeds. Again the influence of the singer at the Augsburg fair is very obvious.

Fig. 15. The hanging of Mack the Knife just before he is reprieved by the Queen's mounted messenger in *The Threepenny Opera*.

Germany's financial and political stability became ever shakier, and the Nazis began to appeal to even wider sections of the German population, Brecht sought to have his art serve the purpose of the communists who were, in his view, the main force capable of stopping Hitler's advance. But in the midst of his didactic/political work, at Aufricht's urging, Brecht attempted with Weill to repeat the winning formula of *The Threepenny Opera* with a play called *Happy End*. When the play failed (largely because of Brecht's very half-hearted efforts on its behalf), he disowned it and insisted that the play be attributed to Elisabeth Hauptmann[51] without, however, Brecht giving up his share of the royalties. Aufricht was so furious about Brecht's behavior that he had nothing to do with Brecht for the next two years.

In his personal life Brecht's activities of the same period led to tremendous unhappiness for several of his closest personal associates. Simultaneously conducting, as usual, a number of love affairs, Brecht arranged a discount system with his tailor who provided the prescribed costume for his women. Those having an affair with Brecht were required to wear a close-fitting woolen coat that reached almost to the ankles. The coat was never to be buttoned, but was to be held closed with one's elbow across the stomach. Thus all of Brecht's mistresses were highly visible to one another and to every one else in Berlin. In April 1929 Brecht suddenly married Helene Weigel but on the same day attended a rendezvous with Carola Neher at a Berlin train station. He handed Neher a bouquet (was it the wedding bouquet being recycled?) and announced of the marriage: "It couldn't be avoided, but it doesn't mean anything." Neher threw away the bouquet. For Elisabeth Hauptmann the shock of the marriage was so great that she attempted suicide. For Marieluise Fleisser the shock was almost equally severe. She persisted, however, in continuing at least to work with Brecht on the staging of her play *The Army Engineers of Ingolstadt*. Brecht's staging of the play was so explicit sexually and shocking, however, that newspapers throughout Germany attacked Fleisser for her indelicacy as a woman in writing it. She was so crushed by the criticism that she shut herself away for a period seeing no one, not even Brecht. Brecht seems to have taken this personally. One day he telephoned her, "in a voice thin like a whip," to say that her mail was piling up at his apartment (though married he continued to live separately from Weigel). When Fleisser went to get the mail from Brecht and read the filth that was written about her in the letters, Brecht remained silent, "his eyes full with a satanic gleam." In her lightly disguised memoire written in the third person, she remembers:

His look was a knife, it killed something inside her at this critical moment. Precisely from him could she receive such a wound. She had so much at that moment, through him also, as without him it would never have happened. She came to this position as a virgin gets a child. She had given something, something a person does not give lightly, she had imagined something, and now must feel the shame. She could at least expect a word if only one, she could expect that it was not a robot that stood there used to coldness of the emotions. He did not speak and she left "and in her anger she cut into her own flesh."[52]

She, like Hauptmann, would survive, but unlike Hauptmann it took many years before she could face Brecht again. The pain of the relationship still had not faded when I spoke with Fleisser in November 1973 in Berlin.

Very shortly after Brecht's marriage to Weigel, Berlin lurched appreciably closer to the abyss and Brecht was there to observe it. The economist Fritz Sternberg, who was close to Brecht in this period, remembers Brecht coming to see him on May Day 1929. From the window of Sternberg's third-floor apartment overlooking the German Communist Party headquarters in the Karl-Liebknecht Building, they watched with horror the confrontation between Communist demonstrators and the Berlin police during an illegal demonstration. Sternberg recalls:

As far as we could tell the people [the demonstrators] were unarmed. The police shot repeatedly. At first we believed that these were simply warning shots. Then we saw demonstrators collapse and saw them carried away later on stretchers. As I recall, there were more than twenty deaths among the demonstrators in Berlin. As Brecht heard the shots and saw that people were hit, he got whiter in the face than I had ever seen him before in my life. I believe it was this experience among others that drove him ever more strongly towards the Communists.[53]

As Sternberg noted later with disgust, the antithetical positions of the Communist Party and the very strong Social Democratic Party forced a person to make a choice, since the two parties were not working together yet to oppose the Nazis. Their energies were largely spent in fighting one another. When Brecht observed the hundreds of thousands who turned out for the one rally jointly planned by the Social Democrats with an invited speaker from the Communist Party, he spoke to Sternberg of the need for the two parties to work together. Sternberg replied that he did not feel that the Communist Party would participate in any alliance unless they could control and direct it.[54] Forced therefore to choose, Brecht chose to support the German Communist Party even though he never joined it and thus retained his right as an individual to reject party discipline. In politics, as in his professional and personal life, he wanted plenty of room for his own tastes and idiosyncrasies. This would now be clear in all the works staged before he went into exile in early 1933.

Undeterred by the faint-hearted moments of valued collaborators who for some reason failed to understand Brecht's very Macheath like approach to "love," Brecht went back to work and soon Elisabeth Hauptmann went back to work with him, as did Carola Neher. Never willing to apologize, Brecht nevertheless required forgiveness and, astonishingly often, he was forgiven. Years later Weigel is reputed to have said of Brecht: "He was always loyal. The trouble was that he was always loyal to so many at once!" And in turn, Weigel was loyal to Brecht. She fed and comforted Brecht's lovers who would visit her and Brecht's first wife, the opera singer Marianne Zoff. And Brecht himself would drop in on Weigel or Zoff or other lovers quite unannounced, often simply to be fed. He required the food he had known in Augsburg and to help ensure that he got just that, he brought his father's maid, Marie Hold, to Berlin to keep house. With ample money from his book contracts and from *The Threepenny Opera*, with his semi-punk, semi-proletarian clothes hand-made by the same tailor (originally from Augsburg) who made his mistress's coats, Brecht drove around Berlin in his large car, with rounds of visits to former mistresses almost as regular as Macheath's schedule at Turnbridge. If Berlin in 1929 was in desperate straits as the death of the stabilizing statesman Stresemann and the Stock Market crash combined to provide fuel for resurgent nationalism, and civil war continued between the Communist Party and the Social Democrats, Brecht personally was at the height of his wealth and fame, and could afford to pick and choose the projects he wanted to work on. Life in 1929 in Berlin was quite *gemütlich* for Bert Brecht.

In the summer of 1929, Brecht returned to the musical festival at Baden-Baden (where he and Weill had succeeded so well with the *Mahagonny Songspiel*) with several new musical pieces in the new "didactic" mode. These were: *The Berlin Requiem* (for radio, in collaboration with Kurt Weill); *Lindbergh's Flight* (collaborators: Weill, Hindemith and Hauptmann); and the *Baden-Baden Cantata of Acquiescence* (in collaboration with Hauptmann, Hindemith and Slatan Dudow). None of these works was a traditional "play" as such. None was designed for performance in a regular theatre with a standard proscenium arch. The very shape of the didactic works of this period was, as Klaus Völker has pointed out, determined by the use of music.[55] *The Berlin Requiem* is simply a loose series of poems (mainly on the theme of death) set to suitably sombre music by Kurt Weill. *Lindbergh's Flight* consists of some seventeen sections of "Brecht's" irregular and unrhymed verse, with most of the sections set to music by Weill but with four sections composed by Paul Hindemith. The score calls for a tenor (Lindbergh), for bass and baritone solos, and for a mixed choir (figs. 16 and 17). Designed either for concert platform performance or for radio transmission, the text was to provide (according to Brecht) self-instruction for the singers. The whole plot is described by John Willett in four sentences: "A flier (Lindbergh) describes his preparations for his solo flight of 1927 across the Atlantic. His enemies – Fog, Snowstorm, Sleep – express their determination to beat him; ships at sea and both continents make reports: all through the mouth of the chorus. Against this he repeats his aim (to overcome the primitive) and also his fears. He lands, and the work ends in praise of man's achievement of flying."[56] Ideally, the audience (if any) should have the score and should (as the background projection instructs) "loudly sing along." The third piece is similar in form, tone and function: *Baden-Baden Cantata of Acquiescence*. When it opens on a concert platform, strewn perhaps with pieces of a wrecked aeroplane, we find four airmen who have crashed and are in deadly danger. The chorus is asked, should one help? The unequivocal answer is No! Power matters most in a world scheme dictated to by powerful interests. The pilot opposes this point of view and is sent off the platform in disgrace. The chorus tells the remaining fliers to organize to change the world while they themselves renounce the world. In the actual performance (conducted by Hindemith but with Brecht himself on the concert platform), the scene with three clowns described in chapter 2 above was added. As noted earlier, when the wooden limbs of the clown were sawn off, several people in the audience are reported to have fainted (see fig. 7). When scenes of dead bodies were projected on a screen

Fig. 16. The modernistic setting for the July 28, 1929 premiere at the Baden-Baden Music Festival of *The Flight Over the Ocean*.

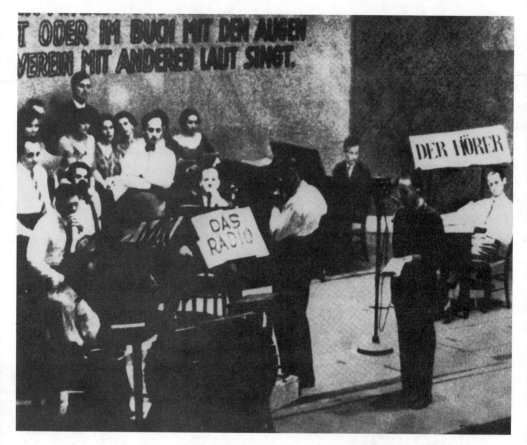

Fig. 17. *The Flight Over the Ocean* (originally called *Lindbergh's Flight*) as produced by Brecht at the Baden-Baden festival in July 1929. In the photograph Brecht himself can be clearly seen standing, book in hand, under the sign *Der Hörer*. A large sign behind the cast urges spectators to follow the text in their programs and to sing along loudly.

and the audience made complaining noises, Brecht personally and very loudly instructed the announcer to tell the projectionist: "Repeat showing of the ill-received portrayal of death."[57] This was too much for Gerhart Hauptmann, dean of German playwrights, who stormed out of the festival hall. Finally the anger of the audience and of Hindemith, who felt that he had been misused by Brecht, led to the permanent closing down of the Baden-Baden festival as a whole. Part of the festival would move the next year to Berlin but "the program committee," all too conscious of the rise in strength of the radical right and fearing Nazi attacks, would in future scrutinize warily anything connected with Brecht. And Brecht, more and more deeply committed to his own concept of Marxist didacticism, would respond the next year with an even more explicitly political work.

Brecht's first production in 1930 was another didactic work, *The Yes Sayer*, revised because of adverse comments in 1929 from students about *The No Sayer*. Produced in a progressive school in Berlin, these pieces were very similar in form, tone, and didactic purpose to the 1929 Baden-Baden works. The one major contrast was that where all conclusions were specifically spelled out in Baden-Baden, in Berlin Brecht was willing to accept two different endings. As with all "Brecht's" work in this period it is difficult to overestimate Elisabeth Hauptmann's role. In a Berlin interview with me in 1972, she stated flatly that she had written 80% of *The Yes Sayer*. At the same interview she told me that she had written a substantial portion of *The Measures Taken* and that when she prepared the text, as usual, for publication (Brecht did not usually bother with such mundane details) she had simply forgotten to list her own name on the title page. A standing joke circulated in Berlin in the late twenties ran: "Who is the play by?" "Brecht." "Then, who is the play by?" Had the question been honestly answered, in many instances the answer would have been: by Hauptmann. I am convinced that there is no major text of the period 1924–33 that does not contain considerable parts written by Hauptmann.

The only stage production done by Brecht in 1930 after his completion of *The Yes Sayer/No Sayer* was a concert platform version, with a massed choir of several hundred voices, of *The Measures Taken* (fig. 18). The score begins in triple fortissimo to clearly argue for organized Comintern involvement in international revolutionary movements. Ernst Busch, later to become a mainstay of the Berlin Ensemble after 1948, played the part of the young comrade. According to him, there were very few rehearsals of the piece and the leading actors/singers virtually directed themselves. By late 1930 it was clear that the time for productions with open-ended conclusions was over.

The 1931 revival of *A Man's a Man*, directed by Brecht with Peter Lorre and Helene Weigel playing the leads was virtually Brecht's swansong in the prewar Berlin commercial theatre. But this was a brilliant swansong indeed and one that both sums up Brecht's pre-1933 theatrical practice and anticipates significant parts of his post-exile work with the Berlin Ensemble. John Willett judges this production to be "the most completely original of his productions in the ordinary theatre."[58] The acting in the production, consistent with the text of the play, was deliberately exaggerated, disjointed and impersonal. For instance, when Peter Lorre was supposed instantaneously to express chalk-white fear at the prospect of his imminent execution, following Brecht's own suggestion, he turned his back on the audience, dipped his hands in a bowl of white chalk, smeared it on his face, and abruptly turned again to confront the audience! The scenery consisted of fragments enhanced by Neher's screen projections of enormous caricatures. The music (since lost) was by Weill. The Russian playwright Sergei Tretiakov, already a close associate of Meyerhold in Moscow and who was to become a close personal friend of Brecht, described the production admiringly: "Giant soldiers armed to the teeth and wearing jackets caked with lime, blood and excrement stalk about the stage holding on to wires to

Fig. 18. *The Measures Taken* as first produced at the Grosses Schauspielhaus, Berlin, on December 10, 1930, with the Arbeiterchor Gross-Berlin conducted by Rankl. The stark platform with its restraining rope is reminiscent of the boxing ring used in the *Little Mahagonny* production at Baden-Baden in the summer of 1927.

keep them from falling off the stilts inside their trouser legs"[59] (fig. 19). Tretiakov felt that this production compared favorably with the very best work then being done in the Soviet Union by Meyerhold. Tretiakov's observation that Brecht's work in 1933 was similar in tone, content and style to that of the Russian avant-garde, the so-called "Formalists" (Tretiakov himself among them) is thoroughly appropriate. It is interesting to note also that just as Brecht's work was on the brink of being snuffed out on German-language stages by Hitler with his hatred of progressive elements in the arts, so, in the Soviet Union, "the Formalists" were on the brink of annihilation as Stalin's comparable cultural policies led directly to the death, or silencing, of virtually all of Brecht's closest friends there. And so complete would become the destruction of even our memory of the Russian avant-garde that stage techniques developed by Meyerhold in Russia before Brecht was in his teens, are now imprinted in our memory as Brechtian theory.

The parallels between Russian work of the first one-third of the twentieth century and Brecht's pre-exile work in Munich and Berlin are numerous and striking but a close examination of all but one strand of the connection would take us too far afield here. However, to understand what Brecht was doing

Fig. 19. The figures on stilts in the 1931 production of *A Man's A Man*, directed by Brecht.

with the 1931 *A Man's a Man* production in Berlin, it is helpful to have some knowledge of montage techniques as they had been developed in the Russian and the American film, and then to illustrate this point by looking closely at Peter Lorre's role of Galy Gay and how this was received by the critics. I know of no clearer example of the application of montage theory and techniques to stage acting.

Montage theory as developed most explicitly by Sergei Eisenstein (who was to become Brecht's friend pointed out (in a well-known example) that if one shows as one fragment a photo of a woman dressed in black and then follows this fragment with another fragment, a photo of a grave, that the viewer of these two discreet fragments would then mentally telescope them into an image of a widow. The spectator, in other words, provides continuity where actual continuity is lacking within the film itself. In the reading of "the text" by the spectator, the whole (the widow) is greater than the sum of the parts (the woman, the grave). Earlier in film history, the American director, D.W. Griffith had introduced (seen and carefully studied by the Russian avant-garde) a technique of film cutting that jumped from scene to scene deliberately leaving out segments of the action and relying on the spectator to make an unbroken transition from scene A to B to C etc. Again, discreet elements are telescoped to provide satisfying wholes for the spectator, just as, in the film process itself, a series of still pictures shown in rapid sequence is linked by the spectator into a sense of linked and continuous movement. In *A Man's a Man*, Brecht insisted on Peter Lorre (usually as much of a method actor, incidentally, as Ernst Busch or Charles Laughton – other actors used and admired by Brecht) acting in a manner best described as a clear stage analogue to film montage practice.

When a number of critics, including both Ihering and Kerr, complained that Lorre's performance (see fig. 20) was exaggerated, disjointed and impersonal, Brecht immediately jumped to Lorre's and the production's defense. In a key sentence Brecht argued that the unity of type or character in the role came about "despite, or rather by means of interruptions and jumps." If we look at this sentence at all closely we see that it is saying two logically contradictory things: (1) unity comes about despite interruptions and jumps, but (2) unity comes by means of interruptions and jumps. This is typical Brecht. He insists on having things both ways. Continuity is *both* despite the breaks and because of the breaks. Now what this formulation might lack in terms of strict logic it gains enormously in carrying our thinking into an area where we can accept a stage equivalent of the indeterminacy principle in contemporary physics where the movement of particles can be explained by two mutually exclusive but simultaneous sets of interpretations. Or, returning to the example of film, the combined image of "the widow" is

Fig. 20. Peter Lorre literally armed to the teeth in the 1931 revival of *A Man's A Man*.

conjured up because of the fragments *and* in spite of the fragments. Cutting swiftly from one frame to another not only divided the action but it also and simultaneously, in Brecht's view, drew it closely together. In response to the challenge that the Brechtian actor (in this case Peter Lorre) was "short winded and episodic" Brecht replied that this view did not take adequate note of the fact that this actor "links all these single episodes together and absorbs them in the combined flow of his role." Again, one sees here similarity to film practice. As we know, the film actor must act in a whole series of discrete segments often shot completely out of the sequence in which they will be used in the finished film. But these discrete segments in a finished film are linked together and absorbed in the combined flow of the role.

The lesson for the student looking at a great Brechtian actor in performance is to look not just for the breaks, the elements that break the production down into clearly marked segments, but also to be alert to the way in which these same elements often work simultaneously to establish strong continuity in a role and/or in a production as a whole. Michael Patterson, in a long essay on the 1931 Brecht production of *A Man's a Man*, is particularly good in noting how several scenes involve a race against the clock and this, of necessity, created "conventional dramatic suspense."[60] The point that Patterson makes here is one that can be generalized to virtually all Brecht's productions. I know of none of Brecht's major plays that does not contain at least one scene (often more) of conventional dramatic suspense. Actors and directors working with Brecht need to remember that the breaks in a typical script or production are always offset by carefully structured elements to establish their continuity and build bridges across the gaps. To return to Peter Lorre, it is essential to note that his playing of the role was an attempt to match stress on breaks with stress on continuity, according to the director's instructions. As a side note for the working actor, it is worth pointing out that precisely this combination was used by the psychopath in Fritz Lang's famous film *M*. An often unnoticed benefit of the Brechtian acting style is the ease with which the Brechtian actor can pass from a stage to a film set. In both settings a role is broken down into individual segments but nevertheless forms a whole in the finished work.

The technical interest of the 1931 production of *A Man's a Man* with its use of whiteface reminiscent of the soldiers in the Munich *Edward II* and the use of half-masks which anticipate the Berlin Ensemble *Caucasian Chalk Circle* did not prevent Lion Feuchtwanger pointing out that the central element in this play is a "rather childish derivation from Kipling." The violence towards women and the brutal macho quality of the text[61] are all too similar to the world of Brecht's *Baal*, *In the Jungle of the Cities*, and *The Threepenny Opera*. And though he would write years later, after Hitler came to power, about the proto-fascist elements in *A Man's a Man*, it is not at all clear that the 1931 production of the play was done in such a way that the production was clearly anti-fascist in tone. With hindsight Brecht was able to see in the play the increasingly ugly face of brown-shirted Berlin. And though he was generally and accurately seen as being anti-fascist in 1931 the production was at best ambivalent. But the mood was now so ugly that unless a director was actually pro-fascist no production could survive for long. Despite constant intimidation, Brecht and his collaborators kept working and were able to complete in 1931–2 a remarkable film on unemployment in Berlin. This film, with the untranslatable title *Kuhle Wampe*, the name of a Berlin suburb (it was called *Whither Germany?* in England and USA), had a great deal of trouble with the German censors. Only after substantial cuts were made was it released for general showing. When Brecht took the film to Moscow for its premiere in 1932, he was deeply disappointed by the negative response of the Russian audiences. This reaction was particularly serious as the situation in Berlin was now such that thoughts of exile must have crossed the minds of some writers and the USSR was a potential haven for writers on the far left. The fact that the film shows no realization of the Nazi menace seems remarkable to us with our hindsight as to how close Hitler was in 1932 to seizing supreme power in Germany.

By late 1931, it was a bold theatre manager indeed who was willing to mount a Brecht production. Despite this risk and despite the way Brecht had treated him in the *Happy End* fiasco of 1929, Ernst Josef Aufricht, the original backer of *The Threepenny Opera*, agreed to put on not one but two Brecht productions: the full-scale *Mahagonny Opera* (developed from the original *Little Mahagonny* and an explicit work of communist propaganda), "Brecht's" dramatic adaptation of Gorki's novel, *Mother*. These were very bold choices in Berlin in late 1931. When the *Mahagonny Opera* had had its premiere in Leipzig in March 1930 it triggered one of the worst riots in theatre history. After the massive demonstration and the panic of the first night, for subsequent performances the house lights had been kept on and a solid phalanx of police had lined opera house walls. Outside the opera house, Nazi brown shirts had kept a close eye on those attending the performance of this sexually explicit work. Explicit erotic pictures had been projected in the opera house even though a few lines such as the brothel keeper, Begbick's lines: "Let the tips of your fingers/Stroke the tips of her breasts/And wait for the quivering of her flesh," and Begbick's Latin sex therapy lesson: *"Introducto pene frontem in fronte ponens requiescat"*[62] had been cut at the insistence of the publisher of the book and score, Universal-Edition of Vienna. To do this piece in Berlin in 1931, a piece with music by a Jewish composer and libretto by the communist Brecht was an act that bordered on madness. Then also to present *Mother*, with its exhortative choruses (set to music by Hanns Eisler, composer of the Comintern Anthem with songs such "In Praise of Communism," and "Arise, the Party is in Danger!", was to directly challenge Hitler's domination of Berlin.

Backed by a banker who was in love with the cabaret singer Trude Hesterberg (who was to play Madame Begbick in the *Mahagonny* production), Aufricht made every effort, through *Mahagonny*, to repeat the winning formula of *The Threepenny Opera*. Weill for the music, Neher for the sets, Lenya to sing, Paulsen (the original Mack the Knife) and Weigel in prominent roles. Brecht was to co-direct with Caspar Neher since Engel was no longer available for such provocative productions. The sources of stage lighting clearly visible to the audience and orchestra and the back screen projections were also a very familiar part of Brecht productions.

During rehearsals the animosity between Weill and Brecht came out into the open. Brecht knocked the camera out of the hands of a photographer who wanted to photograph them together. Totally unable to agree on the relative importance of the words and the music, librettist and composer called in lawyers to mediate *during rehearsals*. Furious at Weill, Brecht shouted that he was going to throw this "false Richard Strauss" down the stairs. The rehearsals could not move forward at all until Aufricht had the bright idea of essentially buying Brecht off by giving him space and a budget to start rehearsing *Mother* with Helene Weigel in the lead. That left Caspar Neher, a friend of both the composer and the playwright, as the actual director of *Mahagonny*. With the co-director downstairs in the cellar of the theatre, Aufricht was able to influence the production in ways that Brecht would probably not have allowed. Aufricht persuaded Neher to drop the projections of the text between scenes and to have these spoken by an actor dressed in a dinner jacket. The chorus was explicitly modeled on the New York City Rockettes! With the Rockettes upstairs and "In Praise of Communism," in the cellar, all funded by a banker bachelor madly in love with a cabaret artist – here was a precise reflection of the forces at work in the Berlin theatre in 1931.

When *Mahagonny* opened it was the greatest possible success that one could expect. It ran for fifty performances. Lenya, looking back on that production recalled:

Today, I have but to meet a true Berliner of that time, a survivor of that truly glorious public, to hear him say: "Yes, yes, the *Dreigroschenoper* was wonderful of course, but *Mahagonny*" and there follows a silence, a meaning beyond words that I do understand. There were those who came night after night, *Mahagonny* addicts, who tell me they would leave the theatre in a kind of trance and walk the streets, Kurt's insidious bittersweet melodies repeating over and over inside their heads.[63]

Aufricht in retrospect saw less of a rosy glow than Lenya, he saw the production as made incredibly rich by Weill's musical imagination but also Brecht's text as "a Walpurgis Night of injustice, horror, and brutality, that announced themselves as elements of the approaching future."[64] As Aufricht was well aware, Brecht, described by Ihering as being "saturated with the horror of our time," had again captured that horror. The hurricane that threatens Mahagonny and then miraculously passes by "the city of nets," would not pass by Berlin.

Whipping up hysteria by brilliantly using the technological means provided by radio and film and flying all over Germany in his own private aircraft, the erstwhile "silly looking young man" of Munich was everywhere at once as he practiced his enormously successful brand of political theatre. Advertising posters proclaimed Hitler as "Germany's last hope," as the German communist leader Ernst Thälmann struggled desperately to provide a viable counter-force to Hitler's awesome propaganda machine. Open street battles between Nazis and communists now became a commonplace and the death toll mounted on both sides. It was in this atmosphere that Brecht and Weigel took their production of *Mother* out of the Berlin commercial theatre, where it had a short run, into the working-class districts of Berlin. On makeshift platforms and illuminated by lights run from a car battery, the production was sufficiently austere and flexible that it could be packed up instantly if escape from the Nazi thugs became necessary. Under these circumstances Brecht began an affair with Margarete Steffin, a young working-class woman from Berlin who would follow Brecht into exile and in many ways replace Elisabeth Hauptmann. Meanwhile, Berlin papers such as *Germania* and *Katholisches Kirchenblatt* asked "how long will the police presidium allow this to continue?"[65] The answer was, not for long. Finally, Helene Weigel was taken from the stage and arrested by the police who were nominally neutral but increasingly dominated by Nazi elements. Fortunately, Weigel was soon released, but the battle for Berlin was essentially now over. Hitler with his macho and racist thugs had taken control and before he would be forced to relinquish it, Berlin would be a vast heap of rubble covering the rotting dead. The poet Zech's admonition "Berlin, Stop! Come to your senses. You're dancing with Death" had been ignored.

4   Brecht in exile: 1933–1947

We are exiles, outlaws. We live uneasily as near the border as we may awaiting the day of our return.

Bertolt Brecht[1]

At the time of the Reichstag Fire in early 1933, Brecht was in hospital. Fearing that his apartment might be being watched by the Gestapo, he went straight to the railway station from the hospital to take a train to Prague. He was accompanied by Helene Weigel and their son, Stefan, then eight years old. Their other child, Barbara (then two) would be brought out of Germany later. Brecht's papers were to be picked up from the apartment by Elisabeth Hauptmann. The risk of being picked up by the Nazi police did not deter her from carrying out Brecht's wish. Although she was detained briefly, she did succeed in getting the most important papers out of Germany. Brecht, like many of the other exiles, felt that the self-styled Thousand Year Reich would be very shortlived and that those opposed to Hitler would be able to return and take up their lives where they had left off. The thing to do was not only to stay as close as possible to the German border but also to try to hasten the day of return by continuing the anti-Nazi propaganda effort.

The visit to Prague was brief. The German-language theatre was far too conservative for Brecht's taste. The family then went on to Vienna where they stayed with relatives. Money was now to become something of a problem as the firm of Felix Bloch Erben in Berlin which had been paying Brecht large monthly sums while getting very little in return and which had been trying for months to change its business arrangements with him, chose the month of February 1933 to insist that substantial changes be made. These changes radically altered Brecht's financial well-being even before the Nazis in later years could begin to sequester Brecht's accounts even for major assets such as royalties for *The Threepenny Opera* stage-play and film. Wanting to remain close to Germany and, if possible, earn money in a German-language theatre, Weigel stayed on in Vienna to look out for opportunities, while Brecht went off to Zurich to investigate the possibility of establishing a foothold in the German-speaking part of Switzerland. Neither Vienna nor Zurich looked any more promising than Prague. Nazi elements were very active in Vienna, and the Swiss theatre was more comfortable than experimental. As Klaus Völker notes in his biography of Brecht, Helene Weigel "received an invitation from the Danish writer Karin Michaelis to bring Brecht and the children to visit her at her home in Thurö."[2] The "visit" to Thurö was to last until April 1939.

Before Brecht moved "permanently" to Thurö in June 1933, despite all the past tension between Brecht and Weill, on Weill's initiative the two collaborators got together in Paris to mount a collaborative effort to repeat the winning *Threepenny Opera* formula (Brecht, Weill, Neher, Lenya) that would earn them both some real money. The prospects for success looked excellent as first Weill and then Brecht were taken up by Parisian artists and socialites. They immediately produced a chamber music version of *The Little Mahagonny* which "was an incredible success both at the Vicomtesse de Noailles's Salon and at the Salle Gaveau the next day."[3] Encouraged by this response and supported by people such as George Balanchine, Ernst Josef Aufricht (who was also in exile by this time), the Vicomtesse de Noailles, the Princess Edmonde de Polignac (heiress to the Singer family fortune), Count Harry Kessler from Berlin and the film-maker Jean Renoir, the collaborators got down to work on a draft of a ballet called *The Seven Deadly Sins*. Despite all these preparations, and with an excellent "libretto" by Brecht and a fine score by Weill, Brecht reported to Helene Weigel (already in Denmark) that "the ballet went very well, but was not very important."[4] It was not the goldmine that had been expected. Brecht's thoughts now turned to Denmark and by the end of June, 1933, he had already moved there.

Though Brecht did not make even a small fortune with *The Seven Deadly Sins* in Paris, it is clear that by the end of 1933, with money from her Viennese relatives and what he had saved from his "luxurious literary life" in Berlin, combined with an advance from the Amsterdam publisher of his new work *The Threepenny Novel*, Brecht and Weigel were fairly comfortably off and settled in Denmark.[5] In August they bought their own house outright and had it remodeled by a Danish architect. There was also the full-time family maid/housekeeper, Marie Hold; and a little later they were joined by Margarete Steffin, Brecht's full-time secretary/mistress/collaborator. Later, another mistress/secretary/collaborator joined the group, the wealthy "Red Ruth" Berlau, an actress with the Royal Theatre of Copenhagen. During this time Brecht made a quick trip to Paris in the company of Margarete Steffin.

While in Paris he worked very hard to establish a material base for the Brecht entourage. Using past contacts to the full, he not only began to negotiate contracts with "bourgeois" publishers and theatres in France, Holland and England, but also worked out a contract with Johannes R. Becher to have a number of his works published in Moscow. His letter to Moscow confirming these arrangements specified that the royalty checks be sent not to Weigel at home in Thurö but to Steffin, in Paris.

Brecht's financial dealings in Paris reveal a pattern which would remain significant until his death. Certainly he was deeply committed to the struggle *against* Hitler and *for* the eventual world-wide triumph of socialism but, at the same time, he was as devoted as Mack the Knife to taking as large a cut as possible from the bank accounts of the non-socialist world. He continued to do this up until his death in August 1956. He courted both sides, retaining his Austrian passport and yet receiving the Stalin Prize in Moscow in December 1954. In 1933, not really knowing how long he would be in exile and not knowing where his greatest chance of safety and material success might be, he realized that he must keep all his options open — both socialist and non-socialist. This sceptical duality (or, as some would say, duplicity) is characteristic of virtually all Brecht's best work as a playwright, as a poet, as a drama theorist, and as a director. From his materially comfortable base in Denmark, Brecht could now travel as far afield as New York and Moscow to test receptivity to his work. But, as we shall see, although he had friends in both Moscow and New York who arranged for him to visit both theatre capitals in 1935, these cities were eventually to show (despite extremely promising beginnings) less than wild enthusiasm for his kind of theatre. Comparatively little of Brecht's work was to be published or staged in these years.

In the spring of 1935, accompanied by Steffin who had conveniently learned quite a bit of Russian, Brecht went on an exploratory visit to Leningrad and Moscow. He was welcomed by his friends from the Munich days — Asja Lacis, Bernhard Reich and Carola Neher — and Erwin Piscator from Berlin. This group, allied with Sergei and Olga Tretiakov who were to become his very close friends, ensured that Brecht was introduced to everyone still doing interesting work in theatre and film in Moscow. (At that time all respected figures in progressive film and theatre circles were unanimous in praise of the brilliance and fecundity of the arts in Moscow, and it was not yet wholly clear that 1935 was to be the swansong of Russian experimentation in the arts.) As a prominent member of the European avant-garde, Brecht was made very welcome by his Muscovite counterparts. Two meetings in particular in Moscow shed light on his own work. He was taken to meet the Russian aesthetician Schklovski. Directly after this meeting and almost certainly influenced directly by Schklovski's own term "priem ostrannenija" (rendering strange, making unusual), Brecht used the expression *Verfremdung*. He then went to see an example of *Verfremdung* in acting: a performance by the Chinese actor Mei Lan-fan. Brecht marveled at the fact that this male actor, performing in a western dinnerjacket, created extremely powerful women's parts.

The term *Verfremdung*, once adopted by Brecht, would lead to endless confusion particularly when translated into English as "alienation" or into

French as "distanciation." What Brecht himself originally had in mind, wholly consistent with his Russian source, was something richly and provocatively ambivalent. The German term as used by Brecht could be seen as a one-word summation of the preface to Wordsworth and Coleridge's *Lyrical Ballads*, where it is argued that the Ballads render the strange familiar and render the familiar strange. In Brecht's terms, an object can become invisible either because it is too strange or because it is too familiar. The paradoxical trick is to disrupt the viewer's normal or run of the mill perception by introducing elements that will suddenly cause the viewer to see familiar objects in a strange way and to see strange objects in a familiar way. The terms "alienation" or "distanciation" only capture one side of the dual formation summed up in the one word *Verfremdung*. Perhaps we should simply speak in English of a V-effect and not try to translate the term. The translations found so far confuse more than they illuminate and have led to substantial misunderstandings of Brecht's work as a director. He has become almost as misunderstood in this as his much-maligned source for the term *Verfremdung*, the Russian "Formalists," who were beginning in 1934 to draw the ire of Stalin and his aesthetic adviser, Zhadanov.

But in spite of the enthusiastic exchange of ideas between Brecht and like-minded Russians, the trip was not very encouraging. He saw that the tide had turned away from the kind of artistic experiments that were similar to his own and that power in the arts as elsewhere was passing to those who would later be called "the Stalinists." The official "socialist realist" cultural policy which had been announced in 1934 by Zhadanov at Stalin's behest was firmly taking hold, and the days of brilliant "Formalist" experimentation were numbered. In the next few years, virtually all of Brecht's closest friends in Moscow would be forced to curtail their experiments and indeed most of them would be murdered or imprisoned by Stalin's secret police. In a later conversation with his friend Walter Benjamin, who said to Brecht "But you have friends in Moscow," Brecht is reported to have responded: "Actually I have no friends there. And the Moscow inhabitants don't have any either – like the dead." But his enemies remained. He told Benjamin bitterly that the surviving Moscow critics all wanted to play the apparatchik, to control others; they constituted a deadly "priestly camarilla" whose "every utterance contained a threat." A revealing letter dated June 8, 1938 from Alfred Kurella (widely thought in émigré circles to be an NKVD informer), who was then on the editorial staff of "Brecht's" journal *Das Wort* (*The Word*) in Moscow, to another *The Word* staff-member, Fritz Erpenbeck, makes it clear that the "camarilla" were not only attempting to set a deadly trap for Brecht but were involving the future head of the government of the German Democratic Republic, Walter Ulbricht, in the plot.[6] When Brecht left Moscow in May,

1935, he already knew that Moscow would not be a healthy place for him. And although in the next few years he would earn a significant part of his living from his work as an editor and writer for Moscow-based journals, it would become ever clearer that Brecht's stage work was basically antithetical to Stalin's conservative cultural policy with its strong endorsement of Stanislavski and literal realism. For Brecht the situation was now extremely complicated. In Moscow he believed he saw the only hope for real political and military opposition to Hitler and the only genuine commitment to improving the lot of the oppressed of the world, but he saw no prospects for furthering his own theatrical work in the "homeland of the revolution." As a consequence, his thoughts now turned to New York.

Knowing by mid-1935 that he, as he put it, "could not get enough sugar for his coffee" in Moscow, Brecht was open to an approach from the left-wing Theatre Union in New York. Interested in a stage adaptation of Gorki's novel, *Mother*, the Theatre Union invited Brecht to New York for consultations during the rehearsals. They never specified whether he was or was not going to be allowed to direct the production. Even before Brecht left Skovsbostrand, however, there were clear signals that the Theatre Union group was not going to be able to accept Brecht's style. The English version of the original German script which they sent to him in Denmark was replete with Stanislavskian color or naturalistic detail which they had added. Alarmed at this text, Brecht sent a verse letter to "the theatre workers" arguing that they should adopt his own style rather than the naturalistic one. The letter concluded with an exhortation: "But even if your audience, the worker, hesitates, you should not follow him but go ahead of him, go ahead of him swiftly, with long strides and absolute faith in his ultimate strength."[7] After continued negotiations, but with his position still very vague, Brecht agreed to an expenses-paid trip to New York. Apparently he thought he could take over the production (as he had sometimes succeeded in doing in Germany) and/or win over the Theatre Union members to his style; they, in turn, thought that Brecht would see reason once he actually got to New York, to adopt their style. Both parties were wrong, and the stage was set for a massive confrontation.

When Brecht first got to New York in late October, 1935 he did manage to get most of his original text restored. In this endeavor he was aided by Hanns Eisler, who had written the music for Brecht's version and who was now lecturing in America. But when the New York theatre people saw what was going on they were appalled. In their view, Brecht and Eisler were completely out of touch with the political and theatrical realities of New York in 1935. Brecht did not help things with his brutal belligerence in the theatre. Convinced that he was the "Einstein of the new stage form,"[8] he demanded obedience and staged temper tantrums in order to get it. Outraged by this, the Theatre Union head then banned both Brecht and Eisler from the theatre and began to rehearse without them. Whatever the shortcomings of the Theatre Union people themselves were, Brecht's intransigence had not helped matters. Nor did he help himself during his New York stay by the way he treated Elisabeth Hauptmann, who had invited Brecht to share her small apartment and agreed to do some typing for him. According to one account, Hauptmann came back to her apartment to find Brecht in bed with a "two hundred and fifty pound woman"⁹ whom he had just met at the Theatre Union. Hauptmann's willingness to continue working under circumstances such as these with the man she had once hoped to marry, is astounding.

Pitched somewhere between Brecht's narrative style and Stanislavski's detailed realism, the final production was a failure with both the critics and the public. Summing up the experience, Brecht wrote to Piscator in Moscow (who was having similar difficulties there and for similar reasons): "All in all an experience, but never have anything to do with so-called theatres of the left! They are run by little cliques, which are dominated by playwrights, and have the worst Broadway producer's manners without their specialized knowledge which, if not very great, is at least something."¹⁰ This summing up contains the seeds of the next stage of Brecht's attempt to re-establish himself in the theatre. Rejected in Moscow by the politically dominant forces and in New York by the left-wing theatre, he now began to wonder if perhaps Broadway producers might not be better. Perhaps their "specialized knowledge" could produce "at least something."

But when Brecht returned to Europe in early 1936 visions of Broadway marquee lights were not yet dancing in his head. For the next two years and more he devoted a great deal of his energy to fighting Hitler and Franco through productions of plays that attacked and ridiculed the fascists. But in late 1936, he was badly scared by the response in Denmark to the ballet *The Seven Deadly Sins* and his anti-racist play *Roundheads and Pointed Heads*. The Danish authorities were so incensed by the cynicism and blatant sexuality of *The Seven Deadly Sins* that the play had to be taken off after two performances at the Riddersalen. There was enough of a fuss in the increasingly right-wing dominated press for Brecht to consider himself fortunate in getting his Danish residence permit renewed at all. The closing of his two Copenhagen productions marked virtually the end of professional productions of Brecht in prewar Europe. Up to the beginning of the war there would now be only isolated émigré productions, as Nazi influence spread to more and more countries; during the war itself, German-language productions were confined largely to neutral Switzerland.

Forced out of the professional theatre in western Europe by the right-wing press, forced out of the left-wing theatre in New York by his own intransigence, and now *persona non grata* in the Moscow theatre because of his "formalism" and "bourgeois decadence,"[11] Brecht, by 1937, was without any professional theatre base. His theoretical position on the downplaying of emotion in the theatre (though he had in fact never successfully excluded emotions in his theatre) was apparently unsuccessful on either the political left or the right. Likewise, his brand of socialism was too much of an aberration for Moscow and yet much too strong for Copenhagen and New York. What is remarkable about this situation is the fact that Brecht went on to use this dangerous crisis in his political and artistic life as a way of breaking through to a different form of playwriting. In just over a year, between November 1938 and May 1940, Brecht (with Margarete Steffin and Ruth Berlau) created the three major plays which (besides *The Threepenny Opera*) have established his international fame: *The Life of Galileo Galilei, Mother Courage and Her Children,* and *The Good Person of Sezuan*. With daily news of the destruction of his Moscow friends and with Hitler's increasing dominance forcing Brecht "to change countries more often than his shoes," his productivity in the period 1938–40 was remarkable.

In his lightly fictionalized memoir of the period, Peter Weiss has left us a remarkable portrait of the way in which Brecht worked and remained so productive in his Scandinavian exile. Berlau was sent off on her motorcycle to research the most diverse topics. Steffin was available twenty-four hours a day "to take dictation." Weigel was to keep the children out of the way and feed the whole entourage at any and all hours. Likening the work to that of a highly efficient factory or assembly line, Weiss writes: "In his full steam ahead factory, he hurried back and forth between all the different departments, here and there giving brief pointers, following the progress of the various products, always checking results and always ready to find new ways to profit from the materials." On this assembly line were "products" such as prose pieces, essays on dramatic form, work on a novel on the life of Julius Caesar, work on "The Refugee Conversations," and on "The Book of Twists and Turns." As Weiss puts it, all this was "directed by a sovereign Brecht who never allowed there to be any doubt that he was there to get the profits from anything produced in his workshop."[12] With the factory ever on the move, he paused in flight in Finland to create with Margarete Steffin and Hella Wuolijoki *Puntila and His Servant Matti*. In March, 1941 in Helsinki, again with Margarete Steffin as a collaborator, he wrote *The Resistible Rise of Arturo Ui*. While declaring that it is "impossible to write without a stage," the Brecht workshop produced and produced brilliantly and with scarcely a pause. By the time Brecht was finally forced out of Europe by Hitler's advancing armies and had crossed the entire breadth of the USSR to sail from Vladivostock to

California in 1941, he had in his suitcases virtually all the plays which, in postwar United States and European productions under his direction, would catapult him back to world fame and exert a lasting influence on the modern theatre.

But after his arrival in California on July 21, 1941 accompanied by Helene Weigel, the children and Ruth Berlau (Margarete Steffin had begun the journey with the party but had died of tuberculosis in Moscow), it would be six years before Brecht was able to mount a major production of any of the plays he had brought with him. The American years – with the exception of the last year of Brecht's stay in America – would not, except indirectly, significantly advance Brecht's career as a stage director. The explicitly pro-communist and anti-fascist plays designed for staging by amateurs on bare platforms that Brecht was interested in at the time he left Berlin, would give way to works with large casts and a heavy dependence on major stars which required large expenditure for set, costumes, stage requisites and so on. Brecht himself, recognizing this major shift in his own playwriting and staging, would be forced to modify his theoretical essays radically to fit them more closely to his own new stage practice. As he was wont to say (in English): "The proof of the pudding is in the eating."

This shift in Brecht's practice and theory in the exile years seems perfectly understandable when one considers the vast difference in resources available to him and the different pressures placed upon him at the different stages of his life, yet somehow confusion seems generally to reign when students, actors, and directors talk about his work. The discussion usually fails to recognize that Munich in 1923, when Hitler was largely viewed as a bad joke, was radically different from Berlin in 1933, with Hitler as Chancellor and with brownshirts controlling the streets and the theatres; and that this in turn was different from Hollywood and New York in 1943, or Berlin again in 1953 with Brecht and Helene Weigel becoming established as *the* leading theatre people both in the German Democratic Republic and the rest of the world. When critics and directors take a theoretical pronouncement made in 1923 and try to have it fit Brecht's plays of 1933, 1943 or 1953, they fail. Much epic confusion (pun intended) caused by this mis-match approach could be avoided if those looking at a Brecht play of any period would simply match it up with Brecht's theoretical pronouncements of that same period, for there is usually a good match between his contemporary theory and practice. Again and again with actors and scholars one hears a recitation of the epic catechism (usually drawn from the 1930 notes to the *Mahagonny* opera) combined with floundering attempts to fit plays like *Galileo* and *Mother Courage* on this procrustean bed. In some ways Brecht himself is to blame for this state of affairs, but in other ways he made serious and sustained efforts to clear up confusion resulting from the term "epic theatre." What seems to have happened historically is that at the time Brecht arrived in America in 1941 he himself was still using "epic" to describe both his Berlin "platform plays" and the very different works he had written in that intense period of creativity in Scandinavia from 1938 to 1940 as well as the later *Puntila* and the final major work (written in American exile) *The Caucasian Chalk Circle*. But friends in America did not accept this. Charles Laughton saw a great play in *Galileo* and had no real interest in talking about what he considered to be largely unintelligible and/or irrelevant theory. Lion Feuchtwanger, Brecht's mentor from the Munich days, and now on a first-name basis with the most powerful people in Hollywood, was much blunter with Brecht and told him that if Brecht mentioned "epic" just one more time in his presence "he could kiss his ass." And the young UCLA instructor, Eric Bentley, not the least bit overawed by Brecht, found the director's own explanations of epic theory inadequate and told Brecht so. In a letter written in response to a Brecht letter in 1946 Bentley stated flatly:

You have a conception of art which few understand. I think I am probably not one of the few. You will have to explain yourself. The explanation you gave in "Writing the Truth: Five Difficulties" was not enough. I felt that you brushed aside all modern art except your own kind. I felt that you brushed it aside; you did not really cope with it. I would welcome two things: a brief account of your philosophy of art and – but this can wait a little – an account of Epic Theatre that deals with some of the difficulties . . .

These are troublesome demands. But I think you will do yourself a service if you can help American readers and playgoers to see the differences between "Brechtism" and the impossible vulgarities of "proletarian literature" of which the most impossible is Socialist Realism. Like Shaw you are more eager to explain your politics and your morality than your art. This is your privilege. But I warn you that you will never make any further advance in America unless you can dispel the illusion and doubts that at present surround your kind of enterprise. They will not listen to your message until they are "sold" on your art.[13]

In his book, *Bertolt Brecht in America*, James Lyon maintains that it was this letter which got Brecht to try to clarify his ideas in the first draft of the theoretical essay (published in 1949) *Short Organum for the Theatre*. This new work represented a radical and largely irreconcilable shift from the strident *Mahagonny* notes of 1930. If one tries to understand the theory behind Brecht's post-1938 writing and directing, it is the *Short Organum* rather than the *Mahagonny* notes which should be studied. But, as we shall see later, the greatest actors working under Brecht's own direction in the last decade of his life hardly used theory at all. Almost all their work came out of close practice with Brecht himself. In fact, late in his life as an addition to the *Short Organum*, Brecht himself came to abandon the term "epic theatre" as he realized that it confused more than it clarified. It may sound heretical, as the term is so firmly rooted now in theatre lore, but I think that we should also abandon it. John Willett seems to suggest this possibility when he notes: "The high sounding term of the 1920s has been made to embrace any kind of play that Brecht wrote – taut or loose, realistic or fantastic, didactic or amusing – and some quite ephemeral mannerisms as well."[14] But despite the reservations expressed by Willett, Bentley, Ernst Schumacher, Hans-Dieter Zimmermann and others, still the term has maintained its strange hold. In consequence, virtually nothing has been written on the question of whether in fact fragmentation of action really occurs during most Brecht productions and, *if* it does, does it inhibit emotional identification (Schiller, for instance, argues exactly the opposite in the preface to *The Bride of Messina*.[15] Very little has been done to question Brecht's early hypothesis (and it is only a hypothesis) that the "epic" form necessarily produces cooler responses than material offered in "dramatic" form. The devices that tie the Brecht plays together, particularly in Brecht's own productions, and that consistently aroused strong emotional responses, have been overwhelmingly ignored by academic critics ignorant of Brecht's actual stage practice. As these links were not provided for in the theory of the 1920s, academic critics go to great lengths to avoid seeing them even though they crop up everywhere in Brecht's productions, and it is clear that Brecht knew exactly what he was doing. Fed up with all the various misunderstandings that got in the way of German critics, he advised: "If the critics would view my theatre as spectators do, without first emphasizing my theories, then what they would see would be simply theatre, I hope, of imagination, fun, and intelligence."[16] Let us follow Brecht's advice and take a look at how he produced his plays, beginning with the 1947 Los Angeles and New York production of *Galileo*, the final, but woefully late production of a play written for Broadway, but not scheduled for production there until his days in America were numbered just before he was driven out by the House Unamerican Activities Committee and the FBI.

The years between Brecht's arrival in San Pedro in 1941 and his hurried escape from New York City in 1947, were largely years of frustration as he was unable to establish himself either as a screen writer or to get his plays staged on Broadway in a way that he thought appropriate. Again and again he would get close to selling a "lie" (as he called film scripts), but usually he was unsuccessful. When he did earn some money from a film project, he would heave a sigh of relief and promptly use the money to buy time to write plays, now usually with Broadway in mind. In 1943, the old Berlin *Threepenny Opera* team tried once again to repeat their 1928 success as Aufricht, Weill and Brecht worked together on Brecht's adaptation of Jaroslav Hasek's novel *Schweik*. Aimed at Broadway with Peter Lorre and Lotte Lenya playing the leads, the plan foundered in 1944 as Weill withdrew, saying publicly that he thought the play was not yet ready for Broadway, but privately that Brecht was simply too tricky in his business dealings and that was the real reason for withdrawing his support.[17] The same year, Eric Bentley (who had met Brecht two years before) began work on an adaptation of Brecht's *Private Life of the Master Race* for Broadway. This production closed after a few days. But disappointing as these failures to make it big on Broadway were, in 1944 Brecht had other reasons not to be discouraged and indeed to anticipate a breakthrough. Not only was he working closely with Charles Laughton on *Galileo* as a "vehicle" for his star but he was also working with two other stars at that time, Elisabeth Bergner and Luise Rainer (Academy Award Winner in 1937 and 1938): with Bergner, "to whose strange charm he was not insensitive,"[18] on an adaptation of John Webster's Jacobean classic, *The Duchess of Malfi*; with Rainer on a possible Broadway production of *The Caucasian Chalk Circle*. But despite the involvement of Rainer, the *Chalk Circle* project never made it to Broadway. According to the actress, the reason she dropped the project was that she was not prepared to put up with Brecht's rudeness. He is supposed to have roared at her: "Do you know who I am?" And when she calmly replied "Yes. You are Bertolt Brecht" and then asked him "And do you know who I am?" he is supposed to have replied "yes, you are nothing. Nothing, I say!" In sum, Louise Rainer felt that Brecht was "cruel, selfish, vain – an awful man," and he seemed to sense that she was apathetic towards this man who always had a "harem" around him.[19] The *Malfi* project limped along but also got into trouble in 1946 as Bergner became frightened that with Brecht's reputation as a radical the production was doomed on conservative Broadway. So when the play was brought to New York after extensive tryouts in various cities it was not a success there. Brecht's poem on the episode sums things up rather nicely: "I outdistanced the tiger/I was a meal for the bedbugs/I was eaten up by mediocrity." For the New York critics the *Malfi* production was summed up in one headline as a "Slow, Long and Unimportant Theatre Relic" and Howard Barnes dismissed the production as "a preposterous bore."[20]

The pattern that emerges from this string of "failed" productions tells us a great deal about what Brecht would seek next with his *Galileo* production with Charles Laughton and later with his Berlin Ensemble productions after his return to Europe. Instead of allowing half-hearted modifications of his work, productions pitched somewhere between "the Brecht style" and "the Broadway style," an approach that he clearly felt satisfied nobody and ensured disaster, he would now insist on total control of every facet of a production, with no "Broadway style" compromises. His detractors clearly felt that the failure of *Mother* in New York in 1935 and the "failures" in the mid-forties were because Brecht had not compromised enough. Brecht felt exactly the opposite. His argument became: either go all the way with me in every aspect of the production or simply don't bother. His position was a bold one because by that time his European fame had largely seeped away and he had established a disastrous record in the "American" theatre.

But where Weill, Rainer and Bergner had withdrawn their backing, Laughton, despite frequent misgivings, pressed ahead. The title role of *Galileo* was altogether too seductive to be turned down. And with Laughton in Brecht's corner this meant that the production was, to use Hollywood parlance, "bankable." As the war in Europe ended in 1945, Brecht was frequently asked to release his major plays for European stage production, but he refused. From a letter to Berlau we learn that he had apparently decided that if he was to return to Europe on his own terms as a director, it would be immensely helpful to have had a successful Broadway production of *Galileo*.[21] Although it took some three years from when Brecht began working on an English version of the script with Laughton until it was finally staged on the West Coast and then transferred to Broadway, Brecht never seems to have really faltered in his confidence in the *Galileo* project. Fortunately, extensive research materials are available on the years of preparation and Ruth Berlau's valuable photographic record of the production enables us to see clearly what Brecht was seeking to achieve.

The *Galileo* play, begun in Scandinavia as the news of Nils Bohr's advances in atomic theory were reported in the popular press, was originally a rather positive treatment of the seventeenth-century scientist as a forerunner of Bohr. Later, in exile in California, after the spectral events of Hiroshima and Nagasaki, Brecht saw the work of Galileo and Nils Bohr in a new and awful light. Fortunately for the play, instead of coming down fully on one side or the other for either a good or bad Galileo, there always remained both in the text and in production a person whom Aristotle described as the key figure in tragedy: someone of "sufficient magnitude," a person neither wholly good nor wholly bad. For Laughton in America, and for Ernst Busch in Berlin, the intensely dramatic wars between the positive and negative aspects in *Galileo* were something they insisted on keeping whatever Brecht's view as playwright/director might be. And in the case of Laughton, the opportunity to maintain these contradictions came in the writing as well as the playing, since he made a large contribution to the creation of the English-language text which then formed the basis of the Berlin Ensemble German-language text. It is no accident that the English-language *Galileo* is both reminiscent of sixteenth-century chronicle plays and also drenched through and through with seventeenth-century turns of phrase. Set in the early seventeenth century, the script is much enriched by Laughton's sensitivity both to

Shakespeare as a linguistic model and to the King James Version of the Bible, a text equally appreciated by Brecht.

In formal terms the play has much more in common with Shakespeare than it does with the theoretical models envisaged by Brecht in the late twenties. To his credit, Brecht recognized all this. As early as February 1939 he had noted in his *Working Journal*:

Technically, *Galileo* is a large step backwards; like *Frau Carrar's Rifles* it is much too opportunistic. This work would have to be completely rewritten if one wished to have this "breeze from new coasts," this red sunrise of science.

The new play, Brecht went on, would have to be something as follows:

everything more direct, without the interiors, the "atmosphere," the emotional involvement. And everything directed towards a planetary demonstration. The divisions could remain, even the basic character of Galileo, but the work, the pleasant work, can only be done with proper contact with a physical stage.[22]

Yet, as Ernst Schumacher has noted in his thorough examination of the various versions of the *Galileo* text,[23] even when Brecht had "proper contact with the physical stage," first in America with Laughton and then in East Berlin with the Ensemble, he failed to make any essential structural changes in the play (perhaps in the latter case because of his failing health). Instead, Brecht kept in each later version all the interior scenes and all the "atmosphere" of the Danish original. Evidently, almost the entire burden of preventing audience identification with *Galileo* was to come not from the text but from the production, especially the Berlin Ensemble production in which Ernst Busch almost singlehandedly attempted to stamp out any good qualities in the role of the great scientist. In view of Brecht's failure to introduce substantial structural changes, we detect more resignation than surprise in an observation he made in January 1945: "In *Galileo*, with its interiors and atmosphere, the structure of the scenes, which is taken from the epic theater, seems strangely theatrical."[24] Some six months later Brecht was prepared to state flatly: "Formally I do not defend this play very strongly."[25] In a number of notes (written in English) on the American version of the play, Brecht sets up the following chart to illustrate the symmetrical structure of the play:

similia in (1) and (12).
there is a morning in (1), and an evening in (12)
there is a gift of an astronomical model in (1), of a goose in (12)
There ist [sic] a lecture for Andrea, the boy in (1), and a lecture for Andrea, the man in (12)
there is a woman going around watching [sic] in (1), and a woman going around watching in (12)[26]

Ernst Schumacher observes of this orderly little table which he found in the Brecht Archive: "Symmetry is an essential feature of the classical drama," and then goes on: "The uses of symmetry in *Galileo* underline, as structural elements of his dramaturgy, the 'conservative' character of the work."[27] Taking his cue from Brecht's own notebooks, Schumacher notes: "In the first scene, in the morning, the beginning not only of a new day, but also of a new era, the bed is being made in Galileo's room. In the next to last scene, [the last scene in the Ensemble version] in the evening, not only of a day, but in the evening of a life of high ideals, the bed is being prepared for the night. In the first scene Galileo is "singing" the "aria" of the new era. In the next to last scene he expresses his conviction that this new era has begun, even if it looks like the old."[28] It is clear that Brecht knew that his *Life of Galileo* is classically circular in structure.

It should not really surprise us that this finely wrought play, constructed as it is from only the most telling episodes in the life of the great but cowardly Galileo, should move us profoundly as we see the many faceted figure pass from health, vigor and hope to blindness, old age and bitter cynicism about himself and about the role of physics in the new world that he recognizes on the horizon. Precisely because Brecht gives us a figure, like ourselves "neither wholly good nor wholly bad," we respond this way to him. In the final American and German versions, enough of the "good" Galileo of the first Danish version still shines through the dark layers painted over him in successive versions for the portrait to have considerable depth and ambience. The character becomes most sympathetic precisely because he has such depth.

After a series of false starts with Orson Welles, Elia Kazan, Mike Todd and Alfred Lunt, a nominal director for the 1947 *Galileo* production was found in Joseph Losey who was answerable to the producer John Houseman. Brecht had met Losey originally in Moscow in 1935 and Losey had gone on to work on Hallie Flanagan's "Living Newspapers" and in the mid-forties was doing some successful Broadway work. Though Losey was little known at the time, the combination of knowledge of Moscow experimental staging of 1935, the "epic" work with Flanagan, and Losey's knowledge of Broadway, was exactly appropriate from Brecht's point of view. Furthermore, the *de facto* director would actually be Brecht, with Laughton also playing a directorial role.

When rehearsals began on the June 24, 1947 the cast promptly recognized who was in charge. Brecht and Laughton had done most of the casting with the assistance of Joseph Losey. All other production choices were made in the same way. The threesome agreed to hire a former co-worker of Losey's, Robert Davison, to design costumes and sets, with much of that actual costume-making to be carried out by Helene Weigel. The choreographer, Anna Sokolow, was hired and quickly fired. According to one eyewitness,

Brecht told her: "We want none of your tawdry Broadway dances in the production."[29] James Lyon's detailed and valuable account of the rehearsal period relates that Brecht's dismissal of Anna Sokolow was but one of his numerous outbursts of anger and frustration. After one big row with Joseph Losey, and Losey's storming out of the theatre, Charles Laughton telephoned him to ask him to come back. Losey said he would if Brecht apologized for what he had said. After checking with Brecht, Laughton called Losey back again with the following message: "Brecht says please come back, and he also says you should know Brecht never apologizes."[30] Losey returned anyway. One of the main backers of the production, T. Edward Hambleton (who matched Charles Laughton's $25,000), reported to Professor Lyon that Brecht "would snap back in his usual fashion at people involved in the production end of the play. For instance, he would shout about the primitive, ill-painted stage properties. In fact, said Hambleton, Brecht did a great deal of screaming throughout rehearsals about the costumes, about the scenery, and about everything."[31] What Brecht sought was total control of every aspect of the production. He would accept and indeed welcome good suggestions from others, but there was never a moment's doubt as to who was in charge.

Given Brecht's dominance of the production and insistence on a non-Stanislavskian approach to acting, it is of importance to note that the Stanislavskian approach, or "method acting," was the starting point for virtually every actor in the production – from Brecht's co-director Charles Laughton down. Brecht's ability to work with Laughton is particularly remarkable as the great British actor was absolutely notorious in Hollywood for delaying productions while he got into "the right mood for a part." Curt Bois, an actor much admired by Brecht, had a bit-part in the Hollywood production of "The Hunchback of Notre Dame," starring Charles Laughton. Illustrating Laughton's "method" approach to roles, Bois recalls the following incident on the Notre Dame set: Laughton was supposed to run down a narrow, dark alley. Next to the camera a horse stood patiently waiting. Laughton only needed to run. "Bill," he said to Wilhelm Dieterle [the director], "I've got to get into the mood for running." "Yes, of course Charles, get into the mood." Ten minutes later Dieterle tentatively asked: "Charles? Are you in the mood now?" "Yes, Bill, I think so." Dieterle: "Action!" Laughton raced off. The patient horse went mad, smashed the camera and broke the script clerk's arm. Shooting had to be stopped.[32] But during the *Galileo* production (probably because of the years of work with Brecht in actually creating the English text of the play) Laughton was so caught up with the part of Galileo and had such a good intuitive grasp of Galileo's complexities and inconsistencies that he did not need to delay rehearsals to feel his way into the part. Other actors, in fact, had more difficulty in grasping the style of acting that Brecht was seeking. And generally Brecht was of very little help as he was usually more given to explaining what he did not want (sentimentality or private or personal feelings) rather than explaining what he did want. When the "method" actors came to Losey and asked "what's our motivation" in a particular scene, Losey passed the question to Brecht who supposedly answered that Losey should ask the actors: "What's the motivation of a tightrope walker not to fall off the high wire?"[33] In another case, Losey, trying to follow Brecht's directions, found fault with Eda Reiss Marin's playing of Mrs Sarti but could not, apparently, explain what it was that he wanted instead. In this case it was Brecht and Weigel who worked with the actress privately and by getting her to rehearse the role using a Brooklyn Jewish accent were able to teach her to understand "estrangement" and play the part to Brecht's and Losey's satisfaction. But conversely, when the writer Abe Burrows was brought in to help write some catchy lyrics for the ballad singer in the play, he recalls the following less than fruitful encounter with Brecht:

BURROWS: Tell me, Bert, how does this street singer feel about Galileo?
BRECHT: He feels nothing.
BURROWS: (hesitantly) I mean . . . is he praising Galileo?
BRECHT: No.
BURROWS: What do the pamphlets he's selling say about Galileo?
BRECHT: They just tell about him.
BURROWS: (puzzled) Are they for him or against him?
BRECHT: It doesn't matter.
BURROWS: Well, just tell me one thing Bert. Why is the man singing a song?
BRECHT: Because I want him to.[34]

Nonetheless Burrows still tried to write the songs, but his versions of them were never used. This in itself is fairly typical of most Brecht productions: many, many suggestions are made by a host of potential collaborators, and Brecht would somehow make every individual contributor feel that he or she had some sort of exclusive "contract" for their contribution. Then he would ruthlessly reject most if not all of the unwittingly competing "solutions." Yet, somehow, despite repeatedly treating his friends and collaborators in this way, a surprising number of them were willing to continue working with him. Whether as lover or as co-worker you had a contract with Brecht only as long as he said you had a contract. These were usually one-way contracts with all the restraints on you and virtually none on him.

Gathered around the playwright/director in Los Angeles were a crowd of people who were to do Brecht's bidding apparently with little regard for their own time, or for any of their personal or private needs. Helene Weigel was mainly in charge of making the costumes for the production and, as noted above, also served as unofficial acting coach. Ruth Berlau, Brecht's long-term collaborator and mistress, was in charge (over Laughton's objections) of making an exhaustive and valuable photographic record of the production. At least one other mistress was also always present. These three women were all expected by Brecht to be tolerant of one another and of him. They were given strict instructions not to be selfish and not to put their own needs before his.

For those concerned with trying to maintain some sense of schedule and of budgeting responsibility, Brecht's working "method" was a continuous nightmare. With a cast of fifty.and some ninety costumes, he rearranged elements as freely as he had at the Chamber Theatre in Munich in 1924 where, it will be recalled, during the *Edward II* production he cheerfully threw entire sets and costumes away from one day to the next with complete disregard for cost. In Los Angeles, the person charged with the responsibility of trying to keep Brecht within his $50,000 budget was Kate Drain Lawson, who was John Houseman's (the show's budgeting director) executive director in Los Angeles. James Lyon reports that a memo was sent by Lawson to Houseman on July 15 in which she detailed what was happening. As Lyon describes it, her memo said "that Brecht's continuous alterations of costumes, culminating in fourteen changes on July 9, had caused an immense amount of extra work in the costume shop, and that two extra people had to be hired to keep up. Further, Brecht had made twenty additions to the props and one addition to and one major alteration in the set during this time. Now Lawson had received plans for the ballad singer's wife's costume, and she was distressed to hear that there also might be an additional child. Brecht was experimenting and changing without regard for deadlines or expenses."[35] If we bear in mind the fact that Brecht not only made this many prop and costume changes but that the props had to be of museum quality and the costumes close approximations of costumes in paintings by Brueghel, Michelangelo and Leonardo da Vinci (but suitably worn), then we have some sense of the problems involved. There was a real aesthetic logic in all this for Brecht. Of course, if a set change was made, this would in turn require elaborate costume changes to fit visually with the new set. Of course, changes in the lyrics of the songs would then require changes in the music. New lines for the text would require new blocking which in turn would cause there to be changes made in the lighting and so on and so forth. But apparently Brecht was the only one with an overall sense of where things were going and how all these changes would ultimately tie together; for everyone else, much faith was required in order to believe that Brecht actually knew what he was doing and that everything would indeed eventually come together as a satisfying whole. Meanwhile apparent chaos reigned as the premiere date neared and then had to be postponed from July 24 until July 30.

Behind the chaos was an enormous amount of theatrical discipline: Brecht juggled antithetical pieces which he knew would eventually emerge as a synthesis. To see how this synthesis was achieved we need to go through the thesis/antithesis process. Let me try to illustrate this by tracing two complex elements through the production as a whole: (1) the use of costumes in the play, and (2) the use of music as an element that both divides and knits together the action.

Similar to Brecht's own analysis of the circular structure of the play itself, with the end bringing us back to the beginning, is his analysis of the linking and developmental role of the costumes. The costumes are consciously used to underline this circularity. Brecht himself pointed out that he used colors to trace a deliberate rise and fall in Galileo's fortunes. At the opening, rather muted colors – white, yellow and grey – were to suggest both a sense of a new day dawning and the modest circumstances in which we initially find the scholar-scientist. But then Brecht notes: "all the scenes taken together must have their own development in terms of color."[36] As Galileo is called to court, the colors literally as well as figuratively become richer. In one scene silver and pearl grey are played off against the brown and black of the next scene. A riot of color marks the carnival scenes, but, after this high point, the color scheme again reverts to the muted tones with which the play began and which matches Galileo's "impoverished" environment at play's end as he lives out his life as a prisoner of the Inquisition.

The rising and falling color scheme is matched by the use of music. First there is the rhymed introduction set to music by Hanns Eisler and sung by three boy-sopranos which leads into each individual scene. Then, superimposed on this basic and continuous rhythmic line, is the music of the carnival scenes which marks the high point of the action. Each "line" of the play (the character of Galileo himself, the music, the colors, the growing size of the cast) follows a classic curve of ascending complexity, then a rapidly descending curve towards the play's end. This powerfully synthesized line is deliberately reinforced by the eye, the ear, the mind, the pulse, and the foot tapping to the rhythms of the music.

But while a set of threads tie the scenes together and accelerate the emotional thrust of the play, all this occurs within a setting which is highly reminiscent of Brecht's theatre of bare platforms, of a half curtain and of the back screen˙projections that marked his highly politicized theatre of the period from about 1929 to 1933. We can ask ourselves whether these devices actually served to offset the main emotional drive of the play taken as a whole. Is there any reason why the huge projections of torture instruments (fig. 21) looming over Galileo in the tension-charged recantation scene, should have reduced emotion in the spectators? And the half-curtain at the

Coronet theatre that was opened and shut by a small "page" boy is difficult to imagine as a device with sufficient theatrical force to undercut emotional involvement. Indeed, one can, of course, view the half-curtain as a way of maintaining continuity in a production, since it does not slice the spectator off completely from the stage as the solid "Naturalist" curtain (or "guillotine," as Brecht himself called it) had done. And platforms *per se* would not seem to have had much of a function in cutting off emotional involvement.[37] In the 1947 production the platforms were used as a way of highlighting a specific action such as the robing of the Pope in scene 12 or when Galileo is "invited to Rome" by the Inquisition at the end of scene 11. In the latter scene, the stage directions call for the messenger to come down the steps, a gesture which clearly signals another repetition of the underlying pattern of the play. Using Gombrich's model of "the minimal image" (discussed at length in chapter 2 above) needed to trigger a response, it is really difficult to imagine that Brecht's 1947 production of *Galileo* did not more than meet this minimal standard. When the play ends with the nearly blind Galileo confronting Andrea and giving him the illicit *Discorsi*, the foundation of a new science, it is difficult to imagine a spectator maintaining much emotional distance. Perhaps the emotion of this scene might have then been undercut by playing the final scene of the book text, Andrea's crossing of the frontier, but this scene was not played in either the Coronet or the Berlin Ensemble production. In fact it has almost never been played in the professional theatre. The theatrical instincts of Brecht and Laughton were sound.

Given the differences between Charles Laughton's "method" acting techniques and Brecht's theoretical opposition to such an approach it should not surprise us that when the production opened on July 30, 1947, it showed elements of both approaches. Lacking the sumptuous sets usually used on Broadway in the 1940s for historical plays, the production looked forbiddingly stark to the national reviewers (though the local reviewers accepted this innovation). And though the play ran for a month with good audiences at the Coronet, Laughton's co-backer, Hambleton, had considerable doubts as to whether the play was ready for Broadway. According to Charles Laughton's biographer, Charles Higham, Hambleton (among others) "felt that it was a mistake to open in New York before drastic improvements had been made. Though he liked the simplicity and beauty of the production, he felt that it lacked passion, excitement, color, that it was too restrained and cerebral to appeal to Broadway audiences."[38] Another complicating factor for Hambleton was the fact that another Galileo play, Barry Stavis's *Lamp at Midnight* had opened on Broadway and had been well-reviewed by the highly influential Brooks Atkinson of the *New York Times*. In contrast, the normally   ecstatic   trade   magazine   *Variety*   had   denounced   the

Laughton/Brecht *Galileo* as drab and boring. And as though this were not enough, in the midst of the deliberations as to whether the *Galileo* production should or should not be taken to Broadway, both Brecht and Hanns Eisler, became objects of investigation by the notorious House Unamerican Activities Committee. Despite all these negative signs, soon after Brecht's appearance before HUAC and his fleeing to France the very next day, *Galileo* was taken to New York and opened at the Maxine Elliott Theatre on December 7, 1947. Despite a rather bad Brooks Atkinson review, the play had good audiences for its three week run but had to close as the Theatre was committed for another production. No other suitable New York venue was available and Charles Laughton was getting very cold feet. Again, Broadway

Fig. 21. Charles Laughton in the title role of *The Life of Galileo*. Beverly Hills production, July 30, 1947. Director of record was Joseph Losey but much of the actual directorial work was done by Brecht and by Charles Laughton. Over Laughton's left shoulder we see one of the instruments of torture that was shown to him to help force him to recant.

had proved to be an inhospitable environment both for Brecht's plays and for his style as a director.

But as these events occured in New York, Brecht was already hard at work in Europe attempting to find out where the climate might be most hospitable for him. In Paris he met with his old friend the novelist Anna Seghers who described Berlin as a "Witches Sabbath," advising him how to handle the situation in Berlin and telling him what difficulties he would meet with there. As Klaus Völker reports of the Seghers meeting:

His talk with her convinced him that, if he wished to maintain contact with the theatres in all the zones of Germany, he would have to have "a residence outside Germany." Although the "iron curtain" had not yet fallen, it was already clear that there were going to be two ideologically opposed German states. As far as opportunities for work in Berlin were concerned, Brecht received the impression that it would only be possible to accomplish anything there as a member of a powerful group: "One cannot exist there on one's own, or almost on one's own." Anna Seghers told him of spying and intrigues. In order to keep her Mexican passport (acquired during her own exile from the Third Reich) she did not live in the Russian sector but in Zehlendorf, in Herbert Ihering's house. She expressed a fully justified fear that if she did otherwise she would lose her readers in the Western Zone. On the other hand it was only in the Russian sector that workers returning from exile were given the privileges "without which work is impossible."[39]

Led on by the will o' the wisp of a major success on Broadway, Brecht had stayed on in America far longer than many of the other exiles. In Berlin the old clique that had so bitterly opposed him in Moscow in the mid-thirties had used the postwar years very effectively and now controlled the main cultural organs in the Soviet Zone. The curious combination of Stanislavski and Socialist Realism were the official watchwords throughout eastern Europe. In the west, as a stateless person in bad odor with the FBI, Brecht was totally unwelcome in the American Zone and hardly more welcome in the other Allied Zones. In Paris itself he was not impressed with what he saw in the theatre. In his notebook on November 11, 1947 he wrote scathingly: "evenings at Barrault's theatre 'the trial' Andre Gide's [another old enemy of Brecht's] adaptation of Kafka – brilliant production, numerous tricks, instead of a presentation of confusion a confused presentation as attempt to transmit fear to the audience – de gaulle ante portas."[40] With very few options open to him, Brecht decided that his best prospect was Zurich with its German-language theatre which had done three world premieres of his big exile plays during the war and where a number of his friends were still active. Brecht's son Stefan had stayed behind in America to study Hegel at Harvard, never, as it turned out, to live in Europe again.

In Zurich Brecht was met on November 5 by his old Augsburg friend and collaborator, Caspar Neher, who had remained in Germany during the Hitler years. He began to discuss prospects for Swiss productions of his plays at the

Zurich Schauspielhaus, while simultaneously looking into his chances for getting a visa from the American authorities to work with Erich Engel in Munich and perhaps to work in Austria (in Salzburg and Vienna). As negotiations dragged on with the Austrian authorities, the Americans flatly refused him a visa. In Switzerland, things were not very heartening either. Those in charge of the Schauspielhaus were not enthusiastic about having Brecht do the *Galileo* he proposed to them. They had done the world premiere of the play during the war and did not wish to revive it. They were not impressed with Brecht's credentials as a director (they surely knew about the New York reviews of *Galileo*) and they had no parts to offer Helene Weigel; perhaps they viewed her as an unknown quantity because of her forced absence from the stage during her years of exile. Neher did not like the atmosphere in Zurich at all and observed: "We have witnessed the destruction of Europe. It has passed over us and here in Switzerland they have the most antiquated theatre imaginable. No thinking is done."[41] Brecht does not seem to have been as despondent about the Swiss theatre as Neher, and, when Brecht was offered a small theatre in the provincial town of Chur to do a guest production of a play of his own choosing, he jumped at the chance, dragging the reluctant Neher along with him.

After consideration of a number of texts (among the plays considered were: *Antigone, Phaedra, Macbeth, Mother Courage,* and *Saint Joan of the Stockyards*), Brecht decided to adapt Hölderlin's nineteenth-century version of Sophocles' *Antigone,* Hegel's favorite play. It is clear that what Brecht had in mind doing this play in Chur was another *Versuch*: another exercise to get ready for what he hoped might be a triumphant return to Berlin for him and Helene Weigel and Caspar Neher. The adaptation of Hölderlin was quickly prepared and rehearsals began in Zurich in mid-January 1948. Weigel was selected to play Antigone and a Swiss actor named Hans Gaugler to play Kreon. At exactly the right moment, Ruth Berlau, who had done the photos of the *Galileo* production in America and who had earlier photographed Brecht productions in Scandinavia, arrived to make a photographic record of *Antigone.* I have described at length in *The Essential Brecht* the changes Brecht made in the Sophocles/Hölderlin text. All that needs to be repeated here for an understanding of Brecht's concept of the play is that he clearly saw Kreon as Hitler and that he saw the ways in which Polynices and Eteocles are killed (one by Kreon's own hands) as a direct reflection of Hitler's attack on Stalingrad.

Brecht's staging of *Antigone* largely followed Caspar Neher's sketches. Sitting in a semicircle on simple benches before an almost colorless backdrop, the actors in Chur simply arose and came forward to act their roles in a square playing area that was marked by four posts on which were hung the skulls of horses (figs. 22 and 23). Ruth Berlau recalls that the complete heads of just slaughtered horses were actually delivered to the theatre and there boiled by Brecht and Neher in huge laundry tubs. The boiled skulls were then painted a bloody red and mounted on posts. The only other items on stage were, on one side, a large square gong, and on the other a rack containing masks set on long poles. The chorus held these masks in front of them during long choral odes and then replaced them in the rack. The tempo of the production was extremely fast and no curtain was used at all as scene followed scene with great rapidity. The acting, partly because of and partly in spite of the pace of the production, was deliberately stylized and no attempt was made at "realistic" portraiture in the manner of Stanislavski. The role of Kreon was deliberately the most stylized, with his makeup suggesting Hitler and his movements (frequently going over into exaggerated dance steps) suggesting the kind of bloody clown Brecht presents in his *Schweik* adaptation and in *Arturo Ui*. As Frank Jones has suggested, this treatment of Kreon characterizes the play as something very close to melodrama, "with all the black on one side and all the white on the other"[42] (fig. 24).

It is perhaps unfair to link the partially melodramatic style of this new production (with all the pejorative connotations of melodrama) with the "new playing style." Despite the claim that he is presenting a new playing style, it is virtually certain that Brecht was fully aware in 1947–8 that the style was not so much new as a renaissance (with some modifications) of many aspects of the stage style of fifth-century Athens – the stage style that Aristotle knew and praised. By 1948, with the staging of *Antigone* and the composition of the *Short Organum*, Brecht has beaten a skilled retreat from much of his earlier iconoclasm. The author of the 1927 essay, "Should We Not Destroy Aesthetics?" now consciously attempts to generate a consistent aesthetic, and says specifically that his earlier attacks on many aesthetic criteria had been determined by the heat of the battle and the fact that his opponents had pre-empted much of the necessary vocabulary for their own reactionary purposes. "We," announces the now regal Brecht in the preface to the *Short Organum*, "despite general dismay, therefore revoke our [earlier] intention to emigrate from the realm of the pleasurable, and we hereby announce, to even greater dismay, our intention of taking up residence there." In section 4 he comes perilously close to praising "the catharsis of which Aristotle writes." In section 9 he speaks of improbability on the stage as being perfectly admissible as long as it "remains of a constant kind." By the time he reaches section 12 Brecht has mellowed enough to speak of the "great Shakespeare" and to state further: "And according to Aristotle – and we agree there – the plot is the soul of the drama." The *Short Organum* then closes (and we are reminded of Aristotle's preference of "poetry" to "history") with

Fig. 22. Caspar Neher's sketch for the basic scene design for the Chur, Switzerland, February 1948 production of *Antigone*.

Fig. 23. The almost exact stage realization of Neher's sketch for the February 1948 production of *Antigone* in Chur, Switzerland. Directed by Brecht. Helene Weigel, after a long absence from the professional stage returned to play the lead.

the observation: "If art does mirror life, it does it with special mirrors."[43] It is clear both from the production of a classic text and from the new tone of the *Short Organum* that Brecht in 1948, self-consciously on the brink of becoming a classic himself, had begun to treat his great forerunners in dramaturgy and stage theory (particularly Aristotle and Shakespeare) with considerable respect. Nevertheless, it must be granted that Brecht was still very reluctant to admit to the similarity of his own work to that of other classical writers. On the one hand (considering his earlier iconoclastic statements), it would have hurt his pride to retreat too openly, and on the other, the classical writers had served other masters than the proletariat that Brecht was hoping to serve upon his return to East Berlin. Yet however reluctant he may have been, and however devious he was in admitting to similarities to other writers, he did now seek consistently to point out in what ways other dramatists and theorists had anticipated him.

Perfectly aware by 1948 that not only were there narrative, epic and lyric elements in the Greek drama, and that the use of choral odes to interrupt the action was a definite anticipation of key elements in his epic theatre, Brecht was also surely aware that both Goethe and Schiller had anticipated him in noting and commenting favorably upon these facets of Greek drama. Yet Brecht writes: "Hellenic dramaturgy sought, through a certain amount of

Fig. 24. *Antigone*, Chur, 1948. A rather melodramatic moment as a dying messenger staggers in to report the fall of the city.

usage of *Verfremdung*, and particularly through the segments devoted to the chorus, to save some freedom of [rational] calculation, freedom that Schiller did not know how to secure."[44] One may be permitted to wonder here why there is any reference to Schiller at all, if, as a footnote seeks to establish, the Schiller of the Goethe–Schiller *Correspondence* is really inept. Surely Brecht knew by 1948 that, important though the *Correspondence* was to the history of German criticism, it was of less importance to the history of thought on the epic than works such as Schiller's essays "On Naive and Sentimental Poetry" and on the role of the chorus in Greek tragedy, and Goethe's on the dramatic and the epic modes. Viewed in the larger context of the theoretical writings of Goethe and Schiller, Brecht's citation from the *Correspondence* reveals either a general ignorance of their writings or a deliberate piece of tendentious citation to prove both their ignorance and his own originality. The similarities between Brecht's own theory and, for example, the following hypothesis from Schiller, are so striking that it is difficult to believe he could in 1948 have been unaware of it:

Just as the chorus brings life to the language, it brings calm to the action – but it is the lovely and lofty calm that is essential to a pure work of art. For the soul of the spectator should retain its freedom even in the midst of the most violent passion; this does not mean that it should be robbed of impressions, but rather that it should always clearly and serenely distinguish between itself and the emotions which it suffers. Thus, the common judgement against the chorus (that it destroys illusion and disrupts the emotive hold of the play on its audience) can be used as the chorus' highest recommendation. This is because the genuine artist wishes to avoid the blind power of emotion and deliberately spurns the creation of illusion. Should the blows with which tragedy strikes our hearts strike uninterruptedly, then suffering would win the victory over action. We would become one with the tragic material rather than rise above it. The chorus holds the individual parts of the tragedy apart and enters between passionate outbursts with soothing contemplation, and it is because of this that freedom is restored to us, freedom that would otherwise be lost in a storm of emotions.[45]

Schiller, it would seem, knew a thing or two about *Verfremdung*, about "a feeling of distance," about pacing of a drama, about deliberate episodic fragmentation. It is clear from Brecht's own copious production notes that his use of the chorus in Chur was a return in some particulars to the theoretical function assigned to it by Schiller, and a return in practice to the oldest of western dramatic modes, the drama Aristotle was thinking of when he formulated his *Poetics*.

As surely as Brecht must have known by 1948 that the German classics had anticipated many of his theoretical points, he must have known also that his earlier view of a theatrical audience sitting hypnotized in a darkened auditorium and creeping into the skins of the characters on the stage described only a very narrow, specifically late-nineteenth-century segment of the history of the theatre. Certainly he knew by this time that neither the Greek nor the Elizabethan theatre (to cite but two prominent examples) fitted his general description. Despite Brecht's claim to be presenting "a new playing style," I see no major differences in probable effect between the style of his Chur presentation and well-known classical Greek theatrical practice. One does not need a profound scholarly knowledge of Greek theatre to recognize that Brecht had come perilously close to returning to the very theatrical mode that he most despised in the 1920s. If anything, Brecht's production of *Antigone* in the small Swiss theatre may have been considerably less epic than *Antigone* in its original setting. How hypnotized, we might wonder, was any member of the Greek audience of some 14,000 who knew the mythological background of the tale inside out? Did the all-male Greek casts with their broad gestures and loud voices hypnotize those huge assemblies? Did the long choral odes, delivered by as many as fifty strong voices, break the action or did they intensify it? We know only that these elements are all "epic" as Brecht defined the term; we do not know with any certainty whether they succeeded any more in the Greek world in achieving a *Verfremdungseffekt* than they did in Brecht's theatre. We might assume that despite the considerably larger number of "epic" elements in Greek dramaturgy and performance the audiences were as profoundly moved as Brecht's audiences, twenty-five centuries later, tended to be.

From what we can reconstruct of Brecht's 1948 production of his version of *Antigone*, we know that he was able to recapture many powerful and essential features of the original Greek play in its original setting. Freeing himself from the burdensome limitations of strict Naturalism in acting and in settings, getting rid of the curtain between the actors and the audience, using a unit set that required absolutely no changes that would interrupt the action, Brecht used mime and mask, choral ode and dance for broad and specifically theatrical effects. The result was, as even many fairly hostile reviewers granted, rather fine theatre. Whatever the drawbacks of the clumsily reworked text (hidden, in all probability, by the sheer pace of the performance), the staging not only recalled the 1924 production of *Edward II* and the 1932 production of *Mother* but pointed ahead to Berlin and to the great productions of the exile plays that would make Brecht, as playwright and as director, world famous. We underestimate Brecht's humor if we overlook the conscious irony of the grandmaster of anti-Aristotelian "epic theatre," as he prepared himself for his last major period of work in the physical theatre by adapting and indeed intensifying an Aristotelian text, and presenting that text in a largely traditional style. Brecht is never more modern than when he uses devices from the past.

The very brief run of the play in Chur (four performances only) and with only one matinée performance in Zurich (far fewer than Brecht had hoped for) had served its primary purpose: (1) to try out on a small scale the kind of work he would do later with a full ensemble and (2) to give Helene Weigel an opportunity to reappear after her long forced absence from the professional stage. And though Brecht did stay on in Switzerland until October 1948, his continued presence there was less for what Switzerland could offer him than for the fact that he was being offered very little of a concrete nature elsewhere.

While staying on in Zurich and from there conducting exploratory negotiations with theatres in Austria, Munich and Berlin, Brecht was heavily involved in a production of *Puntila*, the play he had co-authored with Hella Wuolijoki and Margarete Steffin during the Finnish period of his exile. Whether by design or default he apparently neglected to tell the Schauspielhaus that a co-author was involved, and so at first Wuolijoki's name appeared nowhere on the contract or on the theatre marquee. This was finally corrected only after Wuolijoki's daughter personally complained about it in Zurich.

The Zurich *Puntila* production, like the California *Galileo*, was not officially directed by Brecht (the director on record for *Puntila* was Kurt Hirschfeld) as Brecht's working papers for Switzerland were not in order with the Swiss officials. The records of the production are quite sparse and there is no published "model book" for the Zurich *Puntila* that compares to the one Ruth Berlau prepared for *Antigone* (and would prepare later for Berlin Ensemble productions) even though Berlau and at least one other photographer did photograph a number of scenes from the *Puntila* production. From what is known of the production it is clear that Brecht viewed it as another "exercise," as a way of beginning to train some actors who potentially could then move with time to wherever he might settle after leaving Zurich. But though he considered the Zurich facilities inadequate to his needs, nevertheless Brecht was able to achieve results that were artistically satisfactory both to him and to the public and many of the theatre critics. Brecht's own diary entry for June 10, 1948, describes his work on *Puntila* as follows:

Puntila und sein Knecht Matti is staged at the Schauspielhaus, assisted by Hirschfeld, at first fears because of Steckel's vitality; he charges off with the force of a tank and the sensitivity of a mimosa. by using old credits and medium of rapidly sketched basic stage arrangements which unchain the actors, discussion time was reduced to approximately three minutes in four weeks. that is important. certain novelties (first phase: naturalness, social characterization, epic "standbys," clear telling of the basic story line etc.) can only be striven after practically through trying them out. there are more difficulties with the outmoded lighting facilities at the theatre than with the actors as one cannot uniformly light the stage brightly as one has to try to bring out facial features with flood lights; the photos that ruth [Berlau] made during the performance show that the floodlights blur the

Fig. 25. *Puntila*, Zurich, 1948. The drunken Puntila, on top of a mountain made of furniture, shows Matti (Gustav Knuth) the glorious forests on Puntila's vast estate.

facial features and make seeing difficult. the set designer teo otto is a talented student of [Caspar] Neher. i took up again Neher's Drums in the Night moon from the Munich performance [September 1922]. as background we used a large wall covered in birch bark against which, made up like advertising signs for business, we hung up emblems for the sun, the moon and various small clouds (made of copper or laquered wood) and this wall was strongly lighted for day scenes and weakly lighted for night scenes (naturally we never used any colored light). that is a solution for landscapes (fig. 25).[46]

But despite the fact of the relative success of *Puntila* Brecht became more and more aware that he could not stay on in Zurich where he was "only a guest," but he needed his own theatre where he would be free to begin to rebuild German acting, set design and directing which, in his view, was as badly in need of rebuilding as the ruined German cities themselves. He was appalled when he saw in Zurich the work of Walter Richter and Will Quadflieg "who brought with them the style of the Berliner Staatstheater under the Nazis." Brecht noted with disgust: "Before I even see the ruined theatres I see the ruined acting."[47] In August, after his first visit since 1933 to a theatre on German soil, Brecht raged to his companions about the actors and complained about "their effrontery in simply carrying on as if nothing had been destroyed but their theatre buildings, their starry-eyed attitude to art, their premature conclusion of peace with their own country – all this was worse than he had feared".[48] His fears were increased rather than lessened when he met with two people whose work he much admired, the directors Fritz Kortner and Berthold Viertel, who had devastating things to say about the theatre that was arising from the rubble of the Third Reich. By the fall of 1948 Brecht was fully aware of the enormous scale of the task that lay ahead of them. Lured by an offer to stage *Mother Courage* in a guest production at Berlin's German Theatre and the possibility of later establishing their own ensemble, Brecht and Weigel decided to return to what was at that time the Soviet Sector of divided Berlin. On Sunday, October 10, 1948, Weigel and Brecht left Zurich bound for Berlin.

5   Berlin: an etching by Churchill based on an idea of Hitler's[1]

After brief stopovers in Salzburg and in Prague, Brecht and Helene Weigel arrived at the Czech–German border on October 22, 1948. The arrival was a big event in the Soviet Zone and Brecht and Weigel were surrounded by photographers and reporters. Many old friends were also there to meet them, but old enemies were there too, many of them in important positions; from these positions they could make Brecht's work in Berlin as difficult as possible. Symptomatic of his mixed reception was the fact that after he had been greeted by old friends such as Herbert Ihering and Wolfgang Langhoff, the next evening he was taken to see *Haben*, a rather uninspired play by one of his bitterest enemies, a member of the Moscow camarilla of the 1930s, Julius Hay. The signal was clear: this is the official standard for plays in the Soviet Zone. Brecht noted bitterly in his diary: "evening, premiere of Hay's *Haben* in the German Theatre, miserable performance, hysterically inhibited, totally unrealistic."[2] But while he wrote this in his diary, Brecht, with his "nose for a talent," had observed in the otherwise miserable performance of *Haben* one bright spot: the next day he asked the young and not conventionally beautiful actress Angelika Hurwicz to come to his room at the Hotel Adlon to talk about a part in *Mother Courage* which he planned to do as a guest production in Wolfgang Langhoff's German Theatre. Bold as always in spotting talent Brecht told Hurwicz there and then that he wanted her for the *Courage* production. This erstwhile unnoticed actress who had performed in a wandering troupe in Hitler's Germany and who, after the war ended, had walked to Berlin in the hopes of being able to act there would now, under Brecht's tutelage, become a mainstay of his theatre, playing Kattrin in *Mother Courage* and Grusche in the *Caucasian Chalk Circle*. Always on the lookout for new talent and tireless and ingenious in promoting his own schemes, Brecht began at once to try by telephone and through numerous letters to attract both well-established stars and raw beginners to Berlin to join a company which existed mainly at this time in Brecht's imagination. His only "guarantee" had been one guest production of a play at Langhoff's German Theatre. All future negotiations with East Berlin authorities to establish a genuine repertory company with its own budget in its own theatre would remain extremely tentative for a number of tense months. His fights with the Moscow group in the thirties over definitions of Realism had not been forgotten and his private opposition to the official policy of supporting

Stanislavski was widely known. In addition, his five-fold no, when he had been asked before the House Unamerican Activities Committee in the United States as to whether he had ever been a communist party member,[3] may well have helped him before HUAC but was scarcely a recommendation to communist East Berlin. For the "Ulbricht group" (as they were at first known officially) who had returned to Berlin in the chaotic days before the city finally fell to the Red Army, Brecht's comparatively late and circumspect return from the centre of capitalism was greeted with very mixed feelings. Certainly he was well known in the German-speaking world, and his return to the Soviet Zone could possibly be used as an effective weapon in the cultural department of the cold war, but this also meant dealing with Brecht and his wayward ideas on a day to day basis, hardly a cheerful prospect for his old enemies, such as the critic Erpenbeck, the playwright Hay, politicians Kurella and Ulbricht, and the highly influential Hungarian critic, an implacable enemy from the thirties, Georg Lukács. For these people who had survived in Moscow under Stalin's iron "control of the arts," Brecht was literally "a bourgeois decadent," with no sense whatsoever of party discipline, with an entirely wrong aesthetic position, an entirely wrong moral position (the then rather prudish Soviet Sector disapproved of his perpetual harem), an abrasive personality and a totally exaggerated sense of his own importance. Looking back on the first period in Berlin, Brecht himself said later: "My remarks on the deplorable artistic state of the theatre in the former capital of the Reich, were brushed aside as the more or less offensive carpings of a place-seeking artist who overrated himself."[4] To succeed at all in Berlin he knew that he had to identify people already there who could help him and that he also needed to import as many allies as possible from theatres in America, in the western zones of Germany, and from the Austrian and Swiss German-language theatre. While working very hard to succeed in Berlin, he would also work hard to create other options in the West just in case he was unable to establish his own theatre on his own terms in the Soviet Zone.

Brecht felt that his main chance for success in Berlin would be an exemplary production of one of his major plays written in exile. For his opening shot in the Berlin campaign he chose a play of protracted war and of fragile peace, his chronicle of the Thirty Years War, *Mother Courage and Her Children*, with Helene Weigel in the title role.

When Brecht started rehearsing *Mother Courage* in borrowed space he did not begin his production from scratch but used as a model the extensive photographic records that had been made of the play's world premiere in neutral Zurich during the war. This production, with Therese Giehse (an actress much admired and already used by Brecht in the Zurich production of *Puntila*) in the lead and designed by Teo Otto (who was retained for the

Berlin revival), contained much that Brecht felt could be used. He was particularly taken with the dominant stage requisite of the Zurich production: the actual wagon that Giehse had dragged across the war ravaged landscape. Brecht took over Teo Otto's design for the wagon (fig. 26) and with this design he also adopted much of the stage movement or blocking of the Zurich production. Later, using Ruth Berlau's photos of the Berlin production, Brecht would create the so-called *Courage* "model book"[5] which he then insisted should be used as a guide by other directors wishing to stage his play. But in late 1948 it was Brecht himself who was using a model and staying remarkably close to the key visual elements of the Zurich production. In his view the use of a model was not really a limitation on creativity, but rather something that was ecologically sound, the recycling of elements of proven utility.

While rehearsing *Mother Courage* several hours a day under extremely awkward circumstances with borrowed actors and in borrowed space, Brecht and Weigel were also working behind the scenes to get official authorization and a permanent home for their own ensemble. One day, during *Mother Courage* rehearsals, Brecht was summoned to a meeting of some of the key theatre and political people of the Soviet Zone of Berlin. The mayor, Friedrich

Fig. 26. The original design for Mother Courage's wagon by Teo Otto for the world premiere of the play: Zurich, 1941. Directed by Lindtberg. The lead role was played by Therese Giehse, one of Brecht's favorite actresses.

Ebert, was present, but as Brecht notes in his diary, "he said neither hello nor goodbye to me, never addressed me directly and only spoke once, a sceptical sentence in which he spoke of certain unclear projects that could destroy existing arrangements."[6] Other politicians at the meeting were almost equally discouraging. As Brecht noted: "for the first time I begin to smell the stinking breath of the provinces here." Fortunately, though the German politicians were distinctly discouraging, a number of old friends in theatre circles rallied round in support. Very importantly, Wolfgang Langhoff, head of the German Theatre, agreed to let Brecht and a Brecht/Weigel Ensemble share the German Theatre with him until such time as another theatre could be rebuilt among the rubble and made available for Brecht and Weigel. Fortunately also, the key Soviet cultural official in Berlin, Alexander Dymschitz, despite his general subscription to Stalinist dicta in the arts, came out on the side of Brecht.[7] On one side of the fray were powerful enemies and on the other were powerful friends but the outcome of this battle could not be predicted at the time Brecht was rehearsing *Mother Courage*. The battle for and against Brecht would be decided by the success or failure of the production with its Berlin theatre audience.

In many ways the rehearsals were very like the ones conducted in Munich for Brecht's first production, *Edward II*. Again there was no attempt to create anything approaching the kind of set favored by Stanislavski. The backdrop was a huge semi-circle of plain canvas. Brecht observed of the bland cyclorama: "No doubt the sight of the cyclorama behind a completely empty stage (in the prologue and in the seventh and last scene), creates the illusion of a flat landscape with the sky above it. There is a reason to have no objection to this, because there needs to be some stirring of poetic feelings in the spectator if this illusion is to come to be."[8] In contrast, props were carefully crafted to reflect real use and were modeled closely on those that had been used in the Zurich production. Brecht felt that no such illusion could be created with props. He wrote:

though one has in large matters (the cyclorama) a certain beautiful vagueness, one does not have this in small matters. In a Realistic presentation it is important to have meticulously worked out details of costumes and of props as here the imagination (fantasy) of the spectator can add nothing. The tools and the eating utensils must be created most lovingly. Also, naturally the costumes must not be allowed to look like festivals where people wear national costumes but rather must show individual characteristics such as those of class. They are worn short or long, are made of cheaper or more expensive material, are looked after better or worse, etc. etc.[9]

The care used with the selection of props then carried over in rehearsals into the careful and proper, skilled and "natural" use of them. As with the careful rehearsal of the "hanging scene" in *Edward II* in Munich in 1924, all scenes requiring particular skills (woodchopping, haggling over prices, plucking a chicken etc.) were rehearsed until the actors could exhibit the appropriate level of technical skill in carrying out these tasks in a natural and straightforward way.

In working with these actors (Weigel as Mother Courage, Angelika Hurwicz as Kattrin and Paul Bildt as the cook), there was almost no discussion of theory. What Brecht was seeking was something that Eric Bentley has described as "Naturalism" in his "voice work with actors." The actors were not to shout, posture, or be noble, but rather to speak as naturally as they would to their spouse at breakfast. To help actors become less "theatrical" and more natural in their speech patterns, the rehearsals would sometimes be conducted in the third person, as an actor, instead of merely speaking his line, would introduce it with "he said", "she said" etc. Also, to help actors avoid the artificiality of German "stage speech," Brecht would ask them not to speak high German but to speak their lines in their own native dialect. Angelika Hurwicz, who had not worked with Brecht before was worried that "now Brecht had certainly gone crazy"[10] and that he was going to ask for third-person delivery in actual performance. Her fears were unfounded. These techniques were confined to rehearsals and were dropped as soon as the actors were able to speak their lines in a natural "uncramped" way.[11] Years later Angelika Hurwicz recalled how much she enjoyed these rehearsals. She said it was "like a seminar but where nothing was demanded."[12]

If, despite Brecht's own hostility towards the word, one can describe his voice with actors as "naturalistic," one certainly cannot apply this term to his blocking. In this area he was given to stage movement that can best be described as stylized or emphatically dramatic. He felt that most actors tended, by excessive movement and by moving while speaking, to detract from the story line and to lead to devaluation of movement on stage. In a long note on this question Brecht wrote:

Positions should be retained as long as there is no compelling reason for changing them – and a desire for variety is not a compelling reason. If one gives in to a desire for variety, the consequence is devaluation of all movement on the stage; the spectator ceases to look for a specific meaning behind each movement, he stops taking movement seriously. But, especially at the crucial points in the action, the full impact of a change of position must not be weakened. Legitimate variety is obtained by ascertaining the crucial points and planning the arrangement around them. For example, the recruiters have been listening to Mother Courage; she has succeeded in diverting and entertaining them with her talk and so putting them in a good humor; so far there has been only one ominous circumstance: the sergeant has asked for her papers; but he has not examined them – his only purpose was to prolong their stay. She takes the next step (physically too: she goes up to the sergeant, takes hold of his belt buckle and says: "I bet you could do with a belt-buckle?"), she tries to sell them something, and that is when the recruiters spring into action. The sergeant says ominously: "I could do with something else" and along with the recruiter goes over to the sons at the cart's shaft. The recruiters look the sons over as they would horses. The crucial point is accented when the sergeant goes back to Mother Courage, comes to a standstill before her, and asks: "Why are they dodging their military service?" (The effect of such movements should not be weakened by having the actors speak during them.) If changes are needed to make certain developments clear to the audience, the movement must be utilized to express something significant for the action and for this particular moment; if nothing of the sort can be found, it is advisable to review the whole arrangement up to this point; it will probably be seen to be at fault, because the sole purpose of an arrangement is to express the action, and the action (it is to be hoped) involves a logical development of incidents, which the arrangement needed only present.[13]

The whole question of movement in Brecht is very closely tied to his predilection for tight groupings on stage. He felt that most actors, in order to draw attention to themselves as individuals, tended to drift away from groups, and that directors had to be very tough about this and insist on allowing actors to move away from one another only when there was an absolutely compelling reason for them to do so. Otherwise they should stay together, in carefully orchestrated groupings as tightly arranged and aesthetically ordered as those on a canvas by Breughel, Brecht's actual model for a number of stage groupings in various plays of the post-exile period. Indeed, if one places photos of a number of his Berlin Ensemble productions side by side (figs. 27, 28 and 29) one can see that such groupings took on a routine or mannered quality and that they cropped up in virtually identical form in one Brecht production after another. But in *Mother Courage*, these highly characteristic and subsequently mannered groupings had a real sense of newness as they were being worked out for the first time in Berlin.

In his *Working Journal* (entry for December 18, 1948) Brecht gives a full description of how he prepared for his daily rehearsals. Living at the old, largely bombed-out Adlon Hotel, he had his own separate room (with Helene Weigel and Ruth Berlau down the hall) so that his privacy and flexibility of sleeping arrangements were ensured. He would begin his day as follows:

Routinely I get up at 5:30 and then, make my coffee or tea on a small spirit stove, read a bit of Lukács or Goethe [the collector]. When I look up I see a large print of Breughel's "Peasant Dance" on the wall. I walk around a bit on the red rug and then sit down to work at the table. Around eight it gets light outside and the ruins begin to emerge [the SS, a day after Hitler's death in the bunker, set the Adlon Hotel on fire and only one wing has been renovated]. After 8 Kuckhahn [an assistant on the production] arrives and orders my breakfast and we prepare for the *Courage* rehearsals. At nine I am at the theatre in my office where Kasproviak waits to take my dictation. Rehearsals begin at 10.[14]

This schedule was followed for some two months before the premiere that was scheduled for early January 1949.

The rehearsal period given over to *Mother Courage* was unusually brief by later Brecht standards. In contrast with almost all his prewar directing work, he made few changes in the actual text of the play during the production. He did not hand actors reams of new text to be learned as quickly as possible. The rehearsals were used to polish the text and this led quite naturally to lines being dropped (some forty or so in the first scene for instance),[15] some rearrangement of scenes and an attempt to cut out lines which suggested that Courage might be a sympathetic figure. The most important rearrangement of scenes occurred at the beginning of the play with the audience first seeing the family with the wagon and then the scene with the recruiters, rather than the other way round. In this way the play began and ended with Paul Dessau's haunting wind arrangement of "Christians Awake," with Brecht's own words suggesting that without Mother Courage the war could not be fought.[16]

The opening song of *Mother Courage* serves a similar function to the *Moritat* of Mack the Knife which opens *The Threepenny Opera*. Courage's song introduces her and serves a highly important and extremely economical expository function. The music (played as is usual in Brecht by a group half visible in one of the stage boxes) serves first to claim the audience's attention. Next, the lyrics give a condensed and brilliantly effective introduction to

Fig. 27. The Berlin Ensemble adaptation of J.M.R. Lenz's play *The Private Tutor*. Directed by Brecht and Neher. Sets by Neher. Berlin, April 15, 1950.

Courage and her role in the war. When the song fades away, we are then ready for the scene with the recruiters and everything that transpires in that scene. Reconstructing what Brecht sought to achieve with this opening scene, it is instructive to work carefully through it (as Brecht did), word by word and movement by movement to see how and why the scene was played in the way it was.

Mother Courage's song (in my translation) runs as follows:

> You Captains, let the drums be stilled
> And let your infantry stop for a bit.
> Mother Courage is arriving with boots
> That they'll run better in.
> With their vermin and the livestock
> Baggage, cannon, and the animals to pull them.
> If they've to march into battle for you
> They'll wanna get good boots.
> *Refrain*: Spring is coming. Christians Awake
>   The snow melts. The dead rest.
>   And whatever hasn't died
>   Will stand up in its socks.
> You Captains, without at least some sausage
> Your men won't march for you into death.
> Let Courage cure them first, with wine,
> Of that which ails body and soul.
> Cannon on an empty stomach
> You Captains, that's not healthy.
> But once they've fed, then with my blessing
> Lead them into the maw of hell.

The sprightly music invites one to sing and to march along but the words tell us with the most brutal clarity where this sprightly march is leading. We are told that without Courage's family, introduced succinctly by her as "business folk," the war cannot be fought. The hyena of the battlefield (as she will be called later in the play) cynically and brutally reveals herself here. The language of her song is a foretaste of the recruiters, and of everyone else in the play, a language described by Hans Mayer as "naked, stripped of all conventions and previously accepted principles."[17] There is also no hint here of this being a war fought for religious principle.

Whether the audience actually registered at a conscious level the naked brutality of Courage any more than the 1928 audience recognized the naked criminality of Mack the Knife is an open question. It may well be that none of the content of the song registered, but Brecht left nothing to chance as he then had the recruiters voicing virtually identical sentiments. Standing together at the front of the stage they chatted casually about the people out there (looking and speaking directly to the theatre audience)[18] who had, so they said, not experienced war recently enough. This, in a Berlin that was still

Fig. 28. The Brecht, Dudow, Eisler, Stark, Weisenborn adaptation of Gorki's novel *Mother*. Directed by Brecht. Set by Neher. Lead role: Helene Weigel. A guest production of the Berlin Ensemble company at the German Theatre, Berlin, January 13, 1951.

Fig. 29. Berlin Ensemble adaptation of Gerhart Hauptmann's *The Beaver Pelt and the Red Rooster*. Directed by Egon Monk. Set by Heinz Pfeiffenberger. Premiere, Berlin, March 24, 1951.

largely a pile of rubble! The text looks simple and direct and yet is reflexive. It undermines itself; it invites the closest attention. The supposedly light banter, resignation, complaint can distract us from the layers of meaning that the text contains. In the world to which Brecht is introducing us here, man, when distinguishable from other beasts at all, is distinguished by the superior ingenuity of his cruelty. The brutal world of Brecht's plays, lyrics, novels and short stories — a world in which man is clearly shown to be more vicious than the great white shark — is revealed in all its ferocity in the dialogue of the recruiters "like a louse running away from scratching." Man, in the image of the metaphor, is a louse. No wonder, says one of the recruiters, gesturing towards the audience, "I've lost my confidence in mankind here." Disgust-edly the sergeant-major castigates peace and declares it to be certainly inferior to war. "In peace," he observes, "people let the cabbages run to seed. People mess around with men and cattle as though they were nothing." Then, confusing people and animals, he points to the town ahead and says "No one knows how many young people and good nags there are in this city up ahead; nobody's even bothered to count." Only in war are "people and animals properly counted and led away, because, as everyone knows, without order, no war!"

After the sententious, topsy-turvy "principles" are enunciated and wholly agreed with by the other recruiter, they spot the wagon of Mother Courage, surely one of the best-known and most powerful requisites of the twentieth-century stage. In a world that confuses animals and people it is significant and convenient in stage terms that the wagon is drawn not by real oxen or horses, but by two young men. On the wagon box sits a cheerful Courage and her "dumb" and ever fearful daughter Kattrin. The soldiers eye the boys as potential cannon-fodder, the commodity in which they trade. Courage views the soldiers as potential purchasers of the goods with which her wagon is loaded. Courage is asked to state her name (received, she says, because of her fearless pursuit of profit at the siege of Riga) and to present her papers. Courage produces her largely meaningless papers with considerable humor and a theatrical flourish. But beneath the surface humor lurks the shark of Brecht's imagery, a shark that bites no matter how humorous the scene may superficially appear. One extraordinary "document" illustrates the duality of her humor. She produces a piece of parchment which "proves" that her Schimmel (a word meaning either a "grey horse" or "mildew"), a horse that she obviously does not possess, is not carrying foot and mouth disease! As her sons have replaced this horse, she, like the recruiters, confuses her own sons with draft animals. This same, highly deliberate confusion was then deepened by the actions of the recruiter in the Berlin production. He walked around the boys like a farmer at a fair contemplating the purchase of a pair of draft animals. He felt their muscles and then remarked with admiration: "I see, these lads have grown up like birch trees, deep-chested, strong legs; why does something like that try to avoid the draft?" He then addressed the young men contemptuously, trying to shame them into abandoning their "animal" condition (as cart pullers) and joining the "human" race of soldiers. After asking the boys for their names the recruiter says: "You might as well be called Jacob Ox and Esau Ox, after all you do pull the wagon." Then, with fake resignation, he concludes: "I guess you'll never get out of harness." The recruiter is literally and figuratively correct. The boys will live and die pulling the wagon of war. They have no more ability to avoid their violent fate than an ox or a horse would have in this ravaged landscape.

Though the recruiter has declared to the boys that they will never get out of harness, his objective, obviously, is to get them out of Courage's harness in order to use them himself. The separating out of one of the sons (cutting out a calf from a protective herd) was carefully underlined by Brecht by his use of the wagon as a screen and by his use of blocking to visually reinforce what is going on in the dialogue. This becomes clear, if we take a close look at the official photographic record of the opening scene as contained in the Berlin Ensemble "model book" for *Mother Courage*. The family first appears as a very tightly knit group, in opposition to the visual clump on the other side of the stage, of the soldiers. In fig. 30 the unity of the family is disturbed as Courage enters what we may call the space of the recruiters and one of the recruiters enters the family space. Visual linkage between the two groups is seen clearly in the next picture (fig. 31) as the wagon's shaft points towards the recruiters, Weigel's arm points in the direction of the wagon and one of her sons is provocatively placed exactly in the middle between the two opposed territories. Alarmingly, in the next picture given in the "model book", both soldiers are in the family space and Courage stands alone in the recruiters' space. Suddenly aware of the real danger Courage hastens back to her space and the recruiters return to theirs, but the distance between the two groups is closer now than it was in the first scene. After the incident of the fortune-telling scene with the crosses which brings the groups closer together (fig. 32), the integrity of the family *vis-à-vis* the soldiers' group is momentarily re-established. For an instant it appears that the Courage group will remain intact. But then as one of the soldiers proposes to buy a belt ("The good people live from business deals, don't they?") the integrity of the family group is literally and figuratively shattered. One of the soldiers enters deep into the family space as he examines a belt behind the wagon, out of the cold wind of April, while, on the other side of the wagon, the other soldier enters the family space only to take Eilif completely away with him into the soldiers' space. The other soldier is left demonstrably in the family space as the wagon

Fig. 30. *Mother Courage*, Berlin, 1949. While Courage tries to sweet talk one of the officers the other one is beginning to sweet talk the boys near the wagon.

Fig. 31. *Mother Courage*, Berlin, 1949. Suddenly aware of the danger, Courage points warningly at her son who stands preening himself exactly half way between the wagon and the recruiters.

Fig. 32. *Mother Courage,* Berlin, 1949. The previously fully unified family begins to lose its visual unity.

itself is now drawn away into what I have defined as the soldiers' space. The scene ends with the declaration: "Those who would live from war, must pay the price." The final vision could virtually be labelled: *quod erat demonstrandum.* Everything that the dialogue has conveyed has been massively reinforced by the gestural exposition of the scene with its extremely strong visual arrangement. The scene has a visual clarity that would enable an alert spectator to read the scene accurately even if that spectator could not hear or understand a word of dialogue.

But this does not mean that the dialogue was neglected. Quite the contrary. A blind spectator listening only to the words of the text could form as clear an impression of the plot development as the deaf spectator. For a spectator with normal vision and hearing there is extremely powerful mutual reinforcement of the scene by its parallel, equally powerful, visual and aural "line." The opening scene is illustrative of the play as a whole. Using the theatrical trick of making Kattrin "dumb," Brecht will throughout the play be able to justify interpreting all major developments in the plot line through Kattrin's necessarily gestural "language." She must always *show* as she can never, in a conventional sense, *say* what is on her sensitive mind. From the first scene to the last, she can provide a mimed commentary on everything that is expressed in the play in words. She will communicate with clarity, force and compassion but she will never use words. In the long history of drama, I know of no silence more eloquent than Kattrin's. Silenced by an act of war (she has not spoken since a soldier "pushed something into her mouth") she is the only one who cries out loudly and consistently against it.

It is possible, of course, to use the example of Kattrin to point to something that is essential to Brecht's style as a director. One does not need to be loud to be "heard." It is possible to get an audience's rapt attention not so much by raising one's voice as by lowering it, or even abandoning one's voice altogether. The opening scene of *Mother Courage* does not need Hitlerian rantings to convey extraordinary power. The horrible fact is that a person (Eilif) is led away to certain death with no outcry at all. It is all rather matter of fact. This is how recruiting is done. When you have lost your child to the military you can still kid yourself, as Courage actually does, that your child might survive. The horror of the scene (might we even speak of "pity and fear"?) is that no universal cry goes up as this young life is lost because of a moment spent bartering over a belt. The moment is a quiet one, a natural one.

At many points in the play, the most shattering moments are marked by an extraordinarily eloquent silence. To understate is not necessarily to cool down a scene; a scene can be made white hot by radical understatement. To miss this rather obvious point would be to miss one of the powerful devices in Brecht's jam-packed bag of highly effective theatrical devices. If the content of your work is in opposition to everything that Hitler represented then let the form of your work also be in signal contrast to Hitler's style of address.

Mother Courage and Her Children opened on January 11, 1949 in a Berlin, viciously described by Brecht as "an etching by Churchill based on an idea of Hitler's," resembling a scene from the Thirty Years War. The city itself was eerie as airplanes thundered overhead all night long to land with supplies in the blockaded western zones. It was a city of almost complete darkness after sunset, as energy supplies in the east and the west were so low that they could not be squandered on a mere amenity such as lights. But at the German Theatre the electrical system was strained to the utmost as the play opened with all lights on full. In the brightest light we would see the darkest horrors of the insanity of war. A mirror was held before the audience in which "they might see their own ugly mug."[19] The effect of the play was shattering. As Weigel bent to drag her tattered and almost empty wagon from the stage, she seemed even more gaunt than in earlier scenes, as she had taken out her false teeth to hollow her cheeks further for this final moment! The audience sat in stunned and mesmerized silence broken only by the sound of their own sobbing. After the final half-curtain had slashed across to close off the scene of unbearable horror the audience sobbed and cheered and clapped themselves to exhaustion.

Fig. 33. *Mother Courage*, Berlin, 1949. All her children now dead, a battered and bedraggled Courage prepares to drag her wagon alone.

The Soviet critic Sachawa, well versed in what Brecht sought to illustrate with his portrait of the capitalist Courage, the hyena of the battlefield, wrote of the final scene of Brecht's production: "The heart of the viewer is unwillingly seized when he sees how hopelessly the wagon has aged, how run down it is, and into what a frightful ruin a formerly energetic, active, and level-headed woman has been changed, who, in spite of her frightful condition, still does not understand its cause: the scene is a terrifying symbol of the tragic fate of an entire people.[20] Sachawa's comments, with their Aristotelian references to terror, pity and the tragic, were not an isolated critical aberration. Viewing the Berlin Ensemble production somewhat later, George Steiner observed: "She (Mother Courage) is so enormously alive in each leathery sinew, so rapacious and unconquerable. She is the salt of the earth, destructive yet zestful. We cannot detach ourselves from the play and merely pass cool judgement on her faults. We too are hitched to the wagon, and it is beneath our feet that the stage turns"[21] (fig. 33).

When one turns from the play as a whole to critical reaction to individual scenes in Brecht's production, critical response is, if anything, even more intense. Albrecht Schöne writes: "Scene Eleven of *Mother Courage* is one of Brecht's best scenes in terms of its effectiveness on the stage. On the roof of a peasant hut dumb Kattrin beats a drum in order to save the children of the city of Halle from a night attack. She is struck by a bullet and the sound of her last drumbeat is echoed by the cannon of the wakening defenders. If anywhere, it is here that Brecht's theory of alienation is itself alienated; here the critical distance of the (calmly) smoking audience is destroyed"[22] (fig. 34). Brecht's principal interpreter in America, Eric Bentley, says flatly of Scene Eleven: "The 'drum' scene is possibly the most powerful scene, emotionally, in twentieth-century drama."[23] Overwhelmed by the response to Kattrin, Brecht – the man who had argued for years for the dominance of reason over emotion in the theatre – said lamely: "Spectators are permitted to identify with Kattrin in this scene. They may identify with this being and note with pleasure that they have such powers even within themselves."[24] So much for the "permitted" emotional response to the "good" Kattrin, but what about the "bad" mother herself and the response she elicits?

For many critics, however aware they may be of the words of a traveling companion of Courage that she is to be seen as a "hyena of the battlefield," the final scene of the play (already discussed in this chapter) and the scene where she must fail to recognize the body of her son Schweizerkäs, run the "drum" scene a close race in terms of emotion. Surely Brecht overestimates his own directorial, or, if you will, dictatorial powers when he maintains, to paraphrase the Brecht of the later years, "Emotions are permitted when I say that they are permitted." His overestimation of his own powers is concretely illustrated by the reaction of George Steiner who says in his *Death of Tragedy*:

There comes a moment in *Mother Courage* when the soldiers carry in the dead body of Schweizerkäs. They suspect that he is the son of Courage but are not quite certain. She must be forced to identify him. I saw Helene Weigel act the scene with the East Berlin ensemble, though acting is a paltry word for the marvel of her incarnation. As the body of her son was laid before her, she merely shook her head in mute denial. The soldiers compelled her to look again. Again she gave no sign of recognition, only a dead stare. As the body was carried off, Weigel looked the other way and tore her mouth wide open. The shape of the gesture was that of the screaming horse in Picasso's Guernica. The sound that came out was raw and terrible beyond any description I could give of it. But, in fact, there was no sound. Nothing. The sound was total silence. It was silence which screamed and screamed through the whole theatre so that the audience lowered its head as before a gust of wind. And that scream inside the silence seemed to me to be the same as Cassandra's when she divines the reek of blood in the house of Atreus. It was the same wild cry with which the tragic imagination first marked our sense of life[25] (fig. 35).

Fig. 34 *Mother Courage*, Berlin, 1949. Scene 11. Angelika Hurwicz as Kattrin drums the nearby town awake. Meanwhile a gun is being set up on a tripod to shoot her down.

It is abundantly clear that Brecht's 1949 production of *Mother Courage and Her Children* is not to be measured by Brecht's crudely anti-Aristotelian yardstick of the twenties. An important shift had taken place. Never one to shrink from contradiction, Brecht could now cheerfully explore ways to reach deeper strata of fear than those accessible using other acting methods. He noted for instance, of Kattrin's drum scene: "It is advantageous (in performance) to avoid the direct or 'immediate impression' of the apparently singular (non-recurrent) event in order to reach a different stratum of fear, where frequent, ever recurring misfortune has forced mankind into ceremonialization of his defense mechanisms, which of course can never save man from actual fear itself. We must break, in performance, through this ceremonialization of defense."[26] Breaking through this ceremony of defense particularly in Berlin where virtually every member of the audience (including Brecht himself!) had lost a family member in the war was vital in Brecht's view if a third world war was to be avoided.

Fig. 35. *Mother Courage*, Berlin, 1949. The sound of silence. "The same wild cry with which the tragic imagination first marked our sense of life."

In many ways there was almost a psychotic response in Berlin to Brecht's anti-war chronicle. The general public loved it and it played to sold-out houses for hundreds of performances. But the response of many communist critics (particularly those who had spent the exile years in the Soviet Union and had seen first-hand Stalin's destruction of all opponents of Socialist Realism) was either cool or savage. Several of the German communist critics saw Brecht as a threat to the very life of the kind of Socialist Realist drama (such as Hay's *Haben*) that they felt was the only true path for communist playwrights to follow. In words that dangerously echoed both Hitler's and Stalin's arch-conservative "aesthetic," Brecht's old enemy Fritz Erpenbeck accused Brecht of losing his way in "volksfremde Dekadenz" ("a decadent alienation from the people").[27] Coming from one of the inner circle of the group which at the height of the purges of his "Formalist" friends in Moscow in the late thirties, Brecht had described as "the Moscow camarilla," he knew that if such a position became entrenched his prospects for establishing his own kind of theatre in Soviet Berlin would be virtually nil. Whether Brecht actually knew it or not in 1949, it was a fact that Erpenbeck was stating a position very close indeed to that of one of the most powerful people in the inner circle of the Soviet Zone, Walter Ulbricht.[28] It was therefore fortunate that Dymschitz was among those who rallied to Brecht's view of what forms progressive Marxist theatre should take. With this Russian ally, dozens of figures in the arts behind them, and with a roaring box-office business to counter claims of their being "alienated from the people," Brecht and Weigel were eventually able to prevail. A few months later, in the late spring of 1949, the creation of the Berlin Ensemble was officially approved and Helene Weigel was named as its head. Brecht's position seems to have been deliberately left rather vague. In fact Brecht wrote a letter dated October 12, 1949 (that is to say, several months after official approval for the creation of the Berlin Ensemble had been given) in which he told the Austrian official who was trying to hire him for the Salzburg Festival, Gottfried von Einem: "I have no kind of official function or responsibility in Berlin and I receive no salary."[29] If this was true at the time Brecht wrote it (and the records at the Berlin Ensemble neither confirm nor deny it), it is possible that behind the scenes he had turned down an offer to take an official role in the Soviet Zone (officially changed in November 1949 to the German Democratic Republic) in order to maintain his flexibility in western Europe. But it would also be possible that the company was put under Weigel's direction rather than Brecht's because of what was perceived as her greater political reliability as a longtime party member. Years later Brecht's daughter Barbara is reported to have claimed that her mother had been Brecht's "politische Richtliniengeberin" — "the giver-of-the-correct-political-line." Until we have a complete and reliable history of the Berlin Ensemble it will be hard to know what actually happened when Brecht and Weigel hammered out their deal with the Soviet authorities.

Regardless of what Brecht's official position was with the Berlin Ensemble, it was clear to everyone in Berlin that Weigel was the administrative head of the embryonic organization and that Brecht was the artistic head of the company. This did not mean that he had no say in administrative matters and Weigel no say in artistic matters, but rather that their roles were complementary and that crossovers took place whenever necessary. The coolness that existed in their domestic arrangements was not allowed to intrude into their professional life. Both were talented professionals and it is difficult to imagine that the Berlin Ensemble could ever have been created without their combined talents. When the first official production of the Berlin Ensemble opened in late 1949, *Puntila and His Servant Matti*, Brecht noted in his diary:

Yesterday evening the *Puntila* premiere with much laughter and many curtain calls. The Russians had turned over the central boxes to the members of the new government [that is, the brand new government of the brand new state: the German Democratic Republic] who laughed and applauded with everyone else. The Berlin Ensemble – (as a kind of trademark for the company we had Picasso's dove of peace sewn into the curtain of the German Theatre) – constitutes a gigantic achievement of Weigel, who obtained the means (to establish the company), got an office building and had a rehearsal stage constructed in it, got travel documents, apartments and (in the Zone) furniture for the actors' apartments, special meals for the entire company – indescribable efforts in a ruined city.[30]

If one remembers that Weigel did all this work while continuing to play Mother Courage (supplier of food and shelter in a war zone), one has some sense of the pace at which she had to work and the essential contribution that she made in moving the Berlin Ensemble in a few short months from ambitious dream to realized achievement.

Meanwhile, as Weigel established a sound material base for the new company, Brecht was equally busy. Riding the wave of his directorial success with *Mother Courage* he was now frequently in demand as a full or part-time director of productions of his big "exile plays" in western Europe. Everywhere he went he would keep his eyes open for talent and would recruit the people he worked with to return to Berlin and work with the Ensemble. He then had to be available in Berlin to work with the new people. With a mixture of talented newcomers and of established international stars, Brecht's objective was to create exemplary productions for the East and the West. The Ensemble was to be a showcase for established figures and an advanced training ground for beginners. Brecht's objective was to create an advanced school of theatre where he could train people to carry his ideas, techniques and high standards beyond his own lifetime in independent work. Needless to say, this vast ambition placed enormous pressure on Brecht's schedule as more and more people sought to work with him. Simultaneously, Brecht the playwright/entrepreneur was anxious to have his plays written in exile ("for the desk drawer") produced in good productions in as many different cities and countries as possible. Negotiating for such productions was time-consuming even though much of this work was delegated to Elisabeth Hauptmann and Ruth Berlau. And of course the reading public could not be forgotten. A new and comprehensive edition of Brecht's complete works was necessary and it needed to be brought out in both western and eastern editions. If all this was to happen, Brecht also had to find time to help form cultural policy in the newly established German Democratic Republic, serving on commissions and attending countless meetings. As though this were not enough, he was also too much a creature of habit as a writer to be able to give up his writing. So time had to be found for him to attempt to describe in his work the socialist reality of his homeland. And to understand contemporary socialist reality he needed a better grasp of the history of practical socialism, which involved talking with people who had known Lenin and Stalin personally, to try to understand better what had happened in the Soviet Union. And in the midst of all this activity, Brecht would not have been Brecht had he not been also maintaining several old love affairs while actively promoting new ones.

As had been true for all stages of Brecht's work as a stage director, the line between his stage work and his love life was hazy at best: a list of present and former mistresses was established on the Berlin Ensemble payroll adminis-tered by Brecht's wife, Helene Weigel. Mainly behind the scenes, but sometimes in public, the tension between Brecht's life as lover and as director would cause (as it had done throughout his career) real difficulties. When Brecht favored one of his lovers with a better role than her stage talents had earned and other members of the Ensemble complained, it fell to Helene Weigel as chief administrative officer to try to resolve the difficulties. Brecht saw this as all in a day's work. "How," he asked of one mistress, "could you complain about my interest in other younger lovers?" Did this mean the rejected lover was frigid? Needless to say, with all this going on behind the scenes at the Ensemble, life there was seldom dull, usually hectic and often impossible.

So complex is this past period of Brecht's life, so numerous are the productions at the Ensemble and so various Brecht's greater or lesser contribution to many of them, that it would require a very long book to do justice to all the different strands of his life in Berlin. If we were to try to understand specifically Brecht's work as a stage director, we can do it best I think *not* by looking at a dozen or so productions in a superficial way, but rather by examining Brecht's role in two major and exemplary productions in detail. These two, *The Caucasian Chalk Circle* and *The Life of Galileo* (regrettably he did not live to stage his own production of *The Good Person of Sezuan*), together with the *Mother Courage* we have just examined, were the productions which established Brecht in international theatre circles as the dominant director in the "fifties and beyond." What did these productions look like? How were they put together?

6 Diary of a production:[1] *The Caucasian Chalk Circle*

The key test always was: does it work on stage? If not, throw it out. If it does work, and if it conflicts with the theory, throw away the theory. The stage solutions found by Brecht and his co-workers were preserved from the mid-thirties on by Ruth Berlau's detailed photographic record of productions. With Brecht's return from exile and his and Weigel's creation of the Berlin Ensemble, a further refinement of the record of productions became both desirable and possible. First, with Hans Bunge's (Brecht's directorial assistant in the production) stenographic record of rehearsals, and then later with Bunge's wire recordings of almost all *The Caucasian Chalk Circle* rehearsals,[2] it became possible to reconstruct much of the rehearsal process itself. As we also have the Berlin Ensemble stage text of the play, Angelika Hurwicz's and Gerda Goedhart's brilliant published commentary,[3] as well as Brecht's own notes, the designer Karl von Appen's commentaries,[4] and Dessau's music, we can piece together virtually every moment of rehearsal that would be the last completed before Brecht's death in Berlin during the *Galileo* rehearsals in 1956. I believe that the text of *The Caucasian Chalk Circle* and Brecht's staging of that text in 1953–4 is the most comprehensive, complete and useful record that we have of his fully mature work as a stage director. We see Brecht here at the absolute peak of his powers. For those interested in how he achieved the Berlin Ensemble theatrical effects that were to bowl over audiences in Paris, Moscow and London, this production provides the greatest number of clues. Here we can see in detail how much of his earlier "epic" theory and uses of *Verfremdung* remain in actual stage practice.

If we look first at the actual text of the play, written, as we may recall, in 1943–5 for staging with Luise Rainer on Broadway, we see at once that it employs many of the devices called for in Brecht's early epic theory, namely fragmentary action, simultaneity of events, extensive use of narrative or "third-person exposition," the use of songs, and finally, the sheer breadth and depth of the materials treated within the play. It will be remembered that the prologue tells us that we are about to watch a performance by amateur actors of an adaptation of a fourteenth-century Chinese play, *The Chalk Circle*. Actually, Brecht's play has but little in common with either the Chinese play itself, or with his friend Klabund's German version of the original Chinese work, or with the more stylized conventions of the Chinese stage. Brecht has switched the locale of the play from China to the crossroads of the East and

West, Soviet Georgia. With the change of locale he throws out the decorous and largely decorative language of both his models, flatly rejects the sentimental tale of a former prostitute who ends up as an empress, and switches the ending of the play so that the bitchy, rich, biological mother of the child loses him in the circle test to the impoverished woman who loved and cared for him after his "real" mother had selfishly abandoned him. Besides throwing out most of the original content, Brecht introduces the long, lovely and involved tale of the cowardly and inebriated, clever and sober judge, Azdak. With all these changes it is clear that Brecht's play has, in terms of content, virtually only the chalk-circle test itself in common with its Chinese and German models.

Those familiar with the placards which introduced Brecht's version of *Edward II* and *Mother Courage*, the traditional chorus in *Antigone*, the use of a chorus and of direct address in *Mother*, the "narrator" Wang in *The Good Person of Sezuan*, and the four-line verses that introduce the separate scenes of *Galileo*, will recognize the singer who links and introduces the tale of the chalk circle as a summing up and extension of all these devices. Abandoning the implicit exposition of an Ibsen play like *The Wild Duck*, Brecht returns (as Henry Goodman has long since noted) to a far more ancient, far more widespread form of dramatic exposition, the explicit method used by the Greeks, by most Oriental playwrights, by the medieval theatre, and by Shakespeare and most of his followers. Volker Klotz has pointed out the similarity of the singer's function in Brecht's play to Aeschylus' use of the chorus.[5] Like the chorus of the great Greek tragedian, Brecht's singer does not act, he plays no part, he simply sings. There is, however, one interesting Brechtian innovation connected with this singer. Although he is basically "outside" the action, he is also right in the middle of it. With his chorus of helpers (singers and musicians), he speaks the thoughts of Grusche when she is forced by circumstances or her own overpowering emotion to remain silent. He assumes at these moments both the ancient function that was served by the overheard monologue or choral ode and the modern function that is called in film "voice-over narration." Throughout the play, the singer introduces and comments upon each scene and, finally, sums up what he (Brecht) believes to be the lesson that the staged presentation should have taught to its kolkhoz and theatre audiences.

When we go on from the text itself to Brecht's magnificent 1954 staging of the play, there is one further point about the singer that deserves mention. Brecht cast the greatest male actor and singer he had available, Ernst Busch, as both the singer "outside" the play *and* as Azdak, a character very much "inside" the play. In performance, therefore, we can postulate an intensification of the specifically dramatic (in Brecht's terms, the non-narrative or non-epic element of the play) at the expense of the purely narrative or epic when Ernst Busch (in the fifth scene)[6] joins the magnificent Grusche (Angelika Hurwicz) in the dramatic plane of the play. Henceforth, the part of the singer, though still of some importance *as a role*, is reduced in stature in Brecht's production as the strongest member of the "narrative" team changes his role and function and lends his enormously powerful personality to the dramatic side of the play. More subtly, of course, his switch in roles tends both to theatricalize the production by stressing role-playing as role-playing and to link the various parts of the play together. Thus, instead of a "new" character, Azdak, first appearing halfway through the play, he is deliberately foreshadowed from the first line on by the voice and gestures of the charismatic Ernst Busch. The roles of singer and of Azdak can, of course, be separated and given to different actors, but then we have a different aesthetic construct from the one Brecht chose to present in 1954. This is a case where the text alone gives only subtle hints of what in performance became a very important move on the part of the creative artist.

Viewed as Brecht staged it, his play moves from the plane of "reality" into the world of the drama in several carefully calibrated stages. First, in the kolkhoz we have a supposed one-for-one relationship of character to player, we have the kolkhoz people themselves, we move then to the play-within-the-play as the kolkhoz workers, with the aid of a professional singer, perform the roles given in the ancient tale. The first part of the play is balanced between action (Grusche) and narration (the professional singer and his amateur helpers). We move deeper (in performance) into action as Busch switches roles in scene 5. From this moment on the performance is dominated by its active (dramatic) rather than passive or narrative (epic) elements. We have been subtly transfered from one plane of action, the kolkhoz, to another, the Circle of Chalk.

Ernst Busch's availability to play both the role of the singer and that of Azdak casts some interesting light on the text of the play. Brecht the playwright/director was fully aware that his text supported the casting move he makes in scene 5. The relative importance of the singer in the two "halves" of the play is demonstrated by a small experiment. Remove all the lines of the singer from scenes 1 to 4[7] and then try to make some sense of the text. Not only would the remainder be barely comprehensible, it would also lack a large measure of poetic power. We would miss, for instance, those heightened scenes where the singer provides the voice-over narration of Grusche's thoughts. We need the singer in these scenes to "give voice" to the "dumb" Grusche. In scenes 5 and 6, however, as the wily and articulate Azdak comes to the fore, we no longer need any voice-over narration: he is perfectly capable of voicing his own thoughts. Except for the short song in the trial scene, where Grusche is again struck dumb with emotion, the singer has but little to do in scenes 5 and 6. The role could be cut in these scenes with almost no damage to the basic plot line. It is not, therefore, simply an accident of Brecht's own production that shifted (with Busch) the balance of the play from the narrative–dramatic to the overwhelmingly dramatic plane in the closing scenes.

The rearrangement of the play so that Ernst Busch's role could be very large is, of course, typical of Brecht's response to actors he liked, but the rearrangement also underscores Brecht's reliance on stars such as Busch, Angelika Hurwicz and Helene Weigel. Brecht's plays, like those of Shakespeare, almost all have a couple of absolutely central roles. At every stage of his career, unless he could cast his key roles with stars, very sensibly Brecht would not even attempt a production. His late-twenties and early-thirties experiments with amateur actors notwithstanding, virtually all of the plays staged by Brecht after his return from exile were vehicles for stars. As Angelika Hurwicz said flatly in an interview with me: "Brecht loved stars."[8] Supposedly fully conscious of the need for seasoned professionals in the main roles, Brecht noted in his diary:

Roles such as those of Azdak and Grusche cannot, in our time, be created by the work of a director. No less than five years at the Berlin Ensemble was necessary in order to give the extraordinary Angelika Hurwicz the necessary prerequisites. And Busch's whole life, from his childhood in a proletarian milieu in Hamburg through the battles of the Weimar Republic and in the Spanish Civil War to the bitter experiences after '45, was necessary in order to create this Azdak.[9]

Though Brecht says very positive things here and elsewhere about the *necessity* of using Busch and Hurwicz, it is of some historical importance to note that Brecht's observation does not square with what he originally tried to do. In our interview Angelika Hurwicz told me that originally Brecht wanted to cast one of his mistresses, Käthe Reichel, as Grusche. However, when Brecht told Busch that he was casting Reichel rather than Hurwicz, Busch is reported to have said "then I will not play in the production." Desperately wanting to retain Busch, Brecht agreed to having Hurwicz play Grusche. But, still determined to give his mistress a major role, Brecht cast Reichel as the Governor's Wife. Ironically, late in the production, as we shall see, even this role was taken away from Reichel and given to Weigel because of an irreconcilable "lovers'" quarrel between Reichel and Brecht, whose attention had begun to drift to yet another member of the Berlin company. Little of this emerges in the historical record of the production as prepared by Bunge but edited by Brecht. Brecht, at this stage, as at every other stage of his life, wanted his own edited version of reality to be the official record.[10]

The 284-page production notebook, prepared by Hans Bunge and regularly checked "for accuracy" by Brecht himself simply confirms the importance of Hurwicz and Busch as though things had always been that way. The first paragraph of the "Diary of a Production" (beginning in early November, 1953) reads:

Finally the decision is made to begin rehearsals of *The Caucasian Chalk Circle*. Brecht will direct the play himself, Dessau will write the music to accompany it, and Karl von Appen will do the sets [and costumes]. The final questions for putting the play into the repertoire were casting questions: is Ernst Busch available to play the double role (especially combined for him) of the singer and of Azdak and is Angelika Hurwicz available to play Grusche? Other difficulties will be resolved during the production itself.[11]

While beginning rehearsals with the actors, Brecht was working out a basic production concept, not with his usual designer Caspar Neher, but with a person Brecht had recruited to the Berlin Ensemble the year before from Dresden, Karl von Appen. During the Third Reich, von Appen had been imprisoned for four years by the Nazis as a German Communist Party member who had been implicated in resistance activities against Hitler. The combination of great talent and his resistance background made von Appen doubly appealing to Brecht.

The basic production concept conveyed to Karl von Appen by the director was contained in just two words: "Nativity Scene." What Brecht apparently had in mind was literally the kind of tableaux "Nativity Scenes" of brightly painted wood that were common in his childhood in southern Germany. The designer understood this to mean that the production should combine the raw simplicity of the Bethlehem stable itself seen in signal contrast with the gaudy pomp of the royal visitors. The "stable," or the set itself, like the Bavarian nativity scenes on which it was to be modeled should be simple and movable, something that could be packed and used again next year, but at the same time these mobile set units needed to convey both the rich grandeur and the humble simplicity of such scenes. Quite consciously Brecht and von Appen discussed the fact that this approach had more in common with the regular practice of Shakespeare's and Molière's theatre and the theatre of the Chinese than it had with the highly technological exhortations of Brecht of the 1920s when he had given the following instructions for set design: "The set designer/builder, as the situation demands, is to replace the floor with treadmills, the background with a film screen, the side sections of the set with an orchestra. The ceiling must become a scaffold for lifts and even simply transfering the whole playing space into the auditorium should be considered."[12] On such stages one was to present, of course, wholly modern and highly technological subjects such as maneuvers on the stock exchange or international sales of oil. Now, in 1954, in a theatre redolent of mahogany and red plush rather than of the bare-bones functionalism of the 1920s, Brecht was frankly and self-consciously turning to Shakespeare's and Molière's theatre and even back to the mystery and passion plays of the middle ages as a model for his own theatre. In *Mother Courage, Galileo* and *The Caucasian Chalk Circle*, Brecht turned for subject matter set in the sixteenth-century or even further back to a medieval model for his new/old stage, and then to the world where he began his directing career in Munich with the sixteenth-century text of Marlowe's *Edward the Second*. After an early identification with the world of the Elizabethan theatre and of country fairs in Bavaria, followed in the twenties in Berlin by a tempestuous love affair with technology whereupon Brecht denounced Shakespeare as having "created a theatre for barbarians," here was Brecht discussing with von Appen (and many others) the extraordinary merits of Shakespeare's play construction and the staging methods of the Elizabethans, a theatre now fully acknowledged by Brecht to be "full of V-Effects." Central to the production concept of *The Caucasian Chalk Circle* (and this is equally true of the Berlin Ensemble *Mother Courage* and *Galileo*) is a clear sense that the set provided must be, in no "fourth wall" sense, "complete," but rather that it must be richly evocative and its very incompleteness must invite the audience to piece out its "imperfections with their own thoughts," to only modestly paraphrase the prologue to Shakespeare's *Henry IV* and *V*.

Many of the set designs provided by von Appen were taken over *in toto* in the production. Examples of this are the design of the cathedral and the palace (figs. 36 and 37) and individual items such as the highly distinctive costumes of the palace guards or Azdak's "Seat of Judgement" (fig. 38). Sometimes the basic design would be modified by Brecht. The best example of this is the famous wedding scene in the production where the wedding guests are crammed into a tiny space. Brecht insisted on this (modeling his own concept on Breughel's "Peasant's Wedding," the picture he kept above his bed) over von Appen's initial objections. There was one design idea offered by von Appen that Brecht rejected totally out-of-hand. Von Appen, perhaps not yet completely grasping the fact that Brecht's theatre was an amalgam of the real (props of museum quality, for instance), and the flatly unreal stylized masks, proposed that the "baby" that Grusche rescues from the palace be not simply the large and inert doll that *was* used in the production (fig. 39) but rather one that was mechanized so it could wave its arms and legs about. Consistent with past practice, Brecht knew that this was a case where more would be less. The doll itself was more than enough "minimal image" to satisfy a theatre audience's needs. At times Brecht himself would have an idea for something which would then be drawn by von Appen and subsequently rejected not on the grounds of von Appen's drawing but by Brecht recognizing that his own

Fig. 38. *The Caucasian Chalk Circle*, Berlin, 1954. Karl von Appen's sketch
for Azdak's portable seat of justice and the portable gallows. The stage
realization of the sketch for the seat of justice can be seen in the
background in the Chalk Circle test scene.

original idea was wrong. The best example of this is an idea that Brecht had
had originally, that the backdrop for the entire play should be a massive "class
picture" painting of all the kolkhoz members (fig. 40). The idea here was two-
fold: first, that the real audience in the theatre should be constantly reminded
that the "Chalk Circle" play was supposedly being done by and for the
kolkhoz members, but secondly, that by completing the circle of the audience
Brecht was attempting to retain, at least in pictorial terms, something of his
idea of a theatre space analogous to a boxing ring surrounded by smoking
spectators. But when Brecht saw the actual designs he rejected this basic idea

Fig. 36. (Opposite, above) *The Caucasian Chalk Circle*, Berlin, 1954. Karl von
Appen's sketch for the basic set units of the play. The steeply rising streets of
the town are painted on the backdrop. The set units used in the play were
designed so that they could be removed from the turntable stage without
needing to stop the movement of the stage.

Fig. 37. (Opposite, below) *The Causasian Chalk Circle*, Berlin, 1954. The stage
realization of von Appen's design for the basic set units. The palace servants
frantically pack. The imperious "Governor's Wife" (played by Helene Weigel)
sits, stage left, on a crouching servant.

Fig. 39. *The Caucasian Chalk Circle*, Berlin, 1954. Grusche (played by
Angelika Hurwicz) pauses briefly on her flight into the Northern
Mountains where she hopes to find a place to stay with her brother.

of an artificial audience facing the real audience not only because it was
literally and figuratively artificial, but also because it would be blocked off
anyway with a whole series of backdrops illustrative of the various stages of
events at the palace and the wanderings of Grusche and of Azdak. So the
"class picture" was displaced by a set of drawings: the town in which the

original revolution takes place (see fig. 57); the backdrop to the hut where Grusche buys the milk; the backdrop of the glacier in "Flight into The Northern Mountains" (fig. 41); and the backdrop to the setting of the kolkhoz in Georgia (fig. 42) etc. These backdrops were deliberately designed to be used without the weights usually inserted at the bottom of such curtains. The idea was that without weights the curtains would billow or float down with a pleasing aesthetic effect. But the backdrops were also designed to serve a vital technical purpose when used with the huge turntable stage that was central to the production (fig. 43). Behind these backdrops which were hung halfway forward on the turntable, rapid changes could be made of the deliberately light and portable set segments. Thus Grusche's march like that of Mother Courage (against the direction of the turntable, keeping her always in the proscenium opening) could bring her "closer" to new scenes that had been loaded on the turntable behind the backdrop without the turntable even being stopped. The advantages of this as a means of radically cutting the actual playing time for what was an extremely long and rather complex play should be obvious to anyone with theatre experience. The backdrops helped the production move lightly and rapidly. Also in this production Brecht and von Appen agreed to dispense with what had become an absolute cliché of "Brechtian" productions, the famous half-curtain. In his superb record of von Appen's productions at the Berlin Ensemble, Friedrich Dieckmann writes:

The production did not use the half- "curtain" – which is after all a polemical instrument whose supporting strings divided up the playing space in an ugly way – that would not have been appropriate to the fairy-tale-like quality of the play. The regular curtain, which completely closed off the stage, was not used to replace the half-curtain rather than being used as a part of scene changes (with the use of the turntable stage most changes were made with the curtain up), the curtain was used to mark certain epic-dramatic caesura. The big curtain was lowered nine times during a performance.[13]

Fig. 40. *The Caucasian Chalk Circle*, Berlin, 1954. The "class picture" not used in the production.

Fig. 41. *The Caucasian Chalk Circle*, Berlin, 1954. Grusche, with the child in her arms, prepares to cross the rickety bridge over the 2,000 foot chasm. A bystander (right) demonstratively turns her back on the suicidal act.

Fig. 42. *The Caucasian Chalk Circle*, Berlin, 1954. The prologue of the play. Two rival claimants to land in the Caucasus meet to resolve the dispute. The mountains of the Caucasus tower in the background. Directed by Brecht. Set and costumes by von Appen. Music by Dessau.

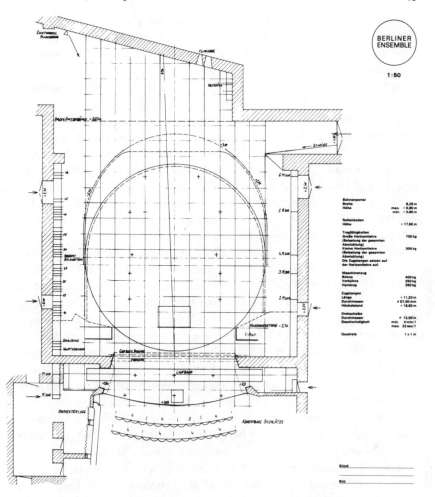

Fig. 43. A technical drawing of the stage at the Am Schiffbauerdamm
Theatre, including the huge turntable. The two rows of seats shown in the
drawing can be removed if a director wishes to add a thrust stage.

The fact that the production was in a sense already set in many major particulars by Brecht and von Appen at the time Brecht met for the first rehearsal with the actors is typical of this and his other major Berlin Ensemble productions, as well as his prewar productions in Munich and Berlin. The designer was expected to attend rehearsals and to be willing to discuss minor and major changes during the months of rehearsals.

The establishment of the visual pattern and of the blocking of the production, then to be tested in rehearsal, was usually supplemented by Brecht's equally intensive work with a composer. For *The Caucasian Chalk Circle*, particularly because of the importance attached to the role of the singer, Brecht worked intensively with Paul Dessau on the score. As with his work with the designer, Brecht accepted much of the composer's work but was not necessarily bound by Dessau's ideas and was perfectly capable of making his own musical suggestions as he had done on previous productions when working with either Hanns Eisler or Kurt Weill. Because Brecht had done his own music for his earliest productions, and because he had actually prepared the text of his plays with a view to setting sections of the work to music, this meant in practical terms that Brecht had enough sensitivity to musical values to be able confidently to override "his" composers whenever he felt they were not catching the exact sense of what he was seeking. First, an artist selected by Brecht would submit a draft treatment. From this Brecht chose the elements that he wished to keep and firmly, and usually politely, rejected those portions which did not seem right to him. New portions were then submitted until the various parts met with Brecht's approval. Then, everything was thoroughly tested in months and months of rehearsals. Some things would survive *in toto*, others would change subtly, and yet others would fail and be rejected. But whatever the fate of a particular song, or a costume, or a backdrop, or a prop in actual rehearsal, it is significant to Brecht's work as a stage director that all style choices remained in his own hands. At each stage, whatever choices were made as to how any given line or scene would be played were measured against the "nativity scene" or folk-music quality of von Appen's and Dessau's work, and though good suggestions from anyone would be welcomed, Brecht was the only person who decided what new ingredient would be added. Frequently, as we shall see as we go through the day-by-day notes on the rehearsals, to anyone but Brecht the situation looked as though the cook had gone mad and chaos reigned. But we see from Hans Bunge's log of the rehearsals and the reviews of the play that this seeming "chaos" was itself part of the production process. Though Brecht himself was fond of arguing theoretically that ideal ensemble work was done by equal partners with no one person being indispensable, the facts of the Berlin Ensemble productions done under Brecht's own direction speak otherwise. Angelika Hurwicz and Gerda Goedhart assess the situation in respect of the *Chalk Circle* productions as follows:

From what point of view was the selection made amidst the heaps of representational material that were offered during rehearsals? To achieve this there are certain methods that can be learned. But there should be no underestimation either of the power of genius that is able to take the conflicting details colored by different temperaments of his co-workers and to finally blend these in a unified whole, or the imponderable element of Brecht's own personal taste, or the unmeasurable quality of the personality of a given actor. In conversation Brecht would grant the weight of these imponderables. In his theoretical writing however he hardly mentioned them at all.[14]

Having mentioned these unique qualities that are imponderables, Hurwicz and Goedhart try to summarize that which is learnable from Brecht's style: "Learnable is the use of the point-of-view: 'what contributes to an understanding of the story?' Learnable is the commandment: 'Even thoughts, even subtle internal developments should be depicted through the gestures and bearing of the actors.'" "In the fulfillment of this commandment," they continue, "lies the most outstanding characteristic of Brecht's production style. Brecht did not put his trust in words on the stage. Brecht's work is in contrast with that of many directors for whom it is a principle of artistic economy to not repeat that which has been stated verbally by gesture and the actor's bearing and the setting."[15] An unstated principle here would seem to be again something I mentioned in an earlier chapter, that the ideal Brecht production should make sense either to the blind or to the deaf. As Goedhart and Hurwicz put it:

The great teacher proceeded on a basis of simple wisdom. His work reminds one of primers in which the meaning of a story could be read from the pictures. When the public complained about not understanding something, Brecht would never raise the acoustic level of the performance but would change the basic arrangement of the actors on the stage. To return once more to Brecht's personal taste: he himself found productions in which he could understand every word to be boring and exhausting. The object of the stage for him was to appeal to the eye of the spectator . . .[16]

But while stressing the importance that Brecht attached to purely visual elements of the production, Hurwicz and Goedhart hasten to point out that Brecht paid the closest possible attention to the aural qualities of the performance also.

Before going through the day-to-day log of the rehearsals, a few additional observations made by Goedhart and Hurwicz may be helpful to a general understanding of the role played in the production process of some rather clichéd "Brechtian" vocabulary such as "epic" and *"Verfremdung."*

As Goedhart and Hurwicz remember it:

That long-awaited word "Verfremdung," was only used once during the *Chalk Circle* rehearsals. In the fourth scene, Grusche, after her long wanderings, arrives exhausted at her brother and his wife's place. This scene struck Brecht as being too agitated, loaded with too much anger aroused by Grusche's condition. He took up as a way of introducing "Verfremdung," the use of the third person, "the man said," "the woman said," that they were to add to their text. Slowed down by this device, the basic situation of the scene became clear. Instead of agitation there was surprise at the unasked for guest, the farm people checking out the situation and looking at its consequences, and the tension between the married couple. Of course a director could achieve the same end through carefully differentiated direction of the dialogue. But it was important for the creative collaboration of the actors themselves that through self-examination they were led to their own discoveries.[17]

As I understand this from my discussions with Ms Hurwicz herself, though *Verfremdung* was useful to an actor on that actor's way to fully understanding the manner in which a scene might be played, the device itself would no longer be visible by the time of the premiere. Returning to Brecht's pudding proverb, *Verfremdung* was an ingredient but an ingredient so skillfully blended in at the time of the premiere that the cook would not take it as a compliment that it could be distinguished by any director when he or she thinks that deliberate style breaks, when hallowed by the word *Verfremdung* or epic, constitute a Brechtian way of working. They do not. To force someone to crunch down on a whole garlic clove instead of detecting its carefully blended presence will alienate rather than helping towards a better understanding of pudding preparation. In a sense, to extend the culinary metaphor further, I would argue strongly that Brecht's work as a director is analogous to the *nouvelle cuisine* of Paul Bocuse and his followers. The heavy dishes of the nineteenth century are replaced by lighter dishes that are at least as satisfying to the palate. Many of the old ingredients are used, of course, but they are used in a different way. We do not do Brecht good service in seeing his creations as being wholly new. We need to revise our thinking.

Similarly, Hurwicz and Goedhart caution us against the way in which most critics writing on Brecht have dealt with the use of songs in his work. They write:

Often the songs are interpreted as V-effects. They interrupt the dialogue; it follows therefore, so the conclusion is drawn, that they also interrupt the action [*Spiel*]. However, Brecht wanted, for instance, in the scene where Grusche again meets her fiance, the actors to mime, with the most polished expression, the text of the singers. Distrust, reproach, disappointment, should be mirrored in their faces. The song as the poetic expression of silence. At the same point [in the play], the singers, as they give expression to the reproachful thoughts of Simon Chachawa, should not sing, as at other times, as though they were telling a tale and were not part of the action, but rather angrily, accusingly.[18]

"This moment," conclude Hurwicz and Goedhart, "cannot be classified under any stylistic principle, it is simply a poetic, beautiful, and self-contained aesthetic moment." But before going more deeply into the superb photographs and commentary provided by Hurwicz and Goedhart let us go through the production itself with Hans Bunge to see not only where the directing went but how it got there.

At the beginning of Bunge's "Diary of a Production" (dated: beginning of November, 1953) he sketches in the background of the production as follows:

Theoretical preparations were virtually non-existent at the beginning of rehearsals. Even though some notes existed that Brecht had written at the time he wrote the play – these made some suggestions on the music, the set, and something on the play itself – Brecht never talked about these notes and appeared to have even forgotten them. The only thing he retained was the text itself. And even this he retained only to the extent that it proved itself in rehearsal. It speaks for the text that the changes made in it were not substantial; the changes made were *not* in the basic story but were only of a linguistic and stylistic nature.[19]

The music for *The Caucasian Chalk Circle* and the set (in the broadest sense) were first created during the rehearsals. But that which was completed at first was then changed many times. Author and director, composer and set designer played off their various suggestions against one another and, in some cases, as temperament and situation dictated, inexorably demanded what they thought was necessary. In a very cursory fashion Brecht gave out preparatory assignments for the production to his assistants. In essence he would say:

"Look about a bit and see what you can find out about social situations and customs in the Caucasus and Grusinia [Georgia]. I haven't concerned myself much with this." The material collected this way was used then only in a supporting way to answer some not very important questions during the production. For instance, we were glad to accept the information that in the Caucasus large flat loaves were baked and that these were broken apart by hand rather than cut at meals. We liked the idea of using this custom during rehearsals of the marriage scene in the play. Nevertheless we decided against using the embracing ceremony that is customary in the Caucasus. We felt that for the governor and the prince to embrace one another on Easter Morning was to invest the action with too much force. This was how arbitrary Brecht was in the uses of real cultural history and how much he was concerned with things from a theatrical viewpoint (that is to say: how to tell the story) and this is what he let guide him. The play is not placed at any particular historical time. The placement of the original old Chinese legend in the Caucasus is not simply an accident, but the reasons for placing it there are not ones that really need to be explained in geographical terms. We decided to answer a certain number of such questions in the program.[20]

The first short day of *Chalk Circle* rehearsals on November 17, 1953 were carried out on a rehearsal stage rather than in the main theatre. Hans Bunge remembers the events of that first and of subsequent days as follows:

Those acting in the second act of the play were asked to attend the rehearsal. Brecht did a brief introduction. He spoke softly and gave the impression that he did not attach much importance to this introduction: "The play is a parable played by a group of collective farmers in order to add emphasis to the decision reached in the introductory scene [on the collective farm]. Through the passage of the major threads of the story (introducing scene [at the collective farm], parable of the chalk circle, the story of the judge [Azdak]) it is possible in the play as a whole to double up and have one actor play a number of roles. Indeed we have to do this because we have too few actors to fill the large number of roles in the play. This therefore demands the use of heavy masks through which also the basic difference between the frozen faces of the upper class figures and the more human faces of the lower classes can be established. Let us begin now with work on the second act because it is the easiest one." What Brecht meant by this was that it was the easiest from the director's point of view as it was the easiest to get an overall view of the scene. Then he indicated that he was basically opposed to a rehearsal in which the actors read their lines and that he preferred that they should essentially describe the story of the play and should have every opportunity to "offer" something themselves. All suggestions would then be tried out on a practical basis. Brecht indicated that he did not want there to be discussions of purely psychological problems. Brecht did not like to see scripts in the hands of his actors and preferred that they wait to be fed their lines by the prompter. The actors moved through the scene as instructions were called out to them from the director's table. They were given great freedom to propose whatever ideas they themselves had.

This was not new at Brecht's rehearsals. Worthier of (more) note is the fact that while working on this play he gave the standing order that actors were to speak loudly: "The music," he said in explanation, "has a folk music quality and is loud and full of movement. We *must* be heard despite this." Later, Brecht stressed that "the whole playing style of this play is fairly crude and is similar to a nativity scene." He also often imitated the way in which clowns act in a circus.

As the rehearsals were conducted on the rehearsal stage (rather than in the main theatre) and the rehearsal stage did not have a turntable [stage], something that is a prerequisite for Grusche's journey, instructions for the stage hands had to be simply noted down for subsequent use on the turntable stage. Stage hands simply carried in an approximation of the necessary scenery, the individual "stations" of Grusche's journey, as the cue line was given. Right from the very beginning Brecht stressed the fact that the actress playing Grusche [Angelika Hurwicz] must be on stage before the hut where she buys the milk, the farmhouse, the glacier and the bridge over the chasm were brought towards her on the turntable stage, so that it would be clear that Grusche's wanderings were in the direction of these various places.

The help given to actors in the building up of their parts was usually more reticent than forthcoming and was usually offered only as a response to the demands of the actors. Brecht preferred to have the actors offer him suggestions. He would then use these suggestions as a model to be tested and accepted or to be altered or even thrown away again. All in all he was alert to whether a proposed arrangement could be translated into stage action. Following the day's rehearsal [conducted between 10 am and 2 pm] Brecht spent part of the evening with his assistants [not with the actors! As this was and is a repertory company the actors would usually be in actual performance in the evening], and in the course of the evening they [Brecht and his assistants] discussed the notes on the play that Brecht had written during his exile years in America. One of the assistants reminded him: "But you said this morning in your introduction 'the play is a parable.'" Brecht answered: "Did I talk about a parable? So? Of course that was wrong. The story of the chalk circle is really an independent story that only has certain parallels with the prologue. So let's drop this parable business." At other times, with the actors and the directorial assistants he would make fun of himself as an author and would ask others to explain the play to him! At one point Brecht the director exclaimed of Brecht the playwright: "One cannot always be guided by what *he* says."[21]

After a few days of such rehearsals with other cast members, Ernst Busch arrived in Berlin from Vienna where he had been playing as a guest artist. With remarkable speed, Busch got into the rhythm of the rehearsals. His long familiarity with Brecht's work, combined with a very strong personality, perhaps accounts for the fact that Busch, whether playing Azdak or Galileo or other roles under Brecht's direction, was never in awe of Brecht and indeed often insisted on his own way even when that way was completely different from Brecht's. It is a tribute to both these strong personalities that each was tolerant of the other. Busch's readiness to make his own suggestions as to how his roles should be played was basically consistent with Brecht's own wishes as a director. As Bunge notes:

Generally speaking Brecht did not like it when actors waited for instructions. He preferred to see the actor present a number of possible ways of playing a scene, rather than the reverse of this where he would demonstrate to the actor a particular way of playing a scene. He was grateful for every suggestion, every impulse coming from the actors on the stage except where these suggestions were based on psychologizing. Occasionally Brecht would change the text of the play if something being improvised on the stage appealed to him more than the original text. Brecht did not interfere with the actors very much. As Brecht himself was wont to say: "It's always good not to say much. Then the actors contribute something themselves because they are not simply waiting for orders."[22]

By the eleventh day of rehearsals Brecht apparently began to worry as to whether they were not making too much progress. The basic style and movement of the production, in a large sense, was already set. As Bunge reports, now when Brecht would be asked about plans for future rehearsals he would look bewildered and say: "Almost everything is already set. I'm really frightened. Here we've had ten straight days of rehearsals to get certain things set and I don't know what's going to happen in the months ahead." Bunge describes the scene:

Today Brecht sits on his director's chair looking as though he did not know what was going on. Yesterday's solutions that seemed firm now looked completely tentative, and he felt bound to not a single gesture, none of the blocking, none of the tonal emphases that had been presented before. He looked at everything with a very critical eye and checked over the basic scene arrangements as the actors played them before him. All of the inter-relationships were checked out, changed, holes filled, new ideas and changes introduced wherever he had second thoughts. His work as a director is dialectics made visible.[23]

These sudden shifts noted by Bunge are basic, I feel, to an understanding both of Brecht's stage work and his personal life which were, always in Brecht, and particularly in *The Caucasian Chalk Circle*, inextricably intertwined. Always a play within a play was being played in real life during the rehearsal period as Brecht would be having an affair with one actress until, with alacrity and with "dialectics made visible," Brecht would suddenly give up a seemingly set relationship and switch over to someone else. It was a carefully maintained convention within the Ensemble that, because Brecht continued to use the polite *Sie* address whether an actress was in or out of his favor, one was not supposed to notice his switches of affection or even to know that any affairs were going on at all. But the personal developments could not really be ignored at all as they then had direct repercussions on the play and resulted in significant changes in the cast during the long rehearsal period. If Brecht was having a bad time with Ruth Berlau then she would disappear for a while as official photographer for the Berlin Ensemble. While never wholly breaking up old arrangements, Brecht's love interests went through a sequence of young women. First Käthe Rülicke, then Käthe Reichel, and lastly Isot Kilian, wife of Brecht's friend, the philosopher Wolfgang Harich. Brecht, knowing himself rather well, is reported by Klaus Völker to have said to Harich: "Divorce her now and you can marry her again in two years."[24] In the administrative offices of the Ensemble Isot Kilian and Käthe Rülicke shared an office and constantly fought over the stewardship of a small change fund (about $100) that Brecht kept there to supply his minor needs such as coffee etc. A change of affection could affect vastly more than the coffee fund however. As rehearsals progressed Brecht's interest in Käthe Rülicke, who was playing the major role of the Governor's Wife, would give way to his interest in Isot Kilian, who would then, despite her limited acting experience, be given a fairly large role in the play's prologue. The various women, as Brecht's interest rose and declined, were admonished to be cheerful about this and preferably not to enter on any new relationships themselves as this would reduce their availability and desirability to Brecht, should he later want to resume the liaison.

By the seventh day of rehearsals, with Hans Bunge writing down the day's events and with Brecht looking over these notes and correcting them,[25] it was decided to have a microphone present to record verbatim everything that went on. On a record of these rehearsals issued by Bunge[26] one can hear very clearly how Brecht worked. At times he guffaws at what he sees and hears. At other times his already high pitched voice rises to a scream uncannily reminiscent of Hitler as he subjects the object of his ire to violent abuse. But then, while everyone else was still shaking from the violence of his rage, Brecht himself was capable of rapidly shifting gears and laughing and going on as though nothing had happened. Was the violent outburst mere acting, or was it the laughter that revealed Brecht's real feelings, or was it both and neither?

A good example of one of Brecht's rapid switches from anger to humor occurred during the evening of the seventy-seventh day of rehearsals as Brecht decided he wanted vastly to improve the scene in which Azdak is installed as judge. Brecht announced to the actors playing the Ironshirts (who were rehearsing in the summer in armor plate weighing over seventy-five pounds): "Now we want to try something else, namely to do the whole installation of Azdak at breakneck speed. Azdak is virtually to be flung onto the judge's seat." Bunge gives some of the background for this decision:

The previous days had been very exhausting both for the actors and the directing staff. Among other signs this came out in a kind of reluctant attitude on the part of the actors playing the palace guards as, in the fourth act, they were supposed to transport the judge from place to place on his judicial chair or litter. The actors either complained that the chair with the judge on it was too heavy or that they couldn't really move properly in their costumes and so on and so forth. Brecht got very angry and stated categorically: "The judge's chair must be carried and with Azdak on it. That must be possible to do because it is necessary that it be done. Then we will have to start doing gymnastics or whatever is necessary until we are able to get the job done. Slowly this is beginning to bore me. You are artists! Not petit bourgeois and cardsharps, who try to make it easy for themselves! Now I am slowly starting to get impatient. I know that it is difficult with the costumes, I have known that for a long time. I now ask you to carry it. I ask you to try it. Now the joking needs to slowly stop. And that's that! All the details, even the smallest, even those that can only be carried out with difficulty. That's it! And if we have to get into a fitness program with masseurs or do something like that in order that people get their bodies into good shape. So repeat the scene now please. And take off your gloves this time otherwise it can't be done. We'll have new handles put on that chair, square ones, so that you can get a better grip."[27]

The rehearsals went on. For a time the rebellion seemed successfully to be averted by Brecht's outburst using the royal, or possibly collegial plural form: "We." None of the actors dared answer Brecht back and point out that if the "we" included Brecht who was averse to all exercise in any non-sexual form, then there would be little chance of getting fit at all. Brecht was a good theoretical lecturer on the values of physical fitness – for others. Meanwhile the nicotine addict Bert Brecht continued to wheeze around with his ever-present smelly cigar. But though the rehearsal with Azdak's chair went on, the battle over the guards' costumes was by no means over. The actors playing the guards continued to complain so much about the heavy and bulky costumes that Brecht finally but reluctantly allowed the heavy plates to be removed. But then he did not like the effect on stage. As Bunge recalls:

"For the premiere," he said, "we'll probably have to put the plates back in. The fourth act, particularly the installation of the judge, has been rehearsed like no other scene in the play. It was good before. Now we have simplified the costumes and the whole act has gone to hell. You act like card players, petit bourgeois – *boring*! You make things easy for yourselves. If you were really able to act and maintain the roles, I might be able to make the costumes smaller for you. But when you play like bit players I have to make the costumes big. Bit players are people who make things easy for themselves from the first moment on. And that's what's happening in your case. That's simply miserable what you're showing right now. Then I am certainly going to need large costumes so that people will see at least something of the actor's art. That's the truth!"[28]

But on the same day, Karl von Appen changed the big pigtail of one of the singers and gave her a thinner pigtail which she liked less. She went to Brecht to complain. He said: "She sings beautifully, let us keep the thick pigtail." The next day again started out badly as Brecht declared:

"The premiere [supposedly only weeks away at this time] is very doubtful. It's been such a pigsty with the workshop. All of the craftspeople have been working on something else without telling us about it. I can't get over this. This is a major scandal. Unless everything is delivered today and works wonderfully there isn't going to be a premiere here. Then we'll simply have a few pre-showings and then stop the whole thing. This is simply out of the question that we are supposed to simply fling the chalk circle on the stage half finished. This greasy mess, this totally rotten . . . This is out of the question. That's that."[29]

Then, without a break, Brecht said, "what's that coming?" and from the wings came the actor with the canvas horse from the caravan scene (fig. 44) who danced his way across the stage. Brecht laughed uproariously. The tension was broken, the outburst forgotten, and the rehearsal broke up with Brecht's instruction for the pre-showing for a selected audience that everyone was to arrive half an hour early for make up: "Anyone not prepared to do this should tell me. We're not cooking a single extra Bratwurst." But in fact the premiere was months away. As with *Edward II* in Munich, the play would be ready only when Brecht said it was ready. Before he would be satisfied hundreds more hours of rehearsal time of the entire Ensemble would be lavished on the play. Over and over again parts would be recast, lines would be rewritten and then these lines thrown out again.

Some of the most interesting work in rehearsal was with Ernst Busch, who had his own strong ideas as to how things should be. At one point, as they were rehearsing the scene around Azdak's hut, Busch entered his hut holding the hare that the script calls for behind his back. Brecht yelled at him that this was all wrong. Busch yelled back but tried out all of Brecht's various other suggestions. Finally, quite amicably, the solution that Brecht had declared would never do, did do. On another occasion, Busch who really worked much of the time in a way indistinguishable from a Stanislavski-trained actor (and we will see this even more clearly in the next chapter with his Galileo), complained about the fact that he and other people in the play were drinking out of bowls. Busch, whose own research had convinced him that wine was drunk out of skins in Grusinia, said that wine should be drunk out of wineskins in the play. Not so said Brecht, "bowls are better." "But they have wineskins in Grusinia," replied Busch. "Fine," said Brecht, "but I am still opposed to it. Much will not ring true when something is too true." But though this particularly overly naturalistic idea of Busch's was rejected, if one goes through all the *Chalk Circle* rehearsals I think it is fair to say that Ernst Busch so consistently made good suggestions about the staging of the play that he deserves almost to be given co-director credit. His active engagement in the process of seeking a correct stage solution, so very similar to Weigel's and Laughton's method of working, marks Busch as a model Brechtian actor.

After one hundred days of rehearsals, the actor playing Simon, Grusche's fiancé, was replaced by Raimund Schelcher, who at once had problems with the scene where he must call across a wide river to Grusche (fig. 45). Brecht went up on stage himself and had Schelcher go down into the auditorium to watch him. The way Brecht played the scene was not to raise his voice to give a sense of distance but to lower his voice and to give his voice a sense of strain. To reinforce this visually he held his hands up like a funnel in front of his mouth.

But the shift in actors for the role of Simon was minor in comparison to what was to happen twelve days later. Käthe Reichel, who had been playing the part of the Governor's Wife and who had begun the part as Brecht's favorite mistress, had been "demoted" from the role of favorite mistress in the course of the long rehearsal period and Brecht's affections had shifted to Isot Kilian. Apparently, Reichel, after unsuccessfully trying to get Brecht to give

Fig. 44. *The Caucasian Chalk Circle*, Berlin, 1954. A classical "progress" of the sort used by Shakespeare closes the play. The "horse" used in the caravan scene is clearly visible at the back of the stage.

up Kilian and telling him he would deeply regret it if he did not, carried out her threat and attempted suicide. Whether by accident or design she was found very shortly after she had taken an overdose of pills and she quickly recovered. But before she was properly recovered, Brecht had replaced her in the role with Helene Weigel, who then proceeded completely to reshape the role without requiring any large changes in the script. Where the younger actress had bustled about the stage sticking her nose in everywhere, the older actress played the role in a much more static but no less effective way. Hans Bunge describes the events after the suicide attempt and Weigel's assumption of the role of the Governor's Wife as follows:

The person who had been playing the Governor's Wife suddenly was ill. One could not count on her recovery by the time of the premiere. Helene Weigel declared her willingness to take over the part and to study it in the days remaining before the announced premiere. At first Weigel rehearsed the part very tentatively. Brecht did not insist on her sticking closely to Reichel's model but gave her every opportunity to present her own interpretation. In the midst of this the astonishing happened. Weigel gave a

Fig. 45. *The Caucasian Chalk Circle*, Berlin, 1954. The singers (left) give voice to Grusche as Simon, across the stage river, demands to know how she is "with child."

completely different version of the role and yet the actors playing the servants hardly had to change at all from the way it had been when they played the scene with Reichel.

Reichel's interpretation depended on movement. She showed enormous strength on stage. Alternatively she spoke loudly and sharply and then quietly and sufferingly while she dominated the stage with her many quick movements. Weigel achieved the impression of being "a born ruler" through an almost opposite method. Instead of the hysterical changes in speech used by Reichel, Weigel used an even, quiet voice. She spoke almost quietly, but in a hard and sharp voice. Instead of flying movement she chose a deliberately static position. She sat in one place for almost the whole scene and controlled the situation from that place. She did not lift a finger to help but rather just gave orders.

A particularly good idea of Weigel's was accepted by Brecht after he had convinced himself that it would be effective on stage: The Governor's Wife was accompanied by a slave who was then used as a human chair. This slave had to always remain close to her mistress and when given a sign was to crouch down so that her back could be used as a seat. Whereas the Reichel–Governor's Wife by reason of her hysteria gave only a limited sense of being dangerous and gave more a sense of the natural stupidity of this highborn woman and was therefore not to be taken very seriously, in contrast the Weigel–Governor's Wife radiated an infectious brutality of stupidity, the dangerousness of which was absolutely convincing.[30]

The work with Weigel illustrates how rapidly progress could be made if the actor was extremely sensitive to Brecht's working methods. However, not every actor had Weigel's or Busch's or Hurwicz's ability to create their own role under Brecht's ever watchful and rigorously selective eye. For many of the "minor" roles in the piece, Brecht had Ruth Berlau and Benno Besson, both of whom were on the directorial staff for this production, conduct separate rehearsals with the actors. A good example of this procedure was what was done with the roles of the woman and the man with whom Grusche decides she will leave the baby. Here, verbatim, is the scene itself and then Brecht's rehearsal of the scene in which the farm woman finds the baby on her doorstep (the scene begins on p. 527 of the Bentley text and p. 169 in Willett):

THE FARM WOMAN: What's this lying here? Man!

THE FARM WOMAN'S HUSBAND: (comes) What's going on? Let me eat my soup.

THE FARM WOMAN: (to the child) Where's your mother? Don't you have one? I think it's a boy. Fine linen, that's a child from a rich family. They've simply put it on the doorstep. There are some clothes.

BRECHT: It's like this, we have, you have let the child lie there much longer Mrs Meier. You have, isn't that so. It is . . . to be done lightly, but people don't express themselves that way. They are astonished and so on, but not as if this were a moment of historical significance.

(*Speaker on tape explains what happens next*): Ruth Berlau has rehearsed this scene separately with the actors.

BERLAU: What we tried to achieve was that it would be light, that . . . when the knock comes, then they would know that somebody must be very close by.

BRECHT: Yes, that's what we were trying to . . .

BERLAU: Yes.

BRECHT: I don't know. So, there's a knock. But in general people don't simply go outdoors when they hear a knock, but rather they open a bit and peer out, particularly in times of disturbance. (Someone in the background objects.)

BRECHT: Yes, there is a knock, she must, yes she must knock, isn't that so. Grusche, otherwise the baby could lie around for hours, could just not be found at all, can't let that happen to the child . . . So she peers out, who's there? She can't simply come running out, I think that's it. That's what makes it look so unconvincing . . . How will you pick up the baby? Eh, how will you actually pick it up?

(*Speaker on tape again explains what has happened*: Grusche has left the child in front of the door and has then hidden herself. The farm woman comes out of the door and finds a curious bundle.

THE FARM WOMAN: What's this lying here? Man!

BRECHT: Mrs Meier, when you find the child you need to play it up a bit. You've got time, take the time that you need for it, won't you, yes, so that you can then bend over, wonder about things, look around, is someone running away, what's going on here? A baby! No. It almost looks now as though you expected to see one there, isn't that so. A whole lot has to be brought out of this small scene. OK, you see a small bundle lying in front of the door isn't that so. Now that is a very unhealthy thing, isn't that so, and it's also dangerous, the baby could be sick with anything on earth: plague, cholera. People are mistrustful they don't just take in even a dog (coughs). In order that that should be really clear, you could perhaps just let it lie there for a while. Who left something lying there? And then must come the moment when one sees, where you actually see the baby as a baby and you begin to get interested in it. And then you'll never give the child up, isn't that so. So that the contrast becomes really strong. Even the beginning, eh, aha! Yes this isn't an everyday thing, nothing was there before. Yes.

(*Speaker*): The farm woman has called to have her husband come out.

FARM MAN, FARM WOMAN: What's happening . . .

(*Speaker*): As the scene is repeated Brecht is still not in agreement with the way in which the farm woman comes out sticking her neck out like a turtle.

BRECHT: When you come out like a turtle, sticking your head out from under your shell that's beautiful but it can be overdone in a way that one wouldn't do it if one would stick one's neck out. Look in the corner!

ACTRESS: Here?

BRECHT: Yes, wherever. Here and there. Just like that carefully. What if someone was out there with a big block of wood with a nail in it. So look out in that way, starting to look back in, about to go back and while you are drawing back you lower your head. You see it. You say without being heard: "Jesus." No one needs to hear that. Then you say normally without any special emphasis: "What's lying here?" Without being forced. Strange dogs, strange cats, strange kids, that's really something: infectious diseases, an epidemic, to invite something like that . . .

THE FARM MAN: If they believe we're going to feed it for them, they're wrong. You take it into town to the priest and that's that.

THE FARM WOMAN: What's the priest supposed to do with it, it needs a mother.

BRECHT: "Intotowntopriestthat'sit." That has to be absolutely, isn't that so, "that'sit!" "that'sit!" You know your wife, isn't that so.

FARM WOMAN: "It's waking up. Don't you think we could keep it?"

FARM MAN: "No."

BRECHT: "Don't you think we could keep it?" Still as though you were against it yourself, isn't that so. You have reservations. You are convincing *yourself*, I'm convincing *myself*. Who am I convincing? Myself. Do you understand? You convince yourself that it's possible that it would work, isn't that so . . .

THE FARM WOMAN: If I bed it down in the corner near the armchair, all I'll need is a basket, and I'll take it with me into the fields. You see, how he smiles? Man, we've got a roof over our head and we can manage it, I don't want to hear anything more about it . . .

BRECHT: In that moment the baby opens it eyes . . . baby wakes up: the case is decided. Now she must remove the barriers . . . No more hesitation but rather you are looking for justification. Yes. It's not that simple. Yes. Naturally it's not easy, isn't that so. But you make it easy. Yes. But you don't say "keep it" right away because you first want to convince him, isn't that so. That's precious isn't that so, precious. "Keep it," there's nothing to that, nothing about the cost. Yes you pick up the child but food, buying it clothes, and milk, then, later comes shoes, isn't that so . . . It's as though travellers were overtaken by rain, are taken into the hut. So, what of it? They wait an hour, the rain ends, they're back on their way. Do you understand? Shall we do it again. I think you can show your determination even sooner. Besides: these are women's things, they don't concern him at all. If you are hindered in your cooking or in your work in the fields, because of the child, that will concern him, isn't that so, the slave to work, but if you can do it all yourself, without it ruining the daily jobs, then it doesn't matter shit to him, isn't that so. Yes. The same way it would be for me.

(*Speaker*): The farm woman goes into the house with the baby.

BRECHT: Before you follow her [to Farm Man], look as if, look completely taken in, look at where she's gone, shake your head and go in, go into the house, isn't that so. Shake your head, that's it, that's it, great. Then look around a bit with the lingering hope of maybe discovering the person who left it [laughter] and can make her responsible. Look further, look, no, no, no, let your eyes wander in the distance but without much hope, isn't that so . . Now the following: if you follow right after her, then people will think there's going to be an argument in there and one can never know, if – who will win out. But if you simply look astonished and then shake your head at the weakness of the female sex, and above everything else at the weakness of the male sex.[31]

The care lavished on these minor roles was, of course, matched by the care lavished on the major role of Grusche. The complexity of the role and Brecht's method of working with an actress to bring out that complexity is exemplified in the following interchange in rehearsals when Brecht suddenly discovered that Angelika Hurwicz, on her own initiative, had reduced the size of the bundle (see fig. 39) that she was carrying in the play. Brecht asked why the size of the bundle had been reduced and the exchange and commentary ran as follows:

HURWICZ: That's only logical. Originally I took a whole bunch of things from the palace. But in the meantime I have had to use things for the baby out of my bundle. Besides that, because it is now cold, I am wearing a shawl around my shoulders, and that shawl was in my bundle before. Besides that I have had to exchange pieces of clothing for the baby. Therefore the bundle must have gotten smaller and I am trying to show that realistically.

BRECHT: You are starting from a position that logical reflection must always be right. But that is by no means the case. Here, for instance, this is based on the presupposition that Grusche hasn't stolen anything during her flight. Probably this would be argued on the basis of Grusche's "character" that for her stealing would be out of the question. And that is dangerous. One should never start out on the basis of a figure's character because a person has no character. For Grusche, given the circumstances under which she lives, the times even demand that she steal, at least when its essential, and this reinforces her "positive character." It is consistent with the main thrust of the play to show what it costs Grusche to take care of the child. So, in future we will make the bundle bigger again, perhaps even make it bigger than it is at the beginning. There is, of course the question of whether our spectators will recognize the background of this measure, but that is not so important. If you think about it, and you could do that anyway if the bundle were smaller, perhaps you will come to a similar conclusion. What is good about what we are doing is that we are creating the basis for a many-layered person, which Grusche is. And what is of interest, at least for the directing staff and all those who think through with us is the conscious use of contradiction.[32]

This "conscious use of contradiction" underlies, I believe, virtually every directorial decision made by Brecht. It is the key to his work as director at every stage of his career. If, in one rehearsal, you have built up so-called "good qualities" in a Grusche, or the farmer who sells her the milk, or Simon her lover, or Azdak, then be sure to bring out so-called "negative" qualities in other rehearsals. Likewise, if you have stressed slowness and deliberate "breaks" in the play in one rehearsal then be sure to build up speed and continuity in other rehearsals. And, as you do this, do not, repeat, do not, resolve the contradictions inherent in the method. Remember always that complex individuals and complex action are made up of multiple layers of contradictions. To reduce those contradictions is to have your characters become cardboard cutouts. The characters themselves may very well not be aware of the contradictions but the director needs to bring them out. It is this quality, I believe, that Andrzej Wirth was trying to describe when he wrote of the "stereometric nature" of Brecht's work. The physics of stereometry is that the two separate eyes see not the same thing but different things and it is the mental super-imposition of one image over another that gives depth to what is seen. I would suggest that there is virtually no character in Brecht (with the exception of a very few out-and-out villains) who are not simultaneously at least two rather different characters. It is this simultaneous difference, these consciously unresolved contradictions that give these characters their depth and stereometric character. How dedicated Brecht was to this principle of simultaneous contradictions is revealed in a remark he made to Eric Bentley about Ernst Busch's playing of Azdak. Apparently, even after a year of rehearsals, Brecht still felt that Busch's Azdak was not contradictory enough. Visiting Brecht in Berlin in June, 1956, Bentley asked Brecht "was Ernst Busch as Azdak exactly what you had in mind?" Brecht's answer was no, Busch was not exactly right, for "he missed the whole tragic side of the role."[33] I am reminded here of Plato's observation to Socrates in the *Symposium*: Socrates, still talking after a whole night of carousing, observes that surely comedy and tragedy are the same thing. For Brecht apparently, the role of Azdak should permit one person to be simultaneously comic and tragic. This wish of Brecht's should caution the actor or director who seeks to find a consistent "line" through a character that this is missing the contradictions desired by Brecht as both director and playwright. *And you build these contradictions in to the performance whether or not your audience is ever consciously aware that the contradictions are there.* As Brecht himself said to Hans Bunge at one point during the *Chalk Circle* rehearsals, when Bunge tried to explain Grusche's motivation from only one point of view: "People don't act on the basis of only one motive, but always out of various motives that are in part contradictory."[34] The 284 pages of the rehearsal notebook show over and over again that *the* key reason why the rehearsals needed to spread over almost a year was because it was necessary to Brecht's mature working method to first develop all possible and probable contradictions of persons and plot and then speed and polish the continuity between the contradictory parts so that the contradictions would be virtually invisible to the ordinary spectator seeing the play once.

This development of the characters took 115 actual rehearsal days (not counting the separate rehearsals of "minor roles" conducted by Ruth Berlau, Benno Besson and Manfred Wekwerth). At this point, Brecht was ready to conduct technical rehearsals with particular emphasis on the lighting. As the assumption is often made that all Brecht called for in lighting a production was all lights at full all the time, it is helpful to see how much care was actually lavished on lighting a Berlin Ensemble production. Just as the work with the actors, the set designer, the stage carpenters, the costumer, the composer, the musicians had all been directed towards the explication or setting out of the basic story line of the play, not surprisingly the same motive guided the work with the lighting. Commenting generally on the lighting rehearsals conducted for several days from September 29, 1954, Hans Bunge writes in his "Diary of a Production":

The director was not interested in special effects with the lighting. Effects were used sparingly and only when the exposition of the plot or fable directly called for them as, for instance, during the closing sequence of the first act to indicate nightfall and the dawn of the next morning as Grusche sits so long with the abandoned baby until she then picks it up and takes it with her. The object here was not to show complete darkness, but rather it was sufficient that one noted the change.[35]

The next day was devoted to lighting Grusche's "Flight into the Northern Mountains" (Act 2). The basic idea of the lighting here, says Bunge, is that it "should be very bright." This relatively simple goal, however, was more difficult to reach than one might think. Bunge writes:

Grusche's path for her wanderings was to be indicated by a semi-circular "path of light" stretching from the backdrop on one side to the apron and then back to the backdrop on the other side. It took us a long time to get this light right so that we would have a silken gleam on the backdrop. Simply using the existent lights we could not get the proper effect at first. Numerous attempts with the use of a fan to get the backdrop to move continuously did not result in the desired effect. The director finally came close to being satisfied by the use of indirect lighting of the backdrop by means of having eight spotlights placed in the fly space behind the backdrop. But this experiment proved that it was necessary to have a series of spots that were free to move so that, by hand, one could quickly move them and make carefully nuanced changes.[36]

Whether or not audiences would be aware of it, it had required complex and continuous maneuvering by the lighting technicians to achieve a supposedly simple or natural effect.

A third day was devoted to lighting the third act and here Brecht wished to achieve a lighting effect noticeably (at least to him) different from the other acts. He called here for the backdrop to not be transparent and to be bathed in "milky white light." In addition he called for there to be distinct lighting differences between the individual scenes of the act; and also the act itself was to be different from other acts. Summing up the complexity of Brecht's directions for the lighting of this act, again we return to the contradictions as they relate to one another. As Bunge puts it: "But it was never merely a question, that would have been an easy goal to strive for, but rather always that the contradictions should add up to a unified whole built of contradictions."[37]

The sophisticated work on the lighting then revealed all kinds of deficiencies in the way in which various sets and costumes worked in the production as a whole. At a full-scale dress rehearsal on November 1, 1954 (the 121st day of rehearsals and almost exactly a full year since rehearsals had begun) Brecht was dissatisfied at the discrepancy between Karl von Appen's drawings and the way these ideas worked when translated into actual sets and costumes by Kurt Palm and his staff. Again Brecht stressed the role of contradictions. He complained that whereas the von Appen drawings had contained many contradictions that nevertheless combined to form a unified whole, this effect had not been achieved on the stage itself. Where in the drawings one had seen a clear space between the curtains hung as flags or backdrops and the other backdrop behind the area of the turntable stage, on the stage itself the two different backdrops blended in with one another. Brecht proposed that the distance between the two backdrops be emphasized by the creation of a dividing "dark corridor." Also unsuccessful in Brecht's view was the way in which the technicians had tried to render von Appen's two clear color-scales. For lighter parts of the play, the mood was to be underscored by the use of lighter tones in the characters' dress and in the color of the backdrops. As the mood of the play darkened, however, the costumes echoed in their dark hues the mood of the play. Only after these colors were emphasized clearly to bring out the connections between color scheme and mood did Brecht declare himself satisfied. Again a great deal of effort and ingenuity is put in to make the final effect one of simplicity and directness. Again complexity and indirectness prove to be essential if the final effect is to be simple and direct. Laughing as he said it, Brecht observed of the dress rehearsal: "One has to pay a colossal amount of attention to accidental results because that's the way one often finds the right solution."[38] So far 125 rehearsal days spread over a year had been used to seek those right solutions. By the time of the premiere on October 7, 1954 there had been 600 rehearsal hours just for the actors. In addition there had been 40 rehearsal days with 100 hours of rehearsal for the orchestra and the singers; 70 rehearsal days with 165 hours for the dancers; 30 days with 60 hours for the scenes with children; and the literally countless hours that went into the original preparation of and frequent complete changes of some 130 costumes, 40 masks, numerous sets and backdrops, and the creation of "museum quality" props.

The October 7, 1954 premiere ran smoothly and the running time of the actual performance was three hours and eighteen minutes, a remarkably fast pace given the complexity of the play itself. On the evening of the premiere Brecht sat with his staff in what would have been the old Royal Box in the Am Schiffbauerdamm Theatre. His running commentary on the actual perform-ance was recorded by a stenographer and then notes were given to appropriate individuals the next morning. He ordered that the hut where Grusche buys the milk be given just a touch of grey coloration by adding a blue gel to one spotlight. At the instant Grusche hits the Ironshirt over the head Brecht ordered (in English) "black-out" in the house. He wanted the light level raised for the bridge scene over the chasm and another black-out as the turntable stage carried the bridge away at the end of the scene. These small changes suggested by Brecht would never really end. When the play was taken to Paris in 1955 for its triumph at the International Theatre Festival he polished it further. In fact, just before he died in August 1956, following Khruschev's denunciation of Stalin at the Twentieth Soviet Communist Party Congress, Brecht polished the play further and wrote lines to reflect changes in the Soviet Union. And on his death bed as the Berlin Ensemble prepared to go to London without him he instructed the company to be "fast, light and strong" in their playing. The instructions for London and for Paris were followed and it is fair to say that with *The Caucasian Chalk Circle* production following hard on the heels of the international success of *Mother Courage and Her Children* in Paris in 1954 Brecht achieved his maximum impact on the international stage. Henceforward no one could afford to ignore him. What sophisticated critics saw was theatre such as it was practiced nowhere else. They saw actors like Busch and Hurwicz who were highly talented but who had figures and faces that would blend in with any crowd of workers. These were not actors' faces, the pretty faces of London's West End, or New York's Broadway or the Boulevard theatres of Paris. And these actors played with a verve and precision that made much other acting suddenly seem stale, slow, imprecise, in the worst sense "theatrical."

Because we have such an extensive photographic record of the Berlin Ensemble production of *The Caucasian Chalk Circle*, together with Angelika Hurwicz's superb commentary, it is possible to reconstruct what it was that audiences saw in Brecht's original production. Again and again our attention is drawn to linkage, to speed, to the unity of what began as contradictions. Hurwicz has us note, for instance, the skilled transition (by means of wrapping the child in a blanket) from the baby that she brings to the mountains (see fig. 39) to the small boy we see in the spring. Hurwicz notes on this scene: "In order to suggest the coldness of the pantry, the child is wrapped in a blanket. But this also serves to make, for the spectator, the transition from infant to larger child less crass or glaring."[39] A little later, in the scene where Grusche is torn between "her" explanation to her returned fiancé, Simon Chachawa, a soldier of the governor, and the threat to "her" child, Brecht does not let her stand there very long, torn between her two loves. He has her dash off after the child and the governor's henchman. Instead of "Naturalistic" delay, a delay that would make her painful psychological choice credible, Brecht had something else in mind. Hurwicz notes: "Brecht avoids developing the scene of Grusche's interesting dilemma. What was of more interest to him was *dramaturgically linking this scene with the later trial scene* [my italics], where Grusche, with all the forcefulness she can muster, will assert her rights to the child.[40]

The small but important details that Brecht used to tie the action together and which are so admirably explicated by Hurwicz's analysis of the photos of the production, are then supported by Brecht's use of the most important technical device available to him first at the German Theatre and later at the Am Schiffbauerdamm Theatre: the huge turntable stage that he had used with such telling effect in his *Mother Courage* production. The basic function of the turntable was to tie the scenes together as closely as possible. The effect sought was flawless continuity and, with this, chronological compression. In effect, therefore, we may postulate that the transitions from scene to scene in

Brecht's "epic" play were far smoother than the kind of delayed changes (necessitated by major set changes) that we see so often in more "Realistic" productions. Brecht's play was not sliced up by the "guillotine" (to use Brecht's own term for the device) of the heavy curtain used even today in many "Naturalist" productions.

The smooth continuum of action established first by Brecht's choice of visual details (wrapping the child in a blanket for the hut scene), secondly by his not permitting "Naturalist" delay (Grusche's swift flight after the child and away from Simon), and thirdly by the use of the turntable stage itself, is then reinforced by the music that Paul Dessau composed (on Brecht's instructions) for this scene. Brecht himself notes of this music: "For the second act ('Flight into the Northern Mountains'), the theatre needs a driving kind of music that will hold this very epic act together."[41] This music tended to reinforce the tension generated by the flight itself. The "Flight into the Northern Mountains" is very much a "chase sequence" in a style close to that of the old American films Brecht so dearly loved, and in his own notes on the play he himself made this connection. Grusche's escape, as the text never for a moment permits us to forget, is a nip-and-tuck affair. What is true of the text is, however, even truer of Brecht's staging. Instead, for instance, of completely stylizing the crossing of the two thousand feet deep chasm (a scene that would probably be done in the Chinese theatre, full as it is of V-effects, solely with gestures and with no props at all), Brecht gave the scene additional emotional drive by introducing an actual rickety bridge.[42] With the soldiers in hot pursuit, Grusche, almost too tired to move at all, approaches the makeshift rope bridge (see fig. 41). Other characters, terrified of the rotten ropes and completely loose end of one side of the bridge, stand around, refusing to attempt to cross and urging Grusche not to try anything so suicidal. Laden as she is with her bundle and her child, the bridge will, they assure her, collapse under their combined weight. But for Grusche to stand there and not cross is perhaps even more suicidal. The soldiers, one of whose heads she has smashed in the previous scene, can be heard approaching and they will, as one bystander assures Grusche and us the audience, "make hamburger out of her" if she is caught. Under these circumstances she is willing to attempt to cross the bridge. Tension mounts as she resolutely decides not to leave the child behind and thus increases the danger considerably. Amid the gasps and prayers of the bystanders she makes the hazardous crossing safely and, just as she reaches the other side and the loose end of the bridge once again dangles over the chasm, the soldiers appear on the side she has just left (fig. 46). The scene and the staging are obviously so designed that we cross that bridge with Grusche; we see the two thousand foot drop below; we feel the breath of the pursuing soldiers on our necks. In a

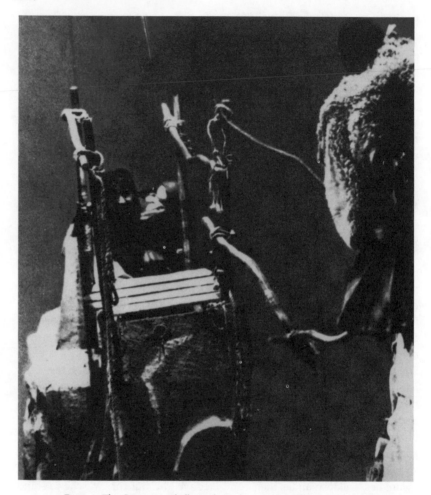

Fig. 46. *The Caucasian Chalk Circle*, Berlin, 1954. At the very instant that Grusche reaches the other side the bridge collapses with a loud roar and the pursuing soldiers watch helplessly as Grusche, on the other side of the chasm, continues her flight with the child.

word, we are forced to identify fully with the heroic Grusche. We then follow her on her seven-day journey as the stage turns (as with Mother Courage) against her progress. We are with her as she reaches her brother's hut, and we are there as, all her heroic efforts and sacrifices notwithstanding, the child is taken from her by the soldiers at the end of the act.

The myriad aesthetic knots introduced deliberately by the playwright–director to offset scenic division and to eliminate breaks between dialogue and song, indicate how far the later Brecht had departed from the earlier theory. The pleasure of the spectator (the guiding principle of the 1948 *Short Organum*) and the pure aesthetic satisfaction that the later Brecht sought and found in the theatre, seemed to have played a greater role here than the early theory with its discrete parts, its anti-aesthetic bias, and its theoretically calm and largely unmoved spectators. Brecht's own reading of the text is specifically dramatic and profoundly moving. The separate parts of the play become in production welded together. Even leaving aside for a moment Brecht's casting innovation of having Busch be both the singer and Azdak, it is obvious, in dramaturgical terms, that the break in the Grusche story, coming at the time it does, hurries us as precipitously as Grusche into the last lap of the play where the destinies of Grusche and Azdak converge in the test of the circle of chalk.

When Brecht shifts the scene to Azdak and the corrupt judge's rise to power, the spectator does not simply forget Grusche or the fact that the poor woman is in danger of losing her child to the wretched governor's wretched wife. Scene 4 (a superb point for an intermission) closes very cleverly with Grusche running after her child, while the singer, using one of the oldest devices known to storytellers in any medium, asks: "What will happen now?" Everything depends on a just judge to decide Grusche's claim to the child; who will that judge be? We are then introduced to the man who is vital to Grusche's cause. Thereafter, with brilliant use of retardation as we are amused and frightened by and for Azdak, as we see Azdak's rise to power and how tenuous his power is, we continue to be nagged by the question: What is going on "back at the ranch?" Will the mad, sensuous, cowardly, brave Azdak be able to save the child for Grusche or will he be removed and slaughtered at whim even before the case comes to trial? If he tries the case, will he be swayed by power or threats from the wealthy wife of the governor or will he stick his neck in a noose in order to save the child for the "true" mother? His earlier decisions in the case of the miraculous ham lead us to hope that he will help the poor and heavy laden; but he is at the same time too cowardly, too whimsical for us to be wholly sure. We are raced by Brecht in the closing two scenes of the play, as surely as Racine ever raced an audience in his climatic and precipitous fifth acts, towards the denouement.

Fig. 47. *The Caucasian Chalk Circle*, Berlin, 1954. The chalk circle test itself. Azdak (Ernst Busch) directs the contestants to try to pull the child out of the circle. The "evil" mother has a tight grip on the child. Grusche holds the child's hand gently and lovingly while the child looks only at her.

When Brecht combines, in his climactic final scene, the chaste and simple Grusche and his bawdy, cowardly, corrupted but kindhearted "judge", and pits Grusche against the grasping "real" mother and her slimy cohorts, he creates a scene of tremendous dramatic intensity (fig. 47). Heinz Politzer, in an essay that asks the question, "How Epic is Brecht's Epic Theatre?", notes of the final scene of the play: "As if to stress the climactic character of this scene, Brecht constructed the two parts of the play so that the life histories of both Grusche and Azdak are crowned by it. The time sequences of both actions converge here and break the parallel structure of the epic drama."[43] It is obvious that if one of the hallmarks of the non-Aristotelian or epic drama is that such drama does not build towards a climax, does not work towards magnificent "curtains," then Brecht's play bears no trace of this hallmark. If prevention of audience identification is necessary, we look in vain for anything in the play to prevent our total subscription to Grusche's feelings and those of the "almost" judge Azdak. Surely Grossvogel is correct when he claims that after the frametale of the kolkhoz is complete, "the conventional dramatic suasion takes over . . ."[44]

Brecht was himself, of course, perfectly aware of the professional polish and expertise that was needed in order to produce the big exile plays properly. This point of view was, of course, shared by others beside Brecht. Angelika Hurwicz herself speaks consistently of the downright luxuriousness of Brecht's work with the Berlin Ensemble on plays such as *The Caucasian Chalk Circle*. It is not every theatre which can permit itself rehearsal periods of up to an entire year and props any one of which would qualify as a "genuine museum piece." Brecht's theatre in the mid-fifties hardly qualified as poor theatre. By 1954 the Ensemble had a budget of three million marks, only one-sixth of which came from box-office revenues from the seven-hundred seat house.[45] This was a theatre which was never asked to sustain itself solely from ticket sales. Only with massive subsidies could Brecht and Weigel maintain a company of some two hundred and twelve people (including fifty-five actors) and rehearsals of full casts including stars for a full year. For theatre on this scale and of this complexity, Brecht's early model where he argued that events on stage were like a simple scene on a street corner is less relevant critically than his later *Small Organum* and that compendium of the Ensemble's practical work in theatre, *Theaterarbeit*. In these works, as Rudolf Frank has pointed out, we find with astonishing frequency words such as "noble, poetic, naive (in the sense the word is used by Schiller), graceful, soft or delicate, sweeping, sublime, charm, distinction, elegance, selectivity, beauty, precision, mythological grandeur, and a sense of reasonableness."[46] It is this vocabulary which helps us to describe Brecht's last and most famous production. Apparently now well beyond the rational pauses his earlier theory had set such store by, Brecht said frankly in 1955: "In order to put a final polish on the production for our visit to Paris, cuts were made in the text and the tempo of the performance was increased." He then added: "The increase in tempo served not only to shorten but even more to enliven the production. The majority of scenes and figures were improved by means of this tempo."[47] As he and the Paris critics watched this precise and highly polished production, they were fully aware that the rather plain caterpillar of the "street scene" had become the lovely butterfly of high dramatic art.

7   I am become death, destroyer of worlds.[1]

It must work on a colossal scale,
like the H-Bomb.[2]

Bertolt Brecht

Work at the Berlin Ensemble resembled in pattern if not in output the work of many repertory companies. While one or more productions were running others were being prepared. Brecht's degree of participation in these productions would vary considerably. Sometimes, as when Benno Besson directed adaptations of Molière's *Don Juan* and Farquhar's *The Recruiting Officer* (titled *Drums and Trumpets* in the Berlin Ensemble adaptation), Brecht would appear only occasionally at rehearsals and would allow newcomers such as Besson, Manfred Wekwerth or Peter Palitzsch a virtually free hand to guide the production. Such productions are perhaps best labeled, to borrow some vocabulary from the other arts, as works from "the Brecht school." Brecht might come in and paint a hand here or a face there, but the basic creation was the work of one or more of a very talented group of young directors. By late 1955, despite already having large productions of such works as *Mother Courage* and *The Caucasian Chalk Circle* and several "smaller" plays from "the Brecht school" in the repertoire,[3] the decision was made to have Brecht himself begin rehearsals of another blockbuster, *The Life of Galileo Galilei*. As was usual with Brecht, the decision to put one of the big plays into production was largely dependent on the availability of a major star. As early as 1951 he had tried to get leading German stars such as Oskar Homolka (Brecht's co-director of *Baal* and the lead player in Berlin in 1926), Fritz Kortner (Shlink in the Berlin 1924 *In the Jungle of the Cities*), or Leonard Steckel, to play the lead. When these attempts failed he put off the production until a major star became available. The star was Ernst Busch, another Brecht standby who had appeared in Brecht's production of *Mother* in pre-exile Berlin and the successful Ensemble production of *The Caucasian Chalk Circle*. Brecht embarked on the 1955 *Galileo* production with a mixture of enthusiasm and reticence. He was worried about the strain that another big production would place on his now rather precariously balanced health. His commitments were already far too many. Work on national committees in the German Democratic Republic took up lots of time, as did his ever-active love life and travels to various political and cultural events. The preparation of his collected works under Elisabeth Hauptmann's capable direction also took some time, as did the constant negotiation of new contracts[4] for reprintings or restagings of his works in various countries and various languages. And though the main administrative burden of the Berlin Ensemble continued to be borne by Helene Weigel, the international success of the Ensemble at the Paris Festival in 1954 had established Brecht as the major force in world theatre; a study visit to the Berlin Ensemble and the Am Schiffbauerdamm Theatre (figs. 48 and 49) had become the goal of virtually everyone in theatre. The stream of visitors was constant and all of them wanted to talk with Brecht. By late 1955 "Brecht" was not just a person anymore, he was an entire industry with franchises being sold everywhere. He was rich and very famous but he was also ill and unhappy in his personal life. Many of the various liaisons from previous years[5] were in considerable disarray and Brecht never seemed to understand why his double standard (any number of simultaneous affairs for him but no others for his partners) was not cheerfully accepted. Surrounded night and day by assistants who Brecht felt, often very unfairly, were almost all old Nazis, Brecht was rarely alone and yet he had few friends he could really trust. Politically he had mixed feelings about the development

Fig. 48. The restored interior of the Am Schiffbauerdamm Theatre. The Schiff was where the original *Threepenny Opera* opened in 1928. It became the home of the Berlin Ensemble in 1954. Picasso's Dove of Peace adorns the curtain.

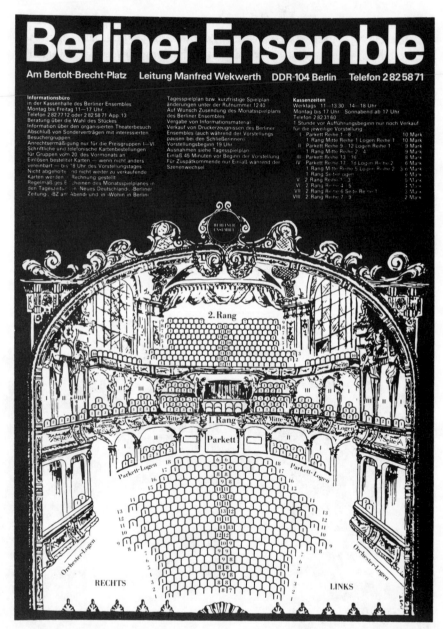

Fig. 49. Seating plan for the Am Schiffbauerdamm Theatre.

of genuine socialism in the German Democratic Republic. He was also deeply pained in the last months of his life by Khruschev's revelations about Stalin at the Twentieth Party Congress. His own late poems on Stalin spoke of "the honored murderer of the people" and referred to Stalin as a Führer. On the positive side of the socialist ledger he looked to China under the leadership of the poet–philosopher–soldier Mao whose poems Brecht had now begun to translate.[6] When his old friend Erwin Leiser came to visit he slipped him a copy of an anti-Stalin poem. In conversations with the old revolutionaries Herta Gordon[7] and Jakob Walcher (who had known Lenin personally) he sought to learn first-hand how Lenin's leadership style differed in positive ways from that of Stalin. Eric Bentley was shocked by his appearance when he visited Brecht in the last months of his life. In his recent memoir Bentley writes:

Brecht presented himself as soon as he knew I was there. A physically shrunken Brecht. A Brecht who had lost his looks. (In his own way, severe, gaunt, a little haughty, Sphinx-like, he had been very good-looking.) Shrunken in the body, swollen somewhat in the face, flaccid. And without that familiar and so distinctive voice. What voice he still had kept sinking to a hoarse whisper. Gallantly – and he did have his own gallantry, had no self-pity that I could ever descry – he bade me welcome back to Berlin. I hope I didn't show signs of shock; but he assumed I *would* show such signs and said his health had not been "too good"; he was "etwas reduziert," (in reduced circumstances). I told him the commonplace thing: that I was very, very glad to see him again. And he saw the reality behind the commonplace. Being a dramatist (*the* dramatist of his time after all) he could read a subtext any time. Seeing my eyes, he also felt all my vibrations. He knew all.[8]

By taking on his lifelong collaborators, Eric Engel as co-director and Caspar Neher as set and costume designer, by relying heavily on the photographic record Berlau had made of the Brecht/Laughton *Galileo* and with his old friend Ernst Busch in the lead role, Brecht was very deliberately setting up a production company that could run reasonably well even if he himself could not always be present. A poem of the final period sums up Brecht's sense of unease and the alienation of Brecht the self-declared spokesperson for the proletariat:

> I sit by the roadside
> The chauffeur changes the tire.
> I do not like where I have come from.
> I do not like where I am going.
> Why do I watch the wheel change
> With impatience?[9]

Wherever he went or stayed the pressure was unrelenting. Whether he recognized it or not, by the last year of his life, Brecht, with Weigel as his business partner, was director of as large a business enterprise as anything that his father had ever managed in Augsburg. His life, with his houses in the

country and one in town, his own BMW two-seater *and* a car driven by an
Ensemble staff member, his huge staff of assistants, his secretaries, his custom-
made clothes, his multiple contracts and bank accounts in various countries,
his dealings with the highest authorities in the German Democratic Republic,
was not the typical life of the member of the proletariat in Berlin in 1955–6.
Though he had declared in an early and famous poem that he had left his own
class, the bourgeoisie, in order to sit down with the workers, most of Brecht's
sitting down at every stage of his life was with lawyers, editors and heads of
theatres, and with international stars of stage and screen. Whether or not he
wanted it to look that way, Bertolt Brecht was a wealthy man and one able to
exercise enormous power over hundreds of employees at his Am
Schiffbauerdamm Theatre. An international celebrity, his every word was
recorded. His own reaction to all of this was as contradictory as any of the
stage characters he had created. Having stated years ago that he was "the
Einstein of the new stage form," he was not about to dispute the fact that his
fame and attendant wealth as a director/playwright was really earned. But at
the same time, he did not want the consequents of fame to have an opulent
look. It mattered very much to him that the car in which he drove about
should be old and look old – the cost of maintaining this "look" might well be
higher than buying a new car, but that would miss the point. His jackets, as
always made to measure, should be buttoned up in such a way that the
custom tailored shirt underneath was not visible. The impression given by his
personal appearance was very like his production style: it might actually cost
an enormous amount but it should look simple, worn, casual, unmannered,
natural. There is a grain of truth in a story that has been told of the early
Brecht, that he had a special gold instrument manufactured to his
specifications, with the sole purpose of pushing dirt *under* his fingernails. This
story is apocryphal[10] but it points to something true: Brecht would spare no
expense to look poor. And, of course, there was drama in this. It had a distinct
shock effect, and in his life and in his art from the earliest productions to the
last, he sought such shock effects. This is nowhere more apparent than in the
Galileo production that he rehearsed virtually until the day of his death.
Rehearsals were begun on December 14, 1955[11] and were continued, with a
break for Brecht to go to Milan in February for Giorgio Strehler's updated
Threepenny Opera, until March 27 when the state of Brecht's health prevented
him from regularly attending rehearsals. Between December and March he
rehearsed only two hours a day for some fifty-nine rehearsal days, most of
which were recorded by Hans Bunge. In addition to the two hours actually
spent with the actors, however, many other hours were spent on discussions
of the use of the Laughton model, and of discussions of set designs and
costumes, on discussions of the play with the staff of assistants and his co-

director, and in discussing technical arrangements with the stage crew. Though other scenes were rehearsed in this period, the two scenes receiving the most attention were the opening and the closing scenes of the stage version of the play:[12] scene 1 (eleven rehearsals) and 13 (nine rehearsals). Most of the rehearsals were tape-recorded and this together with Käthe Rülicke's stenographic notes makes it possible to reconstruct further details of Brecht's working methods as a director (fig. 50). A six-hundred-page transcript of the whole rehearsal period has been prepared by Günter Gläser and may be seen at the Brecht Archive in Berlin.

Brecht's approach at the outset to the figure of Galileo looked deceptively simple. With great satisfaction he recited in English:

> Humpty Dumpty sat on a wall,
> Humpty Dumpty had a great fall,
> All the King's horses and all the King's men
> Could not put Humpty Dumpty together again.

This, he said, contained the essence of the meaning of the play, "for absolutely nothing else happens."[13] He laughed uproariously at this and then quoted another rhyme, this one in German from his friend the Munich comedian Karl Valentin:

> Two boys climbed up a ladder,
> The boy on top was somewhat smarter
> The boy below was somewhat dumber
> Suddenly the ladder fell.[14]

Instead of lofty "scientific" analysis of his text, Brecht stressed with the Humpty Dumpty and Valentin quotations the very down to earth and naive (in a non-pejorative sense) quality of his work. In this, of course, he was returning to a classical tenet of German aesthetics: the "naive" viewed as a positive characteristic of the very greatest literature: the work of Homer and Shakespeare, for example. But Brecht, in simply citing the nursery rhyme and then talking positively about the value of naive simplicity, did not go on to explicate for his audience the parallels between this position and the one advanced by Goethe and Schiller. This connection would have made the discussion both too "theoretical" and even obviously self-serving, and at least in theory Brecht abhorred all theoretical discussion and self-aggrandizement during rehearsals.[15] What would normally happen, however, is that though there would be no theorizing during actual rehearsal, on the evening of the same day when the actors were engaged in other plays, or over the weekend when he talked with his staff of dramaturgical assistants, then he might very well explicate his theoretical position.

For the actors and for Brecht in rehearsal everything finally came down to the practical question: does it work? If it worked it was adopted, and the theory, retroactively and separately, was adapted to fit the actual practice. As early as September, 1920 Brecht had jotted down in his diary the following observation about the usefulness of theories: "A man with one theory is lost. He needs several of them, four, lots! He should stuff them in his pockets like newspapers, hot from the press always, you can live well surrounded by them, there are comfortable lodgings to be found between the theories. If you are to get on you need to know that there are a lot of theories . . ."[16] Epic theory might call for loose and separate scenes. Theatrical practice called for tightly and smoothly linked scenes in which every extraneous word and scene would be dropped. Consequently, scene changes had to be rapid and smooth. With stop-watch in hand, as though he were timing a pit-stop at the Grand Prix in Monte Carlo, Brecht would stop everything to bellow at the

Fig. 50. *The Life of Galileo*, Berlin, 1956. A *Galileo* rehearsal with Brecht (left), Isot Kilian (taking notes), Manfred Wekwerth (seated in background), Ernst Busch (standing, wearing a beret), Hans-Joachim Bunge (seated in foreground) and Käthe Rülicke. After Brecht's death on 14 August, 1956, the production was completed by Erich Engel.

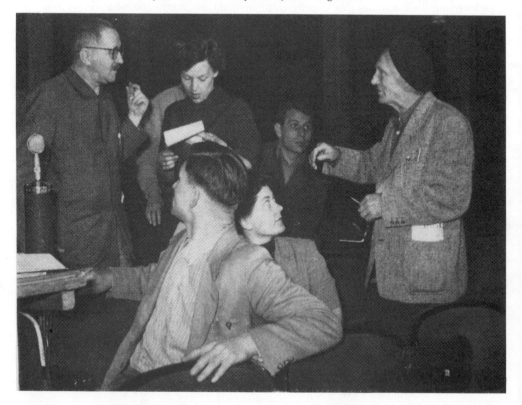

stage hands to speed up the scene changes so they took the absolute minimum time. He sought maximum speed, but it was important to him that these changes must not give a sense of haste, for that would detract from the performance as much as slowness of change would. What was true of Brecht the director's work with the stage crew was equally true of his work with Bertolt Brecht the playwright, and his work with the actors. Again, just as he had in his early productions in Munich, Leipzig and Berlin, Brecht the director would disagree with Brecht the playwright. Typically, at one point in the rehearsals Eckhard Schall told Brecht that Brecht the playwright called for such and such action. Brecht the director reacted, "from him is it, that one writes a great deal of stuff," and the great deal of stuff that "–that one" wrote was promptly thrown out. Yet, on another occasion when Ernst Busch complained that "that one's" physics were flatly wrong in a crucial scene of the play, Brecht replied: "I can't let myself be drawn into a discussion, all this has been checked out by astronomers, please no discussion, it simply is a fact, nothing further Busch, we can't discuss this any further." When Busch insisted on further discussion, Brecht began to look very tired and was unable to work in a concentrated way. When Busch involved himself in directorial details and would make changes in blocking during his absence, Brecht would systematically alter things back again to his own old version.

If one were to summarize the whole rehearsal process, one could note that Brecht began with a large body of material and approached that material in a seemingly leisurely way. Then, during the months of rehearsal, the large body of material (the original text and cast) would be stripped down to the bare essentials of the fable or the story. Simultaneously, the pace of the playing of the individual scenes would be increased so that the actors could race through the whole production. Then, when the transitions were so smooth that they could be done at a run, Brecht would slow the production back down far enough so that things were still done at considerable speed but with a sense of ease. Rather like the artistry of the classical ballet, enormous exertion might lie behind the performance but none of this should be visible for the audience. This final effect should be simple, worn, casual, natural and unmannered, at whatever cost. Yes, there is a basic contradiction inherent in all this, but it must be stressed that Brecht absolutely reveled in such contradictions, for he felt that human behavior is full of such contradictions and that the stage should reflect this fact of real life.[17] Further, as his work was internationally recognized, Brecht was fully aware that many members of his audience spoke no German and were having to follow what was going on without the help of language. He could not, therefore, afford to slow the spoken text down at all as this would have bored the considerable non-German portion of his audience. Speed of movement was essential in keeping the interest of such an audience alive. Nowhere is this more important than in *Galileo* and in Brecht's final production of this play.

When rehearsals of the play began in late 1955 it was clear from the outset that a tremendous amount of detail would be taken over almost *in toto* from the Brecht/Laughton California production of the play. Käthe Rülicke notes: "The arrangement of scene 13 was taken over by Brecht, as was true also of most of the other scenes, from the California production as Brecht used his own earlier production as a model for this one." Rülicke then goes on to note another characteristic of Brecht's directing style on this production: "It is characteristic of Brecht that the blocking arrangements worked out at the first rehearsals hardly ever got changed."[18] Given the fact that so many things were taken over completely from the California model, the leisurely luxury of a rehearsal schedule where fifty-nine days of rehearsals are considered to be only a good start on things is mind boggling. There is in fact one exchange between Busch and Brecht where they have a tongue-in-cheek discussion of the rehearsal schedule that went as follows:

BRECHT (*to Busch*):   In seven years of rehearsals you will have completely faded away.
KILIAN: But we won't rehearse that long!
BRECHT: We don't know that. You know Busch, if in the seven years you're completely faded away there'll be nothing left of you for the dress rehearsal. That's what I think.
BUSCH: Oh well, seven years . . . we'll need only six.
BRECHT: If it's up to me it'll be seven. You are a tempestuous character and naturally you want to do the whole thing in six years. Yes, yes because you are a tempestuous character and a hothead. From now on I'm going to stand around with my hat in my hand collecting lines that we can drop from the text of the play. From now on I'm going to collect them. Do you know what the playing time of *The Good Person (of Sezuan)* was in Rostock?
BUSCH: Three and a half hours – but do you think this play will run that long?
BRECHT: Four hours! Yes that would be lovely.
BUSCH: What? Four hours?
BRECHT: Yes, yes with the intermission. But four hours would be lovely.
BUSCH: You're crazy.
BRECHT: Yes that's true, that's it exactly.[19]

On a less playful note, Brecht recognized that the play was far too long and would really need to be cut. He said to Busch that the opening speech, for instance, was too long and "We'll probably have to cut somewhat." Typical of Busch is his response to this: "OK, when we run it through a couple of times some things will just drop of themselves."[20] This is actually what then usually happened. As the actors worked without either first memorizing lines or with books in their hands, but rather relied on being fed lines by a prompter, they would often just drop "extraneous" lines (lines that did not directly contribute to "the story") and if those lines were not really missed they were then dropped permanently from the stage version of the text. In this manner (as Ernst Schumacher has shown in his superb book-length study of *Galileo*),[21] the dramatic intensity and coherence of the work became more pronounced so that the staged text differed more widely from the "standard" published version of the text, the one that continues to be used by a large majority of academic commentators.[22] Yet the scenes selected, intensified and focussed by Brecht the director, who worked on them virtually until the day of his death, surely have as much of a claim to textual "authority" as the non-stage version as edited by Elisabeth Hauptmann. Looking over the play as a whole, Ernst Schumacher has noted that it does not meet the "epic" standard of discrete and rearrangable parts. He said flatly: "The various scenes are characterized by their relatively closed nature, but they don't simply follow one another like numbers [in a revue], but rather are necessary parts of what has become an organic whole."[23] What was true of the text of the play with its conservative exposition and organic wholeness, became ever more apt in production. As we saw with the *Galileo* production in California, Brecht was very much aware of the classical roundness and organic structure of his play. It is significant that not only was no attempt made to change this organic wholeness in the final months of Brecht's life, but that the last rehearsals actually further enhanced this aspect of the play.

Equally important is the fact that not only did Brecht's final work on the text bring out ever more sharply what he himself called "the conservative nature of the play," but also his work in rehearsals stressed its enormous emotional power. Brecht wanted that emotion there and stressed it again and again.

In discussing the Laughton *Galileo*, I indicated that Laughton's approach to acting was highly emotional; in this and other respects he had a great deal in common with Stanislavski. I believe the same may be said of Ernst Busch in the same role, as indeed it may be said of another international star who often worked with Brecht, Peter Lorre. The composer Hanns Eisler (a good friend of Brecht and Busch) reports that "Busch prepared himself thoroughly for the role of Galileo. He read books about classical and modern astronomy and physics."[24] And even when Busch was not rehearsing he began to look and sound more and more like Galileo. Eisler notes: "it became the most natural thing in the world for him to argue about astronomy, and the jargon of physics and astronomy became part of his ordinary speech."[25] Eisler's account of Busch's preparation for the role then concludes with an anecdote that could almost have been taken from the notebooks of Stanislavski himself: "A friend, who was in Rome at the time told me this story: 'I saw a bust and thought, that's Ernst Busch. How did that bust get here?' So soon? As I came closer I saw that it was a bust of Galileo.' "[26] Clearly, in at least one basic sense, Ernst Busch like Laughton before him did identify with the part of Galileo and did "become" Galileo, all "epic theory" notwithstanding. Significantly, I know of no evidence of Brecht's opposition to this approach. He seems to have been very pleased by Busch's "background homework," and by the fact that Busch's identification with Galileo quite naturally then involved his seeing much of Galileo's activity in a positive light.[27]

From what we know of Busch's work on this role, let us look closely at some specific scenes and speculate on their impact. Let us begin with the recantation scene where Galileo, offstage, publically rejects the most basic element of his own astronomy: the fact that the world moves, rather than being (as the Vatican of that day would have put it) a fixed point at the center of the universe. Let us look at the text and try to see what scope there is for Busch to present the great scientist in a positive way. Some critics have argued that the scene lacks high drama because we do not actually see Galileo make his denial. But this approach ignores the ability of the spectator to imagine the dread that Galileo feels when directly confronted with the brutal torture instruments of the Inquisition. Curiously, whereas in California Brecht had used back screen projection to actually show torture instruments, he dropped them in Berlin. Whether this worked to reduce or enhance the spectator's imaginative involvement is an unanswered question. Further, the spectator's imagination is given a series of powerful pushes by the constant speculation of Galileo's closest associates as they wonder aloud at what horrors the Inquisition might be perpetrating upon him. If we think back a moment either to Shakespeare and the instruction to the audience "to piece out our imperfections with your thoughts," or to Gombrich's idea of the power of "a minimal image" to evoke a full emotional response, then we might wonder whether the pity and fear expressed by Galileo's associates might not trigger a similar response in a general audience viewing the play? If we plot the emotional curve of the scene we can see that it rises steadily as Andrea Federzoni (the lens grinder), the Little Monk, and Galileo's daughter all await the five o'clock bell that is to signal whether or not Galileo has recanted. If it rings at five he has recanted. If it does not ring he will probably be tortured and perhaps even killed. As the clock approaches five, Galileo's daughter's prayers become more and more frenzied and the scientific associates suffer agonies of suspense: will Galileo give in and thus set back all science and scientific morality for centuries to come? When the bell does in fact ring (not before Brecht lets suspense be screwed a notch tighter by not having the bell ring exactly at five), Galileo's daughter rejoices that, in her view, her father's life and soul are saved while Andrea almost collapses in disbelief that a "great man" could do so despicable a thing "in order to save his gut." At precisely this moment, Busch/Galileo enters. Brecht's stage direction tells us that the scientist has been physically broken by the encounter. When he enters he is "completely changed by the trial almost to the point of being unrecognizable."[28] Which way will the audience now incline: will they reject Galileo as Andrea does or accept him as Virginia does? Andrea cries "Unhappy the land that has no heroes," to which Galileo makes a typically Brechtian response: "No, unhappy is the country that needs heroes." We might incline to Andrea's view if we were able to believe Brecht's proposition (made in an essay on the play rather than in the play itself) that Galileo had such a following at this time that he could have successfully defied the church and triggered a popular uprising. However, at the beginning of the recantation scene, Brecht has Andreas say explicitly: "They will kill him. The *Discorsi* will not be completed."[29] This view is supported by the rehearsal transcript. Busch, in discussing how he should look before and after his interrogation, stated that Galileo's hair turns white overnight because "fear penetrated his very bones." There is superb dramatic contradiction here and Brecht deliberately does not resolve it. Galileo and Brecht are both right and wrong. Where Andrea sees recantation as the loss of the *Discorsi*, events in the last scene of the play will show the opposite: recantation permitted the completion of the *Discorsi*, but at a price, a typical Brecht trade-off.

The final scene of the play (the handing over of the *Discorsi*) was specifically viewed by Brecht in rehearsals as a scene with enormous dramatic impact. When Busch and Schall (who played Andrea in the Berlin production) rehearsed the final scene of the play, Brecht repeatedly stressed the kind of power he wanted the scene to generate. According to Brecht's own notes, we find that after Galileo hands over the secretly transcribed *Discorsi* (to transcribe which he has risked his very life and has utterly ruined his eyesight), and delivers judgement on himself (a scene reminiscent in some striking ways to the final scene of *Oedipus The King*), Andrea is so "shaken, he can hardly speak."[30] Andrea must then (with the *Discorsi* hidden beneath his cloak) be almost led from the room as he speaks his last words: "But I cannot think that your murderous analysis will be the last word."[31] From the rehearsal notes it is absolutely clear that Brecht designed the scene to work in a shattering way on Andrea and on the theatre audience. Brecht told Schall that he wanted him to play the scene with the kind of pathos that is associated in the German theatre with the name of Schiller.[32] Of the moment at which the *Discorsi* are handed from Galileo to Andrea, Brecht said that the scene "must have a colossal effect, like the H-Bomb," and that the news of having discovered the laws of motion should be "a hook to the chin." On this discovery "rested," said Brecht, "the H-Bomb." And in order that the scene have an appropriate impact Brecht instructed Busch: "this is the heaviest blow. It would be very lovely here Busch if you were to make a nerve-rattling pause here, as if the whole play had come to a full stop. Very long."[33] Is there scope here may we wonder for an audience to feel both pity and fear? Brecht's choice of the H-Bomb image here and elsewhere is not, of course, accidental. Ever since the news of Hiroshima and Nagasaki had first reached him in California, Brecht had connected Galileo's caving-in before the Inquisition as the great and perhaps ineradicable moral blot on the history of physics *and* the writing of the *Discorsi* as being essential to these developments in modern physics that led to the atomic and hydrogen bombs. For Brecht, therefore, both the recantation scene and the scene in which the *Discorsi* are preserved for posterity should be seen literally and figuratively in the spectral light of Hiroshima and Nagasaki. If contradictions are essential to Brecht's work surely the *Discorsi* scene is the ultimate contradiction. Yes, we are pleased that the itch of knowledge was so strong that Galileo defied the Inquisition *but*, can we ignore what was to come of Galileo's discoveries as the nuclear clock ticks loudly towards midnight? Brecht wants us to believe that Galileo hands Andrea the materials essential to the work done at Los Alamos, the work that led to the first test explosion, and J. Robert Oppenheimer's citation from the *Bhagavad Gita*: "I am become death, the destroyer of worlds."[34] Galileo himself does not ignore the spectral implications of his work. He says specifically: "In time you may discover everything that there is to discover and the advances you will make will only carry you further away from humanity. The chasm between you and humanity can become so great one day that your cries of joy about some new achievement may be answered by a universal cry of horror."[35] It is small wonder that Andrea's response to utterances such as these should be as Brecht wanted them to be: "Shocked, dry, unable to spit. With fear." "Shaken up he can hardly speak." The scene ends with Andrea, hardly able to move by his own volition, being led out by Galileo's daughter Virginia. When she returns, the scene is so arranged as to mirror in a completely symmetrical way the opening scene of the play. While Galileo asks the question "Do you have any idea who sent the goose?" Brecht had Virginia make up Galileo's bed for the night, "the exact opposite of the opening scene which began with Mrs Sarti making the bed after Galileo had got up." "A simple thing," said Brecht about this arrangement (fig. 51).

By the time all these scenic arrangements were in place but, as we can see, after Brecht had established the major aspects of the production, his health began to fail rapidly. In March of 1956 he wrote a letter of apology to Busch about his own inability to continue. In August he did return to the "Schiff" for a couple of days of rehearsals of the plays the Berlin Ensemble was to take to London. He planned to go to Munich on August 14 for consultation with medical specialists, but at noon his Berlin doctors discovered that he was suffering from the effects of a severe heart attack that they estimated had occurred about three days before. Inexplicably he was not hospitalized but sent home again. By the evening of August 14 he had lapsed into unconsciousness. He died shortly before midnight.

After Brecht's death the Galileo production was completed under the direction of Erich Engel, opened in Berlin on January 15, 1957 and was taken on tour to Paris in 1957, to Moscow and Leningrad in 1958 and to various other eastern and western European countries in the following years. For the critics of the fifties, there was much confusion about the emotional quality of this production. Many critics attacked the Berlin Ensemble and accused the company of distorting Brecht's legacy in that they had "dramatized" the play and given it a "tragic focus."[36] These critics wanted the Ensemble to function as what Eric Bentley has aptly called a "fire brigade,"[37] to race to any scene

Fig. 51. *The Life of Galileo*, Berlin, 1956. Note the symmetry of the final scene as envisaged by Brecht. Hunched shoulders of Busch repeat the roundness of the globe (left). The three legs of the globe are repeated in the three candles mounted directly behind Galileo's head.

Fig. 52. *The Life of Galileo*, Berlin, 1956. Ernst Busch as the nearly blind Galileo works on the illegal copy of the *Discorsi*.

that was becoming hot and douse it with lots of cold water to restore a properly scientific "cool" response. All this is fine in theory, but it had absolutely nothing to do with Brecht's actual practice with the Ensemble where, as we have seen, he insisted on heating the final scene of the play to an H-Bomb temperature. For Brecht it was essential to keep the contradictory or dialectical impulses of Galileo intact. As Eric Bentley points out, this means that a spectator can morally disapprove of Galileo and be distanced from him but at the same moment can be drawn close to him by normal human sympathy,[38] something that is almost universally true of Brecht's major characters from every period of his career in the theatre. The complexity of Galileo, so carefully built up by Brecht in rehearsal, is partially captured I think by one Berlin critic, who had done his homework on epic theory of "distancing coolness" etc. This critic wrote:

But besides all this [the theory], what do I actually see on stage during this intellectual battle? I see a man who has weakened his eyes at the telescope and who is now almost blind as a result of working [fig. 52], illegally, by moonlight, in order to make a copy of a work extremely useful to mankind. This is not merely spoken; this is demonstrated. I see further a man ruined by the burden of thought and work that has driven him like an uncontrollable itch into ever more dangerous situations, while, all the time, he is being spied upon by his stupid and shrewish daughter. And I am supposed to hate this man? I don't care how many directives are issued demanding that I do so, I simply cannot![39]

Nor, of course, did Brecht wish to have Galileo wholly condemned. What he wanted, and what the great actor Busch gave him, was a person who remained neither wholly good nor wholly bad. And this did not come about by accident, or by some carelessness on the part of the Ensemble, but had been carefully built into the production by Brecht himself. By the mid-fifties, gone was the stridency of the twenties and very early thirties. Now, to quote from the 1948 *Short Organum*, Brecht was able to speak very cheerfully on the fact that he couldn't imagine an "epic theatre lacking in artistic fantasy, without humor, or the gift of sympathy."[40] Yes, sympathy! As David Grossvogel has asked, quoting this very passage from the *Short Organum*: "How many pages of theory and dogma are subverted by these words? And how far was Brecht, ultimately, from Aristotle, who acknowledged, within a special and very lofty sense, the power of tragedy to teach – anagnorisis?"[41] It is difficult to quarrel with Grossvogel's conclusions. We issue in paradox (Brecht's own native ground): his modernity consists in overwhelming measure in his ability to revivify classical models of play construction and theatrical performance and to make those models live again not as musty artifacts but as highly modern depictions of our own age as mirrored in the past.

Had those critics who objected to the way in which Erich Engel completed the *Galileo* production after Brecht's death not been quite so deafened by Brecht's deliberately overstated slogans of his last pre-exile years in Berlin – those years when he had been more concerned with effectively opposing Hitler than in presenting finely honed aesthetic formulae – they might have heard the much quieter voice of the post-1938 Brecht, the Brecht who wrote *Galileo*, the other famous exile plays, and the *Short Organum for the Theatre*.[42] As Ernst Schumacher points out: "At the time that Brecht wrote the Galileo play, he had already taken a significantly more dialectical position on the problem of identification and of emotional release through events on stage than he had taken in his notes on those plays written before 1933."[43] In support of this contention Schumacher draws our attention to various notes from Brecht's diary of the exile period. We learn, for instance, that in Finland in 1940, Brecht had had to explain to an actor who told him that he understood by the term *Verfremdung* a "performance without emotions," that this was not what he meant at all. The same day he noted in his diary: "On the one hand, even when rational elements are used we find *the act of identification*, and on the other hand, a V-effect can be achieved strictly through the moderate use of emotion."[44] Some eight years then pass between the writing of this diary note and the completion of the semi-Aristotelian *Short Organum*. These eight years mark the gradual but steady whittling away of most of the crude excrescences of the earlier theoretical pronouncements.

If we closely follow Brecht's work through the exile years, looking at the diary entries, the theoretical essays, the recorded conversations, and above all at the plays themselves, we can trace his progress from the anti-Aristotelian notes on the *Mahagonny* opera, to his gradual rapprochement with classical aesthetic theory. It is this Brecht, one drifting, often seemingly against his will, from aesthetic nihilist to warm defender of the "Aesthetic" and the self-conscious author of an aesthetic, it is this man who composes, revises, and begins to stage *The Life of Galileo*. It should not, therefore, have surprised either the Berlin or the Paris critics that the play in the Ensemble's magnificent production could not be fitted to the procrustean bed of Brecht's more extreme anti-aesthetic pronouncements of the late 1920s and the early 1930s. Galileo, as Brecht created him, is a massive, memorable and modern figure, but a figure cut with one eye fixed upon a most ancient and tragic pattern. We should not feel guilty if we are as moved by this as we are by Brecht's great models, the figures of the Greeks and the Elizabethans.

The reverberations of Brecht's play are cosmic. Once again, as had been possible in the drama of the Greek and the Elizabethan periods, a single exemplary figure has been made to reflect the furthest reaches of the known universe. The movement of the planets in space is again linked in the great chain of being with the movement and the destinies of human atoms on the earth. We are led by the logic of the play to believe that Galileo's life is at least as important in the shaping of our destiny as the death of Caesar, Hamlet, Faustus, or Edward II of England. Again, a single guiding world view has been used to help shape historical materials to a clear dramatic and moral purpose. *Galileo* is no more a play for the play's sake than are its great seventeenth-century Christian models. Though there are, of course, things about the play which stamp it as a specifically twentieth-century construct, one wonders if one is not dealing, in *Galileo* and several other plays of the exile period, with a full-blown renascence of the best aspects of seventeenth-century dramaturgy. In the eighteenth century, Johann Elias Schlegel tried to define, as simply as possible, what it was about the English drama which distinguished it from the neoclassical mode. He wrote:

If I am to judge from what I have read of the English stage, I would say that their plays are more imitations of certain persons than imitations of certain actions. They search first for a number of persons whose lives have interconnected. When they have let them talk about the most important events in their lives for long enough to entertain a number of spectators for some hours, or until one reaches a decisive point in their lives or the characters finally die, then one ends the play.[45]

This marvelously naive description of English sixteenth- and seventeenth-century dramaturgy, with its clear recognition of the English departure from the French neoclassical view of Aristotle, fits, in several essential particulars, most major plays of Brecht's exile period. To claim "newness" in either structural or in performance terms for these plays is, to say the least, shortsighted. To pin the "epic theatre" label on these plays is, as later Brecht himself knew, but to give a new and confusing name to a very ancient game. *Galileo*, if we may read it as the very last (if unfinished) aesthetic testament of Brecht as playwright and as director, tells this plainly enough. The Brecht of the chronicle *Life of Galileo* has, similar to this and most of his best plays, come full circle. We are close once again in Brecht's production of *Galileo* to the play and the production with which we began, Brecht's adaptation of *Edward II* in Munich in 1924. From first to last, essentially Brecht had remained the same.

   In the eighteenth century, appalled at the French neoclassical imitations that cluttered the "German" stage, the great German critic Lessing urged a new dramaturgic beginning. He called on playwrights to abandon pallid, imitative, dull, unconvincing refurbishing of Greek plots under the watchful eye of the French Academy and asked German playwrights instead to attempt "to blend the gigantic characters and conflicts of Shakespeare with the restrained, lucid and really classical form of Sophocles."[46] Brecht comes as close as anyone I know to answering Lessing's call. His characters reach that "certain magnitude" that Aristotle called for, without losing a sense of human scale, of human frailty. The plays, in Brecht's productions of them, take us away from the aridity of much Naturalist drama, eschew the bombast of much Expressionism, avoid the pitfalls of the merely symbolic and reintroduce the theatre's ancient and lovely partners: poetry, music, song and dance. All its imprecision notwithstanding, this is perhaps the final justification of Brecht's early iconoclasm and its deliberately provocative product, his epic theatre creed. In his best plays and productions his early iconoclasm and his later stress on clarity and reason are combined not only with a mastery of all major forms of poetic expression but also with a gluttonous (Galilean?) passion for the theatre and an astounding sense of what would work on stage. Open to passion, to chaos, to contradiction, to reason, to gluttony, to knavery, to guile, to simplicity, to the naive and the sophisticated, to Socialism and to Swiss bank accounts, to poverty and to wealth, to genuine communal work and vicious dictatorial tirades, to loyalty to friends and ruthless rejection of friends, the theatre of Brecht reflects both Brecht himself in all *his* turbulence and dynamism and the turbulence and dynamism of the dark years in which he had lived and worked.

The legacy, so full of massive contradictions, has, not surprisingly, evoked massively contradictory responses. Some of the dullest as well as some of the most scintillating moments in the modern theatre can and have been traced directly to Brecht's legacy. Attempts to enshrine Brecht as a classic have usually led to reducing him to a dusty and not particularly noteworthy museum piece similar to the Moscow Art Theatre productions directed by Stanislavski that remained in the repertoire for decades after Stanislavski's death. But when directors have been willing to be as contradictory and as controlled with texts as Brecht was, then quite extraordinary results have been achieved. Brecht remains a "key figure of our time," but a key figure whose legacy can be used either to deaden or to enliven the modern stage. For those interested in the life of the theatre rather than in museums of theatrical history, there is as much to be learned from Brecht's "chaos" as there is to be learned from his "plan." We do him no honor if we do not treat his life in the theatre as a model to be modified and radically changed to reflect the conditions of new times and new places. Would Brecht have done less? Would Brecht have us do less?

Appendix
Bertolt Brecht: A chronology

If a young and talented playwright/director today were to need a model to prepare a campaign to become a major force in one of our contemporary theatrical centres, that playwright/director could do much worse than study the career of Bertolt Brecht as just such a model. What follows here is a brief narrative history of Brecht's background and training that led up to the first stagings of his plays. I then give an annotated list of the productions in which Brecht was in some way involved, and I add some notation of events outside the theatre which nevertheless furthered his theatrical career.

From a practical perspective it is difficult to overestimate the importance to Brecht of his parental home and the material support provided to him. He began his life in a home where all his physical needs were met or could be indulged at virtually no cost to him. Family servants did all the shopping, prepared all the meals and washed all the dishes, while Bertolt Brecht and his younger brother Walter were free to study, to write, to make music and to make love at all hours of the day and night in the largely separate mansard apartment of the Brecht household. The boys were encouraged, in a remarkably tolerant way, to develop their own talents and interests: Bert in drama and Walter, following his father, in the study of the manufacturing of paper.

Mid-way through the war years, Brecht was eligible for the draft into the German army. Through vigorous activity on his son's behalf, Brecht senior was able to obtain deferments of military service for his son so that Brecht junior could complete his gymnasium work in Augsburg, begin writing theatre reviews for the local newspaper, begin actually to write plays, and go on to Munich to study under one of the handful of professors of drama in German universities, Artur Kutscher. From Munich he could return at weekends for rest and relaxation to his father's home (Brecht's mother died, after a long illness, on May 1, 1920) and could leave handwritten scripts there to be typed up by his father's secretaries. With his clearly typed scripts and his contacts with theatrical people established through the Kutscher seminar, Brecht was able to begin to establish a foothold in Munich, at that time second only to Berlin in importance in Germany as a theatrical centre.

With the failure towards the end of the war to obtain another deferment, Brecht senior was at least reassured by the fact that his son was not to be sent to the front but rather assigned as a medical orderly to the military clinic in

Augsburg where he lived at home (with maid service) and wore civilian clothes. Brecht's "military service" did not interrupt his career as he had plenty of time in Augsburg to continue to write, begin to publish and to extend his range of contacts in various theatres and opera houses.

Within a few months of the war's end, Brecht had made the acquaintance of a major force in German theatre of the time, Lion Feuchtwanger, and through Feuchtwanger was able to meet the very people who could best help establish him as a writer of short stories, a playwright and director. He was able to meet the heads of publishing houses in Munich and obtain tentative contracts for the publication of his work, and he met a number of people who not only were to help him in Munich but who also assisted him materially in establishing himself in Berlin.

Though Brecht made one short visit to Berlin in early 1920, his first major assault on the theatrical and political capital of Germany took place in the fall of 1921. It was carefully prepared. He rode into Berlin on a wave of publicity generated by his first non-regional publication, his blatantly homo-erotic and wildly erotic short story "Bargan Lets It Happen," which appeared in September 1921 in the nationally distributed and highly prestigious literary journal *Der Neue Merkur* and caused an immediate furor in literary circles throughout Germany. Brecht's base of operations in Berlin upon his arrival there in early November was the home of the successful Berlin author, Frank Warschauer, who was in an excellent position to help Brecht with introductions to the people who made things happen in theatrical and literary Berlin. Within days Brecht was deep in negotiations with three major publishing houses and shortly he had all three deeply involved in a bidding war for the rights to publish his work that led to a contract paying Brecht, as of January 1, 1922, the then considerable sum of 750 marks a month. A few weeks later he switched contracts and more than doubled his income from these. Money was also available from his father who visited him briefly in Berlin, gave him 1,000 marks and promised a Christmas fare package of smoked turkey and ham. More money came in from an engagement as a singer at Trude Hesterberg's cabaret, "The Untamed Stage." Conducting as usual various love affairs, Brecht also found time to attend rehearsals at Max Reinhardt's theatres and to meet the leading Berlin actors, critics, and directors of the day. Interrupted only by a brief hospital stay in January for (so said Brecht) treatment for malnutrition, but (so said the admitting doctor) for treatment for a venereal "drip," he was by Easter 1922 reasonably well-established in Berlin theatre circles, even if he stylized himself in a poem written in April as "Poor Bert Brecht."

Within months he had received the Kleist Prize, the most prestigious prize for young dramatists in Germany, and theatres were clamoring to put on his plays. The career of Herr Bertolt Brecht was launched. In the years that followed, before he was driven into exile in early 1933, he would become not only very famous but also quite rich, with multiple contracts yielding him several thousand gold marks a month. And in this decade of spectacular success in Berlin, the mansard apartment in Augsburg was always available as a retreat from the cut-throat hustle of Berlin. Also available to Brecht from very early on were a host of admirer/collaborators, bowled over by his charismatic personality, and available to do his bidding. No small part of Brecht's success as a literary figure and a director is directly attributable to that group of dedicated followers who took over a tremendous amount of the dirty work, the gathering of material, the preparation of translations of foreign works, the drafts of major plays, the typing work, the preliminary negotiations with publishers and the torrent of correspondence. And his domestic life, with the maid he brought up from his father's house in Augsburg, his breakfast was made before he got up in the morning and his dishes done after he went to bed at night, also provided the problem-free conditions necessary for creative work.

Here follows an annotated list of the major dates in Brecht's life and theatrical career.

February 10, 1898. Brecht is born into a middle-class family in the small southern German city of Augsburg.

Easter 1917. Brecht completes his pre-university education at Augsburg. In October 1917 he was matriculated at the University of Munich. Ostensibly a student of medicine he actually studied drama and theatre history at the university under the tutelage of Wedekind's biographer, Artur Kutscher.

1918. Brief military service as a medical orderly stationed at his home in Augsburg. Writes his bitter lampoon of the military "The Legend of the Dead Soldier." Already active as a drama critic. Writes *Baal* and begins *Drums in the Night*.

1919. Meets Lion Feuchtwanger who reads and likes Brecht's first two plays. Takes a bit-part in the famous Munich political cabaret of Karl Valentin. Bie Banholzer is pregnant with Brecht's child, Frank, born on July 30th. At end of December, while singing at a bar near Augsburg, Brecht meets Peter Suhrkamp. Many poems, like Brecht's first two plays, frankly extol homosexual relationships.

February 21, 1920. Brecht makes his first visit to Berlin. Frightened by the Kapp Putsch on March 13, Brecht leaves that same day "to protect his father," so he says, in Augsburg.

May 1, 1920. Death of Brecht's mother.

September 1921. Publication of the long short story "Bargan Lets It Happen," in which a pirate captain sacrifices everything for his male lover.

November 1921. Berlin. The twenty-three-year-old Brecht, newly arrived in Berlin, attends Max Reinhardt's rehearsals of Strindberg's *A Dream Play* and begins to gain admission to rehearsals of all the major Berlin directors of this period. In a very short time he gets to know a large number of Berlin's leading actors. Meets and becomes close friends with the playwright Arnolt Bronnen whose plays often dealt with homosexual themes.

Spring 1922. Berlin. Through his new friend, Arnolt Bronnen, Brecht meets the great Berlin theatre critic Herbert Ihering. Ihering mentions that he will be in charge of giving out the highly prestigious Kleist Prize for 1922. Recipients of the prize were virtually thereby guaranteed performances of their plays throughout the German speaking world. Bronnen recommends to Ihering that Brecht be given the prize. Ihering starts to read Brecht's as yet unproduced and unpublished plays, and decides to promote Brecht's career vigorously. In same period Brecht is negotiating with three different Berlin publishers to publish and/or handle the stage rights for his plays. He proves to be a prodigious and formidable negotiator of highly remunerative contracts.

Brecht's first directorial assignment on the professional stage, Arnolt Bronnen's play, *Parricide* ends in a major fight between Brecht and the actors Agnes Straub, Heinrich von Twardowsky and Heinrich George. The directing work is completed by Berthold Viertel who retains much of Brecht's basic stage concept. However, Brecht is now stigmatized as a difficult director to get along with and will have difficulty getting other directing assignments. A pattern develops. Yes people begin to want to stage Brecht's plays but they usually do not want Brecht to direct them himself as further fights are feared.

September 29, 1922. Munich. *Drums in the Night*, directed by Otto Falckenberg, but with Brecht attending the rehearsals, at the Chamber Theatre. The performance was attended by Herbert Ihering who declared in his review of the play, "Overnight the twenty-four-year-old poet Bert Brecht has changed the literary face of Germany." *Baal* and *Drums in the Night* come out in book form.

November 3, 1922. Brecht marries the opera singer Marianne Zoff.

November 13, 1922. Berlin. Ihering announces that Brecht is the 1922 Kleist Prize winner.

December 20, 1922. Berlin. German Theatre production of *Drums in the Night*. Brecht had wanted to direct the play in Berlin himself, but the head of the German Theatre, Felix Hollaender, refused to allow this. After some dispute, Hollaender and Brecht agreed that the Munich director of the play, Otto Falckenberg, should also direct it in Berlin. This solution permitted Brecht to influence strongly the production as he attended a number of rehearsals. As would often be the case from now on, one person would be on record as the director of a production, whereas in reality Brecht himself would virtually direct the play.

March 12, 1923. Birth of Hanne, daughter of Brecht and Marianne Zoff.

May 9, 1923. Munich. Premiere of *In the Jungle [of the Cities]*, at the Residence Theatre, directed by Erich Engel (who was to become a lifelong associate of Brecht) and with sets by Brecht's childhood friend, Caspar Neher. Brecht participated in every stage of the production. Tremendous protests greeted the production and Jacob Geis, Engel's associate director, even lost his job for being the person responsible for putting on such a scandalous work. From now on, virtually no production of a Brecht play in Germany, whether or not it was directed by Brecht himself, failed to cause a major scandal. Brecht relished the publicity and deliberately fashioned such scandals. As a result, however, runs of Brecht plays in the period tended (with the exception of *The Threepenny Opera*) to be very short.

August 1923. Berlin. The new prize winner co-directs with Arnolt Bronnen a production of Hans Henny Jahnn's wildly extravagant play about adolescence, *Pastor Ephraim Magnus*. The author comes to see the play during rehearsals and is appalled that Brecht has changed it virtually beyond recognition. The premiere of the work goes completely unnoticed by the press.

November 8–9, 1923. Munich. Putsch by the stage designer *manqué*, Adolf Hitler.

December 8, 1923. Leipzig. World premiere of *Baal*, directed by Alwin Kronacher but with Brecht attending and taking over many of the key rehearsals. Production seen by the leading Berlin critics, Alfred Kerr and Herbert Ihering who had largely diametrically opposed views of the work. Brecht has already achieved both fame and notoriety.

March 18, 1924. Munich. Premiere of the Brecht/Feuchtwanger adaptation of Christopher Marlowe's *Edward the Second* at the Chamber Theatre. This was Brecht's first completely independent work as a director in the professional theatre. Set by Caspar Neher. Sometime during the rehearsals of the work Brecht meets the Latvian director Asja Lacis and her husband (also a director), Bernhard Reich, who will introduce Brecht to major Russian figures in the Russian theatrical avant-garde. In the same period Brecht meets Helene Weigel whom he will later marry. He also meets the young writer Elisabeth Hauptmann who then was to "co-author" a large number of works with Brecht. The line between "her" work and "his" work is often extremely hard if not impossible to determine.

November 3, 1924. Birth of Brecht and Helene Weigel's son Stefan.

February/March 1925. Berlin. Brecht works on a radical adaptation of

Ferdinand Bruckner's version of *The Lady of the Camelias*. Bruckner is so incensed at what has been done to the play that he threatens to sue those responsible. Directors of record: Bernhard Reich and the famous actress/director, Elisabeth Bergner.

1925. Berlin. Formation of "Group 1925," a group of younger dramatists seeking to substantially change the German theatre. Brecht becomes friends with the heavyweight boxer Samson-Körner and starts to publish a "life" of Samson-Körner in a popular Berlin magazine. Much of Brecht's income derived at this time from journalism and short story writing.

February 14, 1926. Berlin. *Baal* (version revised with Brecht's colleague, Elisabeth Hauptmann), co-directed by Brecht with the actor Oskar Homolka (who also played the title role), sets by Neher, for a single Sunday matinée performance at the "Young Stage." Simultaneously Brecht gains additional public attention with a series of fine short stories published under his name but written in the closest possible association with Elisabeth Hauptmann.

August 14, 1926. Berlin. Brecht publicly attacks in various Berlin publications both Thomas Mann and his son, Klaus Mann. Further publicity is assured by Brecht's being seen regularly with the heavyweight boxer, Samson-Körner.

September 25, 1926. Darmstadt. World premiere of the play *A Man's a Man* (co-worker on the text: E. Hauptmann) directed by Brecht's friend Jacob Geis and with sets by Neher. Brecht begins to study Marx's *Capital*.

January 1927. Berlin. Publication of the deliberately scandalous collection of poems known in English as *The Domestic Breviary*. Though only Brecht's name appeared on the cover some of the poems were by E. Hauptmann.

March 18, 1927. Berlin. Berlin radio, in a production directed by Alfred Braun, broadcasts *A Man's a Man*.

July 17, 1927. Baden-Baden. First Brecht work with Kurt Weill, world premiere of *Mahagonny*. The work was conducted by Ernst Mehlich but largely directed by Brecht. Sets and background projections by Neher. First major success of Lotte Lenya.

Fall 1927. Berlin. Brecht works periodically with Piscator Dramaturgical Collective but it is clear that Brecht is not really comfortable with a group that is not centred on his own dramatic work.

November 2, 1927. Divorce from Marianne Zoff.

November 14, 1927. Berlin. Radio broadcast of the Brecht adaptation of Shakespeare's *Macbeth* directed by Alfred Braun and introduced by Brecht himself.

January 5, 1928. Berlin. Berlin premiere of *A Man's a Man* at the Volksbühne, with the female lead played by Helene Weigel, directed by Erich Engel, and sets by Neher.

January 23, 1928. Berlin. Premiere of the Piscator Collective's adaptation of Jaroslav Hasek's novel *The Good Soldier Schweik*, directed by Piscator with sets by Georg Grosz.

August 31, 1928. Berlin. World premiere at the Am Schiffbauerdamm Theatre (future home, as of 1954, of the Berlin Ensemble) of the Hauptmann/Brecht/Weill/Klammer *The Threepenny Opera* directed by Erich Engel with the active and not always welcome assistance of Brecht. Sets by Neher. First and last Weimar box-office success of the Brecht group. Brecht's financial security assured until 1933.

December 1928. Berlin. Brecht wins the first prize for a short story entitled "The Beast" in a competition organized by *Berlin Illustrierte*. However, as John Willett points out in vol. 12 of the *Brecht Yearbook* (1985), it may very well be that the bulk of the story was actually written by Elisabeth Hauptmann. Published under Brecht's name, however, it helped to keep him in the public eye.

March/April 1929. Berlin. Brecht co-directs with Jacob Geis a deliberately scandalous production of Marieluise Fleisser's *Army Engineers in Ingolstadt* at the Am Schiffbauerdamm Theatre. Brecht's use of a swing in the production was so sexually suggestive that it guaranteed enormous publicity for the production, but it also led to such massive public attacks on Fleisser that the whole course of her life was changed. On April 10, 1929 Brecht and Helene Weigel are married.

Summer 1929. Berlin. Broadcast of Weill/Brecht's *Berlin Requiem*.

July 28, 1929. Baden-Baden. Brecht directs his first two didactic plays: *The Lindbergh Flight* and *The Baden Didactic Play*.

August 31, 1929. Berlin. On the anniversary of the big money-maker, *The Threepenny Opera*, premiere of Elisabeth Hauptmann's play (with music by Weill and some songs by Brecht) *Happy End*. The co-directors, often at bitter odds during rehearsals, were Erich Engel and Brecht. Sets by Neher. The play was a massive failure and the show's backer, Aufricht, lost a great deal of money and was furious with "Brecht" for failing to finish the play properly.

March 9, 1930. Leipzig. Premiere of *The Rise and Fall of the City of Mahagonny* (Hauptmann, Brecht, Weill, Neher). Directed by Walter Brugmann. Conducted by Gustav Brecher. Sets and background projection by Neher. The performances were picketed by uniformed Nazis and the production was only allowed to continue on condition that police line the walls of the Leipzig Opera House and that the house lights be kept on throughout the performances. Right-wing demonstrations by this time were a serious enough factor that any German theatre manager not wholly committed to the left would think twice about putting on anything further by Weill and/or Brecht.

April 1930. The Soviet avant-garde director Meyerhold brings his troupe to Berlin for a number of guest performances. Brecht is particularly impressed with Meyerhold's production of Sergei Tretiakov's play *Roar China*. Tretiakov himself stays for a long period in Germany and becomes a close friend and a promoter/translator for Brecht in the Soviet press.

June 23, 1930. Berlin. The didactic play, *The Yes Sayer* (Hauptman/Brecht with music by Kurt Weill) is produced by Brecht and Weill at Berlin's Central Institute for Training and Teaching using schoolboys and an amateur orchestra. Attacked on various sides, the authors revised the work and produced another version called *The No Sayer*.

October 18, 1930. Birth of Brecht and Weigel's daughter Barbara.

December 10, 1930. Premiere of the Hauptmann/Brecht didactic piece, *The Measures Taken*, with huge Berlin worker's choirs conducted by Rankl.

February 6, 1931. Berlin. Brecht directs *A Man's a Man* with Peter Lorre as Galy Gay. Probably Brecht's finest pre-exile production. Brecht established himself here as being among the front rank of European directors. Tretiakov compared the production favorably with Meyerhold's very best work.

February 19, 1931. Berlin. After a bitter public lawsuit between Brecht/Weill and the firm Nero Film, the Pabst version of *The Threepenny Opera* opens in Berlin.

December 21, 1931. Berlin. Am Schiffbauerdamm Theatre: *The Rise and Fall of the City of Mahagonny* (Brecht/Hauptmann/Weill/Neher) opens, directed for a while by Brecht with Neher and with sets by Neher. Brecht's open battles with Weill got so severe during rehearsals that the production's backer gave Brecht money to go away and direct a production of *Mother* instead. Surprisingly, given the violence of right-wing forces in Berlin at the time, the production ran for some fifty performances and was felt by many knowledgeable theatre people to be superior in many ways even to the legendary *The Threepenny Opera* production at the same theatre in 1928.

January 17, 1932. Berlin. Premiere of *Mother* (a "Brecht Collective" adaptation based on Gorki's novel of the same name), co-directed by Brecht and Emil Burri. After the show closed in a regular theatre, Brecht and Weigel took it on tour to working-class districts of Berlin and produced it, over the protests of fire marshals, on various makeshift stages sometimes using car headlights for illumination.

April 11, 1932. Berlin. Radio broadcast of *St Joan of the Stockyards*, directed by Alfred Braun.

May 30, 1932. Berlin. Opening of censored version of the independently produced film, *Kuhle Wampe*, written by Brecht, Slatan Dudow and Ernst Ottowatt, and directed by Dudow.

February 27, 1933. The Reichstag Fire. Fearing arrest, Brecht fled from Berlin the very next morning.

June 7, 1933. Paris. Premiere of *The Seven Deadly Sins* (Weill/Brecht), choreography by George Balanchine and Boris Kochno, sets by Neher, with Tilly Losch and Lotte Lenya in leading roles. Brecht participated in some of the rehearsals. The basic production was then taken to London for a brief run there. After Paris production Brecht went to Denmark to join Helene Weigel and their two children. With money obtained from Weigel's parents and Brecht's father, they bought a home in Denmark.

1934. Brecht mainly at work on his *Threepenny Novel* from which he derived much of his income for part of 1933 and most of 1934.

Spring 1935. Brecht visits Moscow, and much admires the work of the touring actor Mei Lan-fan. After meeting Schklovski he uses the word *Verfremdung* for the first time, apparently a translation of Schklovski's Russian term *priem ostrannenija*.

June 8, 1935. Brecht's German citizenship is formally removed by the Nazis.

October 1935. Copenhagen. Ruth Berlau's Revolutionary Theatre Group's production of *Mother* in Danish. The lead in the production was played by a genuine worker, Dagmar Andreasen, who cleaned the floors at the local railway station.

November 19, 1935. New York. The "Brecht Collective's" adaptation of Gorki's *Mother*, directed by Victor Wolfson with Brecht fighting with him every inch of the way. Finally Brecht and Hanns Eisler were firmly ushered out of the theatre. The set was by Mordecai (Max) Gorelik who became one of Brecht's strongest supporters in America.

November 4, 1936. Copenhagen. Danish premiere at the Knight's Hall Theatre of *The Roundheads and the Pointed Heads*. The director on record was Per Knutzon but Brecht was present at a number of rehearsals. Set by Svend Johansen. This particular theatre allowed spectators to eat and smoke during performances – a long-time dream of Brecht's. The theatre seated 220 and had a 22-foot-wide stage. In all there were 21 performances of the play.

November 12, 1936. Copenhagen. Danish production of *The Seven Deadly Sins*, with choreography by Harold Landers and set by Svend Johansen. Many of the rehearsals were conducted at Brecht's place at Skovsbostrand, some five hours from Copenhagen by car. The production was viciously attacked by the increasingly right-wing Danish press and had only two performances. So violent were the attacks that Brecht deemed himself to have been lucky to have his Danish residence visa renewed at all.

September 28, 1937. Paris. World Fair production of *The Threepenny Opera*. Director on record, Francesco von Mendelsohn. Brecht attended a number of the rehearsals.

October 16, 1937. Paris. World premiere (in German) of *Mrs Carrar's Rifles*, directed by Slatan Dudow and with Helene Weigel in the title role. Brecht attended a number of the rehearsals and was heavily involved in the original casting of the play.

December 19, 1937. Copenhagen. Danish premiere of *Mrs Carrar's Rifles*, directed by Ruth Berlau with her "Worker's Theatre" ensemble. The title role was played by a real worker, Dagmar Andreasen. Brecht attended a number of the rehearsals. Berlau took a large number of photographs of the production and these photos constituted the first serious attempt at what would later be called "model books" of Brecht productions. Later, on February 14, 1938 in Copenhagen, and using the set and props from the Danish-language production, Brecht and Berlau did a one-performance German-language production of the play with Helene Weigel as Mrs Carrar.

April 23, 1938. Threatened by the Nazis, Brecht moves to Stockholm.

May 21, 1938. Paris. World premiere in German of eight scenes from *The Fear and Misery of the Third Reich*. Directed by Slatan Dudow with Helene Weigel playing "The Jewish Wife." Brecht participated in casting the play and was present for rehearsals.

November 23, 1938. Completes the *Life of Galileo*.

May 20, 1939. Death of Brecht's father.

August 1939. Stockholm. Production of *What is the Price of Iron?*, directed by Brecht and Berlau. Berlau made an extensive photographic record of the production. As one can see from these photographs, the production was done in a knockabout, circus clown style. As the play was highly political throughout, Brecht used the pseudonym John Kent as the author of the play. The play was done with amateur actors at a Stockholm school for adult education.

September 1939. Stockholm. After some preliminary work Brecht begins on the actual writing of *Mother Courage and Her Children*. By early November the play is completed.

April 17, 1940. As the Nazis march into Denmark and Norway Brecht moves first to Helsinki in Finland and then, in July, to the country estate of the Finnish writer Hella Wuolijoki. While in Finland Brecht substantially completes the play, *The Good Person of Sezuan* and writes, with Wuolijoki, *Puntila and His Servant Matti*.

March 10 to April 12, 1941. Finland. Works with Margarette Steffin on the *Resistible Rise of Arturo Ui*.

April 19, 1941. Zurich. While Brecht is far away in Finland preparing to emigrate to the United States, the Zurich Schauspielhaus (one of the last free German-speaking stages in the world) gives the world premiere performance of *Mother Courage and Her Children*. The play was directed by Leopold Lindtberg. The lead was played by Therese Giehse. Sets and costumes were by Teo Otto. Much of the blocking, sets, and costumes were to be used again in Berlin in early 1949 when Brecht directed the play there using Teo Otto as his designer. The most famous stage requisite of all, the wagon of Mother Courage, is permanently identified with this production.

May 15, 1941. Brecht and his family and his two co-workers, Margarete Steffin and Ruth Berlau leave for America via Leningrad, Moscow and Vladivostock. Steffin dies in Moscow but the rest of the group reach California on July 21, 1941. Helped by friends in the cinema industry Brecht establishes himself in California, tries to write suitably commercial film scripts, but concentrates much of his attention on attempting to get his works staged on Broadway. Works on the plays: *Schweik in the Second World War* and on *The Caucasian Chalk Circle* with hopes of having the latter play put on in a big Broadway production. However, only a few scenes of *The Fear and Misery of the Third Reich* are produced in New York but not on Broadway.

October 15, 1946. New York. Opening of John Webster's *The Duchess of Malfi* on Broadway at the Ethel Barrymore Theatre in a production directed by George Rylands, starring Elisabeth Bergner and with music by Benjamin Britten. Brecht, with W.H. Auden and H.R. Hays, had been involved with Bergner in writing a modern adaptation of the play. When Brecht saw the play in tryouts before it came to New York he asked that his name *not* appear on the playbill. Basically, Rylands, who had just completed a successful West End run of the original play in London, brought the costumes, sets, blocking and text over from London and simply copied it as closely as possible in the United States with a different cast. Very little of Brecht's original conception was kept. The most significant Brechtian touch kept in the production was that of having the Black actor, Canada Lee, play the part of Bosola in whiteface. After the play opened on Broadway, Rylands returned to England and Brecht, thereafter, tried to further modify the production which ran for 39 performances.

July 30, 1947. Los Angeles. Premiere of *The Life of Galileo Galilei* in an English-language version prepared jointly by Brecht and the famous film actor, Charles Laughton, who also played the lead in this production and co-directed the play with Brecht, though the director on record was Joseph Losey. After its successful California run the play was taken to Broadway where it opened at the Maxine Elliott Theatre on December 7, 1947. By the time the play opened on Broadway, however, Brecht, following his appearance before the House Unamerican Activities Committee, had hastily returned to Europe. The California and New York productions were extensively photographed by Ruth Berlau.

February 1948. Chur, Switzerland. The premiere of Brecht's adaptation of Hölderlin's translation of of Sophocles' *Antigone*, directed by Brecht, set by Caspar Neher, with the lead played by Helene Weigel. After opening in the provincial town of Chur, the play was taken to Zurich for a single matinée performance. Brecht was disappointed – he had hoped for a far longer run in Zurich. The performance was photographed by Ruth Berlau and a "model book" of the production was published in 1949.

June 5, 1948. Zurich. Brecht and Hella Wuolijoki's play, *Puntila and His Servant Matti* is produced at the Zurich Schauspielhaus. The director of record (because of Brecht's difficulty in getting a Swiss work permit) was Kurt Hirschfeld, but Brecht was in fact largely responsible for the production. The set was by Teo Otto who had designed the wagon and sets for the Zurich 1941 world premiere of *Mother Courage*. The music was by Paul Dessau. The play, by Brecht and Hella Wuolijoki, opened in Berlin on November 12, 1949. Brecht with Erich Engel co-directed the Berlin production of the play as the first official production by the newly authorized Berlin Ensemble. The set was by Neher, and Puntila was played by Leonard Steckel and Matti by Geschonneck.

January 11, 1949. Berlin. *Mother Courage and Her Children* opens, directed by Brecht and Erich Engel with sets by Teo Otto and music by Paul Dessau. The costumes were by Kurt Palm. The lead was played by Helene Weigel with Angelika Hurwicz as Kattrin.

Spring 1949. Brecht goes on a recruiting tour to sign up actors for a proposed Berlin Ensemble. The formal concept and budget for such an Ensemble were approved by late spring. Helene Weigel was appointed administrative head of the Ensemble with Brecht's position with the company described rather vaguely as *Spielleiter*.

April 15, 1950. *The Private Tutor* by J.M.R. Lenz, opens in an adaptation prepared for the Berlin Ensemble by Ruth Berlau, Brecht, Benno Besson, Egon Monk and Caspar Neher. I characterize such adaptations as being "of the Brecht school." The play was directed by Brecht and Neher, with scenery by Neher and the lead played by Hans Gaugler.

October 8, 1950. A new production of *Mother Courage and Her Children* in Munich with Therese Giehse at the Kammerspiel. An assistant director on this production was Eric Bentley. The original Berlin production was taken on tour to Paris in the summer of 1954 where it caused a sensation with international theatre audiences and established Brecht as *the* leading director in postwar Europe.

January 13, 1951. Postwar Berlin premiere of *Mother*, directed by Brecht, set by Neher and music by Hanns Eisler. Helene Weigel played the title role. One of the very few postwar productions of Brecht that used background screen projections.

May 23, 1953. *Katzgraben*, a play by Erwin Strittmater opens. Music by Hanns Eisler, set and costumes by Karl von Appen, directed by Brecht with the assistance of Manfred Wekwerth.

June 17, 1953. East German uprising.

March 19, 1954. Berlin. Opening of *Don Juan* by Molière as adapted by Benno Besson and Elisabeth Hauptmann with some assistance from Brecht. Directed by Besson but with Brecht "interfering" (Besson's description) with the rehearsals periodically. This was first Berlin Ensemble production in the Ensemble's new home, the newly renovated Am Schiffbauerdamm Theatre.

October 7, 1954. The opening of *The Caucasian Chalk Circle*, directed by Brecht assisted by Manfred Wekwerth, with music by Paul Dessau and set and costumes by Karl von Appen. The play was taken on tour to Paris in 1955 and to London in 1956. This production represents Brecht at the height of his powers as a director of a first-rate ensemble.

January 12, 1955. The Berlin premiere of *Winter Battle*, a play by Johannes R. Becher, Minister of Culture of the German Democratic Republic and Brecht's friend since early days in Munich. Directed by Brecht and Manfred Wekwerth.

August 14, 1956. On his deathbed Brecht dictated a will to his childhood friend Dr Otto Mullereisert containing the provision: "I ask my wife, Helene Weigel, to continue to lead the Berlin Ensemble for as long as she believes the style of the theatre can be maintained." Weigel directed the theatre up to her own death on May 6, 1971.

Notes

1 Setting the scene

1 Heinrich Scheuffelhut in W. Frisch and K.W. Obermeier (eds.), *Brecht in Augsburg: Erinnerungen, Dokumente, Texte, Fotos* (Frankfurt: Suhrkamp, 1976), pp. 51–2. Hereafter cited as *Augsburg* with the name of the specific contributor to this useful anthology of views on the early Brecht.
2 *Augsburg*, Hohenester, p. 107.
3 *Augsburg*, Xavier Schaller, pp. 156–7.
4 *Augsburg*, Caspar Neher, pp. 175–6.
5 *Augsburg*, Friedrich Mayer, pp. 136–7.
6 *Augsburg*, Caspar Neher, p. 173.
7 Bertolt Brecht, *Diaries 1920–1922*, trans. and ed. John Willett (London: Eyre Methuen, 1979), p. 41.

2 A monarch stripped of grandeur

1 Brecht, *Diaries*, p. 4.
2 See John Willett, *The Theatre of Bertolt Brecht: A Study from Eight Aspects* (London: Methuen, 1959), p. 105.
3 The scenes were left in no definitive order at the time of Büchner's death.
4 Georg Büchner, *Sämtliche Werke* (Bertelsmann Lesering), p. 194.
5 Lion Feuchtwanger: "Bertolt Brecht Presented to the British", in Hubert Witt, ed., *Brecht as They Knew Him*, trans. John Peet (New York International Publishers, 1974), p. 17. *Spartacus* later became, at Feuchtwanger's suggestion, *Drums in the Night*.
6 Personal letter from Marta Feuchtwanger to John Fuegi.
7 Joachim C. Fest, *Hitler*, trans. Richard and Clara Winston (New York: Vintage, 1975), p. 86. I am also personally indebted to Mr Fest for his willingness to help me trace the close relationship of both Hitler and Brecht to the Munich playwright Hanns Johst.
8 Later both would be driven into exile.
9 Arnolt Bronnen in Witt, ed., *Brecht*, p. 34.
10 Ibid.
11 Bertolt Brecht, *Briefe*, ed. Günther Gläser (Frankfurt am Main: Suhrkamp Verlag, 1981), pp. 80–1. The *Briefe* volume should be used with great care as it contributes only a selection of letters with the selection principle, in my view, leaving a great deal to be desired.
12 Ihering's review appeared in the *Berliner Börsen-Courier*, December 9, 1923 and is conveniently reprinted in Witt, ed., *Brecht*, pp. 35–8.
13 Rudolf Fernau, *Uraufführung von Bert Brechts "Baal" am 8 Dezember 1923* (Berlin: Friedenau, 1971).
14 Fernau, *Brechts "Baal"*, p. 5.
15 Ibid.
16 Hans Natonek, *Neue Leipziger Zeitung*, December 10, 1923.
17 For a detailed discussion of Brecht's lifelong love–hate relationship with Shakespeare see my essay: "The Form and the Pressure: Shakespeare's Haunting of Bertolt Brecht" in *Modern Drama* 15, No. 3, December 1972, pp. 291–303.

18 Opinions differ as to whether Brecht himself was bisexual at the time. Homosexual
    relationships play a very prominent role in *Edward II, In the Jungle of the Cities*, and *Baal* to
    name only the three most obvious examples. But so far, unlike the women who have talked
    or written about their sexual relationships with Brecht, none of his male friends has been as
    frank.

19 The final version of the text is extraordinary in stripping off all grandeur from the "royal"
    personages in the play. The queen, for instance, is presented as a shameless nymphomaniac
    who is addressed thus by her "lover" Mortimer: "With knees spread wide and eyes closed
    you snap at everything and cannot be satisfied, Anna." The king breaks his word of honor
    quite deliberately and ends up in a dungeon that doubles as the castle cesspool. For a full
    discussion of the text of Brecht's *Edward II* see John Fuegi, *The Essential Brecht* (Los Angeles,
    Ca.: Hennessey and Ingalls, 1972), chapter 2.

20 Meyerhold, like many of the major figures of the Russian aesthetic and political avant-
    garde, read and spoke German with ease and followed German experiments very closely.
    As can be expected, the ties with French experimentation in the arts were very close as even
    Nicholas II was a passionate collector of the Parisian avant-garde painters, as the Hermitage
    collection strongly shows with its acquisition of Picassos right up until 1917.

21 Bernhard Reich, *Im Wettlauf mit der Zeit* (Berlin: Henschelverlag, 1970), p. 239.

22 Rudolf Frank, *Spielzeit meines Lebens* (Heidelberg: Verlaghambert Scheider, 1960),
    pp. 271–2.

23 Marieluise Fleisser, *Gesammelte Werke* (Frankfurt: Suhrkamp, 1972), vol. 2, p. 301.

24 Reich, *Wettlauf*, p. 262.

25 Ibid.

26 Reich, *Wettlauf*, p. 255.

27 Eric Bentley, *The Brecht Memoir* (New York: Performing Arts Journal, 1985), p. 60.

28 Reich, *Wettlauf*, p. 255.

29 Ibid.

30 Carl Zuckmayer, *Als wär's ein Stück von mir* (Frankfurt: Fischer, 1966), p. 375.

31 Fleisser, *Gesammelte Werke*, vol. 2, p. 313.

32 Frank, *Spielzeit*, p. 270.

33 Fest, *Hitler*, p. 112.

34 Frank, *Spielzeit*, p. 272.

35 Reich, *Wettlauf*, p. 264.

36 E.H. Gombrich, "Meditations on a Hobby Horse and the Roots of Artistic Form," in
    Meditations on a Hobby Horse and Other Essays on the Theory of Art (London and New York:
    Warburg, 1971).

37 Gombrich, "Meditations," pp. 5–6.

38 Ibid., p. 4.

39 By "presentational style" I mean a style where the actor does not try to "become the part"
    but instead suggests or presents the part to an audience while the actor retains his or her
    own character as a human being.

40 But see also "Rumor, painted full of tongues," who serves a similar function in *The Second
    Part of King Henry the Fourth*.

41 Ibid.

42 For evidence from those who saw the production see Fleisser, Ihering, Lacis, Reich, etc.

43 Hanns Eisler, *Sinn und Form/Brecht Sonderheft II*, ed. Peter Huchel (Berlin: Rütten and
    Loening, 1957), p. 97.

44 Of *Mother Courage*, for instance, Brecht noted ruefully: "The success of the play, that is to
    say the impression it made, was, without doubt, enormous. People pointed to Weigel
    [Brecht's wife who played Courage] on the streets and said: 'There's Courage'. But I don't
    believe now and I did not believe then that Berlin and all the other cities that saw it,

understood the play." Brecht, *Schriften zum Theater*, ed. Werner Hecht (Frankfurt: Suhrkamp, 1964), vol. 6, p. 161.

45 The phrase "mixed mimetic style" is a conscious echo of Erich Auerbach's phrase in his *Mimesis*, a book sent to Brecht by Eric Bentley but perhaps never read.

46 See particularly Brecht's own comments on *The Caucasian Chalk Circle* and *Galileo*.

3 Berlin dances with death

1 Paul Zech, *Vor Cressy an der Marne* (Laon: Revillon, 1918), p. 15.

2 Arnolt Bronnen, *Arnolt Bronnen gibt zu Protokoll* (Hamburg: Rowohlt, 1954) as cited in Ronald Sanders, *The Days Grow Short: The Life and Music of Kurt Weill* (New York: Holt, Rinehart and Winston, 1980) p. 79.

3 Ilya Ehrenburg, *People and Life: 1918–1921*, trans. Anna Bostock and Yvonne Kapp (New York: Alfred A. Knopf, 1962), p. 287.

4 Asja Lacis, *Revolutionaer im Beruf* (Munich: Rogner and Bernhard, 1971), p. 35.

5 Arnolt Bronnen, *Tage mit Bertolt Brecht* (Munich: K. Desch, 1960), p. 30.

6 Ibid., pp. 31–2.

7 Ibid., p. 14.

8 Bertolt Brecht, *Tagebücher 1920–1922, Autobiographische Aufzeichnungen 1920–1954*, ed. Herta Ramthun (Frankfurt: Suhrkamp 1975), p. 157.

9 John Willett, *Eight Aspects*, p. 12.

10 Quoted in Klaus Völker, *Brecht: A Biography*, trans. John Nowell (New York: Seabury Press, 1978), p. 116. My italics.

11 This modest film, entitled: *Mysterien eines Frisiersalons* (*Mysteries of a Barbershop*) has been preserved.

12 Brecht, *Gesammelte Werke*, vol. 18, p. 137.

13 Stephen Heath, for instance, in his tendentious montage of Brecht's remarks on film, manages to ignore this comment by Brecht. See Heath's essay "Lessons From Brecht," in *Screen 15*, No. 2 (Summer 1974), pp. 103–28.

14 Brecht, *Gesammelte Werke*, vol. 18, p. 138.

15 See Lion Feuchtwanger's description of this in his novel *Erfolg* (where "Brecht" has a major role) (Berlin: Gustav Kiepenheuer Verlag, 1930), vol. 2, pp. 15–20.

16 Brecht, *Diaries*, p. 52.

17 Brecht, *Gesammelte Werke*, vol. 18, p. 96.

18 For a detailed and highly laudatory description of Brecht and film see Wolfgang Gersch's *Film bei Brecht* (Berlin: Henschelverlag, 1975). My own sense is that Gersch, like Heath, exaggerates Brecht's own contributions to film theory. I believe that Brecht's scattered comments on film have had an impact in much the way a grain of sand has an impact on an oyster. Brecht's theory as an irritant has helped enormously to generate pearls of international theory but Brecht himself did not create this pearl. Much the same can be said, incidentally, for many of Brecht's highly contradictory theories of staging.

19 Brecht, *Gesammelte Werke*, vol. 15, p. 186.

20 Ibid. p. 173.

21 Ibid.

22 Ibid., pp. 197–8.

23 Elisabeth Hauptmann's diary note for October 1926.

24 Ludwig Hoffman and Daniel Hoffman-Osterwald (eds.) *Deutsches Arbeitertheater 1918–1933* (Berlin: Henschel, 1977), vol. 1, p. 240.

25 Cited in ibid., p. 155.

[26] My reasons for coming to this conclusion have been set forth at some length in my essay "Whodunit: Brecht's Adaptation of Molière's *Don Juan*" in *Comparative Literature Studies*, II, No. 2 (June 1974), pp. 159–72.

[27] Hauptmann would edit "Brecht's" collected works.

[28] In Fleisser's *Gesammelte Werke*, vol. 3, p. 121. See also Fleisser's very unflattering portrait of Brecht as given in her play *Tiefseefisch* (*Deep Sea Fish*), which enraged Brecht and the performance of which he blocked until his death in 1956. At every stage of his life Brecht sought to control the way in which he was seen by the public and he would only authorize portraits that presented him in the kind of light he wanted to be seen in.

[29] Brecht, *Diaries*, p. 112.

[30] If we remember how much was given to Brecht to produce this play in the first place, we can understand that the cost of the production was totally out of proportion to the actual box office receipts. This would remain true up to the end of Brecht's life. According to the official reports of the company only one mark in six was raised at the box office at the Berlin Ensemble! The company was subsidized at a rate of two-and-a-half-million marks a year, an enormous sum for the struggling new state at that time.

[31] Quoted in *Materialien zu Brechts "Baal,"* ed., Dieter Schmidt (Frankfurt: Suhrkamp), pp. 202–3.

[32] Ibid., p. 187.

[33] Bronnen, *Tage*, p. 139.

[34] See Eric Bentley's essay "Brecht und der 'Zonk,'" in *Listen* (March–April 1964). Essay reprinted in Eric Bentley, *The Brecht Commentaries* (New York: Grove Press and London: Methuen, 1981), pp. 114–21.

[35] Klaus Völker has stated flatly that he thinks that it was Brecht's involvement with music at that period that determined the form of the didactic plays. Völker, *Brecht: A Biography*, p. 125.

[36] Quoted in Sanders's, *The Days Grow Short*, p. 92.

[37] See Ernst Josef Aufricht, *Erzähle damit du dein Recht erweist* (Berlin: Propyläen, 1966), p. 64.

[38] This version of the story was given to me by a usually reliable long-time associate of Kurt Weill who claims to have been told this directly by the composer himself. A slightly different version is given by Aufricht in his memoirs *Erzähle*, p. 63.

[39] The details are given in Elisabeth Hauptmann's letter of March 2, 1950 to Kurt Weill, written by her because of what she calls Brecht's "antipathy towards writing." Materials available at the Kurt Weill Foundation for Music, Inc., 142 West End Avenue, Suite 1-R, New York, NY 10023, USA.

[40] Lenya's private letters to Weill are *most* explicit on this point!

[41] Brecht had begun to do this in America much to Weill's annoyance as it was Weill who really knew the ropes of contractual negotiations in the American theatre and he was well-known there. The contract disputes are still not resolved as the heirs continued to exchange acrimonious letters in the summer of 1984.

[42] The limited contract (for eleven years only and excluding the USA) for a film production in Munich for 1958, for instance, specified advances to the heirs of 300,000 German Marks.

[43] Aufricht, *Erzähle*, p. 69.

[44] Völker, *Brecht: A Biography*, p. 128.

[45] Whether it was Brecht or whether it was Weill who came up with the haunting melody for this song is unknown. Both laid claim to it.

[46] The phrase occurs in Bunge's long unpublished transcript of Berlin Ensemble rehearsals.

[47] *Aufricht, Erzähle*, p. 77.

[48] Quoted in Sanders's *The Days Grow Short*, p. 112.

[49] Völker cites this phrase approvingly, *Brecht: A Biography* p. 131. Brecht himself said after

1945 that he had serious doubts about allowing any productions of the play as he felt that unless it was produced as part of a revolutionary movement that the message of the play amounted to pure anarchy. I fully agree with this particular Brecht.

50 Quoted by Völker, ibid., p. 79.

51 The current royalty division however, does not reflect this attribution even though the original contract for the work was exclusively between Elisabeth Hauptmann and the firm of Felix Bloch Erben with a sub-contract separately negotiated between Hauptmann and Weill and Brecht respectively. Appallingly, a recent production of *Happy End* in the United States in Feingold's translation was titled simply as being "by Brecht" with no mention of the real author, Elisabeth Hauptmann. Curiously, Aufricht never seemed to recognize that Brecht was not the author of *Happy End*.

52 Fleisser, *Gesammelte Werke*, vol. 3, pp. 156–9.

53 Fritz Sternberg, *Der Dichter und die Ratio: Erinnerungen an Bertolt Brecht* (Göttingen: Sachse und Pohl, 1963), pp. 24–7.

54 Ibid., pp. 26–7.

55 See Völker, *Brecht: A Biography*, p. 125.

56 Willett, *Eight Aspects*, pp. 33–4.

57 Völker, *Brecht: A Biography*, p. 142.

58 Willett, *Eight Aspects*, p. 148.

59 Sergei Tretiakov quoted by Willett, ibid., p. 148.

60 Michael Patterson, *The Revolution in German Theatre, 1900–1933* (London: Routledge and Kegan Paul, 1981), p. 158.

61 Note particularly not only the macho-eroticism of Fairchild but also the way Galy Gay "forces the mountain pass with his cannon."

62 Quoted in the John Willett and Hans Manheim edition of *The Rise and Fall of the City of Mahagonny* and *The Seven Deadly Sins*, p. 111.

63 "Book" issued with the Columbia Records recording of "Kurt Weill's Mahagonny"!

64 Aufricht, *Erzähle*, p. 128.

65 From Brecht, *Materialien zu Brechts "Die Mutter,"* ed. Werner Hecht (Frankfurt: Suhrkamp, 1969), p. 82.

4 Brecht in exile: 1933–1947

1 Quoted in Völker, *Brecht: A Biography*, p. 173.

2 Ibid., p. 178.

3 Sanders, *The Days Grow Short*, p. 196. It is interesting to note that the people who "take up" Weill and Brecht in Paris in 1933 were the key members of what might be called the Proust circle, those closest to Proust until his death in 1922.

4 Brecht, *Briefe*, vol. 1, p. 165.

5 The full memoirs, after years of being blocked by Barbara Brecht-Schall, are now in print under the title *Brechts Lai-Tu: Erinnerungen und Notate von Ruth Berlau*, ed. Hans Bunge (Darmstadt: Luchterhand, 1985). A briefer version of the same material can be found in "Nach 25 Jahren des Schweigens," *Brecht, Women and Politics*, eds. John Fuegi, Gisela Bahr and John Willett (Michigan: Wayne State University Press, 1985), pp. 11–39, this is volume 12 of *The Brecht Yearbook*.

6 Major source of information is David Pike's huge volume: *German Writers in Soviet Exile: 1933–1945* (Chapel Hill, NC: University of North Carolina Press, 1982). The reference to Ulbricht is on p. 293 of Pike's book. A detailed account of Benjamin's relationship with Brecht is given in Walter Benjamin, *Versuche über Brecht* (Frankfurt: Suhrkamp, 1966).

7 Brecht, *Gesammelte Werke*, vol. 17, p. 1057.

8 Mordecai (Max) Gorelik reports that Brecht made this remark to him. Eric Bentley, who was

not present when the remark was made has told me that he cannot believe that Brecht intended the remark to be taken seriously. When I asked Gorelik about Eric Bentley's comment he told me that he is quite sure that Brecht meant the remark to be taken seriously. There is no evidence I could discover that Brecht made this remark to anyone else.

9   A documentary account of the stormy relationship with the Theatre Union is given by James F. Lyon in his essay: "Der Briefwechsel zwischen Brecht und der New Yorker Theatre Union von 1935", in *Brecht Jahrbuch*, 5 (1975), pp. 136–55. The description of Brecht with his 250-pound friend is found in Berlau's recently published memoirs.

10   Brecht, *Briefe*, vol. 1, pp. 278–9.

11   For a discussion of how dangerous these Moscow attacks were and how they were resumed when Brecht returned to Berlin in 1948, see my essay: "The Soviet Union and Brecht: The Exile's Choice," in *Brecht Heute/Brecht Today: Yearbook of the International Brecht Society*, eds. John Fuegi, et al. (Frankfurt: Athenäum, 1972), vol. 2, pp. 109–21. For further details see also Lew Kopelew, "Brecht und die Russische Theaterrevolution," in *Brecht Heute/Brecht Today*, vol. 3 (1973), pp. 19–38.

12   Peter Weiss, *Die Ästhetik des Widerstands* (Frankfurt: Suhrkamp, 1978), vol. 2, pp. 213–14.

13   Bentley, *Brecht Commentaries*, p. 290.

14   Willett, *Eight Aspects*, p. 187.

15   For a fine polemic against those who automatically assume that Brecht was right in his theories about audience identification see Martin Esslin's essay, "Icon and Self-Portrait: Images of Brecht", in *Encounter* (March 1978), p. 39 where Esslin asks: "Do the alienation effects actually inhibit the spectator from feeling involved? Are the postulated political effects really achieved? Is the consciousness of audience actually affected in the manner postulated by Brecht? Here is a vast field of enquiry which has, as yet, hardly been approached."

16   Quoted in Fuegi, *Essential Brecht*, p. 1.

17   Up to his death Weill continued to be very angry with Brecht about the cavalier and greedy way that Brecht treated *The Threepenny Opera*. In America, without first consulting Weill Brecht tried to have *The Threepenny Opera* mounted by a Black touring company. However laudable the enterprise might have been, Weill was furious at the lack of prior consultation.

18   Völker, *Brecht: A Biography*, p. 303.

19   See James F. Lyon's fine book, *Bertolt Brecht in America* (Princeton, NJ: Princeton University Press, 1980), pp. 124–5.

20   Quoted in ibid., p. 147.

21   Quoted in ibid., p. 174.

22   Brecht, *Arbeitsjournal*, ed. Werner Hecht (Frankfurt: Suhrkamp, 1973), vol. 1, p. 41.

23   Any serious student of *Galileo* can learn extraordinarily much from Ernst Schumacher's superb study: *Drama und Geschichte: Bertolt Brechts "Leben des Galilei" und andere Stücke* (Berlin: Henschelverlag, 1968).

24   Brecht, *Arbeitsjournal*, vol. 1, p. 719.

25   Ibid., p. 747.

26   From Schumacher, *Drama und Geschichte*, p. 284.

27   Ibid.

28   Ibid.

29   Cited by Lyon, *Brecht in America*, p. 186.

30   Ibid.

31   Ibid.

32   Curt Bois, *Zu Wahr, um Schön zu Sein* (Berlin Henschelverlag, 1980), p. 89.

33   Cited by Lyon, *Brecht in America*, p. 187.

34   Ibid.

35   Ibid., p. 193.

[36] Hecht, ed. *Materialien zu Brechts "Leben des Galilei"* (Berlin: Henschelverlag, 1970), p. 44.
[37] Platforms were used very extensively in the Berlin productions of Leopold Jessner long before Brecht moved to Berlin. Jessner did not seem to think that platforms *per se* undercut emotion.
[38] Charles Higham, *Charles Laughton: An Intimate Biography* (New York: Doubleday and Co., 1976), p. 141.
[39] Völker, *Brecht: A Biography*, p. 319.
[40] Brecht, *Arbeitsjournal*, vol. 1, p. 790.
[41] Cited by Völker, *Brecht: A Biography*, p. 322.
[42] Frank Jones, "Tragedy with a Purpose: Bertolt Brecht's *Antigone*," *The Drama Review*, 2, No. 1, (November 1957), p. 43.
[43] Brecht, *Gesammelte Werke*, vol. 16, pp. 661–3.
[44] Ibid., pp. 1213–14.
[45] From an essay by Schiller, first printed as a preface to his play *The Bride of Messina*.
[46] Brecht, *Arbeitsjournal*, vol. 2, p. 832.
[47] Cited by Völker, *Brecht: A Biography*, p. 326.
[48] Ibid.

5 Berlin: An etching by Churchill based on an idea of Hitler's

[1] The title of this chapter is taken from volume 2 of Brecht's own *Arbeitsjournal* and is dated: October 22, 1948.
[2] Ibid., vol. 2, p. 848.
[3] One can hear Brecht's full testimony on Eric Bentley's Folkways record No. *FD*5531 and the less full testimony on the record issued by Hans Bunge: "Bertolt Brecht – Tondokumente" (Litera 8-60-238-239). The text of Brecht's testimony is given in Peter Demetz (ed.), *Brecht. A Collection of Critical Essays* (Englewood Cliffs, NJ: Prentice Hall, 1962).
[4] Dated by Klaus Völker in *Brecht: A Biography*, p. 333.
[5] Actually published in 1961 the book is only available in German. It is worth noting however, as photos speak a more international language, that the model-book photos of the *Mother Courage, Galileo*, and *Antigone* productions can be studied with profit by actors and directors who have no German. For those who wish to delve further, hundreds of unpublished additional photos of the various productions can be seen in the records of the Berlin Ensemble.
[6] Brecht, *Arbeitsjournal*, p. 889.
[7] Dymschitz has now written extensively and positively on Brecht.
[8] Brecht, *Couragemodell 1949* (Berlin: Henschelverlag, 1958).
[9] Ibid.
[10] The comment was made during my November 1982 interview with Angelika Hurwicz.
[11] Much of the confusion about Brechtian terms stems, so I feel, from the distinction between the use of techniques in rehearsal that then became largely invisible during actual performance before audiences. Many critics insist on still being able to see the rehearsal devices in performance and they stress these elements to the virtual exclusion of everything else. Thus the critics end up seeing one thing and audiences end up seeing something quite different. My sympathies lie with the audiences.
[12] My November 1982 interview.
[13] Cited by John Willett in his notes to his translation of Brecht's *Mother Courage and Her Children*, eds. John Willett and Ralph Manheim (London: Eyre Methuen, 1980), pp. 106–7.
[14] Brecht, *Arbeitsjournal*, vol. 2, p. 878.
[15] The stage version of *Mother Courage* is usually ignored by critics despite the fact that this

version has at least as much claim to textual authenticity as the longer version published in the *Gesammelte Werke*.

16 Various recordings of the song are available. The Berlin Ensemble production of *Mother Courage* was also filmed and so students can study this production in detail.

17 Hans Mayer, *Bertolt Brecht und die Tradition* (Pfüllingen, West Germany; Neske, 1961), p. 81.

18 In recently ruined Berlin it would be hard to not see this action as a direct provocation of the audience.

19 Gogol used this formulation in answering critics who saw *Dead Souls* being too bleak a picture of Russia.

20 Boris Sachawa, "Stärken und Schwächen des Brecht' Theater," in *Kunst und Literatur*, 5 (1957), p. 1369.

21 George Steiner, *The Death of Tragedy* (New York: Alfred A. Knopf, 1958), p. 348. Eric Bentley wonders if the final scene of the play could have been suggested to Brecht by the figure of Ma Joad in the film version of *Grapes of Wrath*.

22 Albrecht Schöne, "Bertolt Brecht, Theatertheorie und dramatische Dichtung", in *Euphorion*, 52, No. 3, (1958), p. 290.

23 Eric Bentley, *Seven Plays by Bertolt Brecht* (New York: Grove Press, 1961), p. xiii.

24 Brecht, *Schriften*, vol. 6, p. 131.

25 Steiner, *Tragedy*, pp. 353–4.

26 Brecht, *Schriften*, vol. 6, pp. 133–4.

27 Cited by Werner Mittenzwei in his excellent volume, *Bertolt Brecht: Von der "Massmahme" zu "Leben des Galilei"* (Berlin: Aufbau, 1965).

28 David Pike's *German Writers in Soviet Exile: 1933–1945* shows clearly that Ulbricht was closely connected to the Moscow camarilla of the 1930s that sought by means fair and foul to undermine Brecht's stature as a Marxist artist.

29 Brecht, *Briefe*, p. 619. These volumes are not very complete. The letters are printed accurately but literally hundreds of important items have been left out and the notes that accompany the printed letters conceal as much as they reveal. When I tried to check Brecht's statement against the Berlin Ensemble records I learned that financial records of the early period of the company have not been preserved.

30 Brecht, *Arbeitsjournal*, vol. 2, p. 912.

6 Diary of a production: *The Caucasian Chalk Circle*

1 The title of this chapter is the title used by Hans Bunge for his notes and recordings of the actual rehearsals of *The Caucasian Chalk Circle* in Berlin. I am deeply grateful to Hans Bunge for his willingness to share his work with me and to allow me to use extensive quotations from his invaluable historical record.

2 For excerpts from the actual *Chalk Circle* and *Galileo* rehearsals please see Hans Bunge's record "Bertolt Brecht – Tondokumente" (Litera 8-6-238-239). This record also has Brecht singing two songs from *The Threepenny Opera*.

3 Angelika Hurwicz, *Brecht Inszeniert: "Der kaukasische Kreidekreis"*, photos by Gerda Goedhart (Velber bei Hannover: Friedrich, 1964).

4 See Friedrich Dieckmann's richly illustrated volume: *Karl von Appens Bühnenbilder am Berliner Ensemble* (Berlin: Henschelverlag, 1971).

5 See Volker Klotz's essay in Brecht, *Marerialien zu Brechts "Der kaukasische Kreidekreis"*, ed. Werner Hecht (Frankfurt: Suhrkamp, 1966), p. 141.

6 Those who only read English and are relying on Eric Bentley's "revised English version" of the play in the Grove Press edition may be puzzled here. In many instances Brecht personally gave Bentley different versions of a play from those that he used elsewhere. In Bentley's version of *The Caucasian Chalk Circle* the text is divided into five sections where

Brecht's *Collected Works* text has six sections. Azdak first appears in scene four of Bentley's version.

7 See Brecht, *Materialien "Kreidekreis,"* p. 32.

8 Interview with Angelika Hurwicz in November 1982.

9 Brecht, *Materialien "Kreidekreis,"* p. 34.

10 Comment by Hans Bunge in an interview with me in 1983 in Berlin.

11 Bunge, "Diary of a Production," p. 1.

12 Brecht, *Gesammelte Werke*, vol. 15, p. 440.

13 Dieckmann, *Karl von Appen*, p. 83.

14 Hurwicz, *Brecht Inszeniert*. Pages of text are unnumbered.

15 Ibid.

16 Ibid.

17 Ibid.

18 Ibid.

19 Bunge, "Diary", pp. 1–2.

20 Ibid.

21 Ibid.

22 Ibid., p. 18.

23 Ibid., 15th day, December 8, 1953.

24 Völker, *Brecht: A Biography*. When I recently directly asked Isot Kilian in Berlin about this savage Brecht anecdote, she gave me her own analysis of it. She says that her former husband, Wolfgang Harich, once admitted to her that he had simply invented this anecdote in order to put Brecht in a bad light. The anecdote retained its currency, however, because even if it was (as is very likely) invented by Harich, it described Brecht's usual sexual habits accurately enough that it was widely believed even by such usually accurate scholars as Klaus Völker, p. 349.

25 The notes and the "corrections" are very instructive. In the marginal notes Brecht's concern seems to be with how he will be perceived historically. For instance, where Bunge had originally written that "casting was done by Besson" Brecht changed this to read "casting of minor roles was done by Besson." In my view, Bunge's note was closer to reality than Brecht's "correction."

26 See note 2 above.

27 Bunge, "Diary", pp. 185ff.

28 Ibid.

29 Bunge, "Diary", 78th day of rehearsals.

30 Bunge, "Diary", 112th day (September 9, 1954).

31 Transcript of tape of Berlin Ensemble rehearsal.

32 Ibid.

33 Bentley, *The Brecht Memoirs*, p. 78.

34 Brecht, *Materialien "Kreidekreis,"* p. 64.

35 Bunge, "Diary", 116th day.

36 Bunge, "Diary", 117th day.

37 Bunge, "Diary", 119th day.

38 Bunge, "Diary", 121st day.

39 Hurwicz, *Brecht Inszeniert*.

40 Ibid.

41 Brecht *Materialien "Kreidekreis,"* p. 22. But even here there is a typical Brechtian contradiction. This "driving music" must, at the same time be "light and delicate."

42 The scene is reminiscent of *Edward II* where Brecht has soldiers run at breakneck speed across planks placed high above the stage.

43 *Modern Language Quarterly*, 24 (June 1962), p. 108.

44 David J. Grossvogel, *Four Playwrights and a Postscript: Brecht, Ionesco, Beckett, Genet* (New York: Cornell University Press, 1962), p. 33.

45 I am indebted to Manfred Wekwerth and Frau Schlösser at the Berlin Ensemble who kindly answered, wherever possible, my various questions about administrative and budgeting details at the Berlin Ensemble.

46 Rudolf Frank, "Brecht von Anfang," in *Das Ärgernis Brecht*, eds. Willy Jäggi and Hans Oesch (Basel/Stuttgart: Basilius Presse, 1961), pp. 31–44.

47 Brecht, *Gesammelte Werke*, 17, 1208.

7 I am become death, destroyer of worlds

1 The words are from the Bhagavad Gita and were supposedly quoted by J.R. Oppenheimer as the first atomic test explosion occurred in mid-1945.

2 Brecht, *Materialien zu Brechts "Leben des Galilei,"* ed. Werner Hecht (Frankfurt: Suhrkamp, 1963), p. 141.

3 For a complete list of plays in the repertory at this time see Ruth Berlau and Bertolt Brecht, et al. *Theaterarbeit: 6 Aufführungen des Berliner Ensembles* (Frankfurt: Suhrkamp, 1961).

4 Brecht always paid the closest attention to obtaining the most favorable terms in his contracts. His famous statement about his having "a basic laxity with regard to intellectual property" only applied to the property of others. Brecht protected his own intellectual property with extraordinary care. As "his" intellectual property often subsumed the work of others (Hauptmann, Steffin, Berlau, Wuolijoki etc.), a study needs to be done on the whole question of how much of "Brecht's" writing is in fact Brecht's own writing.

5 Here as elsewhere I am indebted to Hans Bunge for detailed information on the Berlau/ Brecht relationship. For further details see the article "Nach 25 Jahren des Schweigens," in *Brecht, Women and Politics*, pp. 11–39.

6 See particularly Mao's "On Contradiction".

7 Herta Gordon was a personal emissary between the major German revolutionary figures of 1918 (Clara Zetkin, Rosa Luxemburg, and Karl Liebknecht) and Lenin. In this capacity she had personal dealings with Lenin and was mentioned in Lenin's correspondence until she fell into disfavor with the East German communists and her name was removed, so she claimed to Brecht, from a Lenin letter of 1918. Gordon's husband, Jakob Walcher, also had first-hand knowledge of the principal German and Russian revolutionaries as he had co-chaired the Spartakus Conference with Wilhelm Pieck and had negotiated directly with Lenin on the re-establishment of the Comintern. The Walcher/Gordon connection was very strong and of at least as much importance as Brecht's much written about connection with Karl Korsch.

8 Bentley, "The Brecht Memoir", in *Theater* (Spring 1983), p. 24.

9 Brecht, *Gesammelte Werke*.

10 For a whole collection of such stories (each one of which having more than a grain of truth) please see: André Müller and Gerd Semmer's little book: *Geschichten vom Herrn B.* (Frankfurt: Kindler, 1967).

11 Again the record of the rehearsals was prepared by Hans Bunge. Again I am indebted to him for his willingness not only to work through this detailed record with me but to allow me to use that record in writing this book.

12 The stage version of the text was published by Henschelverlag in Berlin in 1970. The play in this version, does *not* have a crossing of the frontier scene. Brecht scholars have largely ignored this very different version.

13 Brecht in *Materialien "Galilei,"* p. 150. But Brecht would not have been Brecht if he had not also declared something quite contradictory to this. Though he claimed the play was a mere illustration of a nursery rhyme he also told his friend and assistant Käthe Rülicke that

Galileo's behavior explained Bucharin's inexplicable behavior at the Moscow Trials. Thus, Galileo is not just Humpty Dumpty but also, if you know how to read the text, another great traitor: Bucharin. The observation occurs on pp. 34–5 of Rülicke's as yet unpublished notes.

14 Brecht, *Materialien "Galilei,"* p. 150.
15 Käthe Rülicke, "Bemerkungen zur Schlusszene", in Brecht, *Materialien "Galilei,"* p. 108.
16 Brecht, *Diaries*, p. 42.
17 As this began long before Brecht began the study of Marxist classics one cannot fully explain these deliberately unresolved contradictions in the early plays by postulating Brecht's conscious use of dialectic but one can suggest that one of the reasons that Marxism was so attractive to Brecht was that it gave such an important theoretical place to contradiction.
18 Rülicke in Brecht, *Materialien "Galilei,"* p. 112.
19 From Hans Bunge's as yet unpublished records of the rehearsals.
20 In fact, when one checks the published stage version one finds that over 173 lines were dropped from the first scene alone!
21 Schumacher, *Drama und Geschichte.*
22 See notes 12 and 20 above.
23 Schumacher in Brecht, *Materialien "Galilei,"* pp. 157–8.
24 Eisler in the foreword to Bertolt Brecht, *Aufbau einer Rolle Galilei–Busch und Laughton,* (Berlin; Henschelverlag, 1956), p. 11.
25 Ibid.
26 Ibid.
27 Busch's building up of the part of Galileo was a curious mixture of identification with Galileo combined with several rehearsals where he would use the third person in relation to the role: "Galileo said, Galileo wrote" etc.
28 Brecht, *Gesammelte Werke*, vol. 3, p. 1329.
29 Ibid., p. 1325.
30 Ibid.
31 Ibid.
32 Brecht, *Materialien 'Galilei,"* p. 137.
33 Ibid., p. 141.
34 See note 1 above. It is worth noting here that over and over again in his last years Brecht sought to try to complete a play to be called the "Life of Einstein," a play in which J. Robert Oppenheimer was to play an important role. Brecht followed both Einstein's and Oppenheimer's career with the closest interest and had the transcript of the Oppenheimer hearing forwarded to him from America.
35 Brecht, *Gesammelte Werke*, vol. 3, pp. 1340–1.
36 The responses of the Paris critics are given in Grossvogel, *Four Playwrights*, p. 40.
37 Preface, of Eric Bentley's *Seven Plays by Bertolt Brecht*, p. xxvii.
38 Ibid.
39 Fritz Erpenbeck, *Aus dem Theaterleben* (Berlin: Aufbau, 1959), p. 333.
40 Cited in Grossvogel, *Four Playwrights*, p. 45.
41 Ibid.
42 Brecht, *Materialien "Galilei,"* p. 161.
43 Ibid.
44 Ibid., pp. 162–3.
45 J.E. Schlegel, in *Meisterwerke Deutscher Literaturkritik*, ed. Hans Mayer (Stuttgart: Goverts, 1962), pp. 107–8.
46 This formulation of Lessing's objectives is by Werner P. Friederich in his *German Literature* (New York: Barnes and Noble, 1948), p. 68.

A Selected Bibliography

The following bibliography can make no claim to completeness except in the specific area of Brecht as a stage director. Those seeking fuller information on either Brecht's own writings or on those who have written about him would be well advised to consult directly the following more comprehensive bibliographies:

Grimm, Reinhold. *Bertolt Brecht*. Stuttgart: Metzler, 1961. This volume is periodically updated and reissued and is perhaps the single most reliable source of bibliographical information on and about Brecht.

Nellhaus, Gerhard. "Bertolt Brecht–Bibliographie." *Sinn und Form/Brecht Sonderheft I*. Ed. Peter Huchel. Berlin: Rütten and Loening, 1949. An important list of articles about Brecht in English.

Nubel, Walter. "Bertolt Brecht–Bibliographie." *Sinn und Form/Brecht Sonderheft II*. Ed. Peter Huchel. Berlin: Rütten and Loening, 1957. This bibliographical list has been much admired for its completeness in the area of Brecht editions.

Petersen, Klaus-Dietrich. *Bertolt-Brecht–Bibliographie*. Bad Homburg: Verlag Gehlen, 1968.

For the reader with little German it may be convenient to note a basic list of those publishers, translators and editors whose work is easily obtainable. Eric Bentley has served as general editor for the Grove Press and has personally translated a large number of Brecht's plays and many of his poems. In England, under the general editorship of John Willett, a large number of plays and significant sections of Brecht's theoretical writings have been published by the Methuen Company. More recently, Methuen in England and Pantheon Books (a division of Random House, New York) have begun publication of many Brecht plays. Edited by Ralph Manheim and John Willett, several volumes of the British and American editions of the plays are now available. Inasmuch as different translators have worked on the American and British editions respectively, this means that a choice of three different versions (Grove, Methuen, and Pantheon) is now available in English for most of Brecht's more important plays.

Auerbach, Erich. *Mimesis: The Representation of Reality in Western Literature*. Princeton, NJ: Princeton University Press, 1953.

Aufricht, Ernst Josef. *Erzähle damit du dein Recht erweist*. Berlin: Propyläen, 1966.

Bach, Rudolf. "Marlowe, Eduard II und Bert Brecht." *Die Rampe*, 7, November 16, 1926, pp. 137–48.

Banholzer, Paula. *Meine Zeit mit Bert Brecht*. Munich: Goldmann, 1981.

Baxandall, Lee. "Brecht on Broadway: A Commercial System at Work." *Prompt*, 5 (1964), pp. 38–40.

Benjamin, Walter. *Schriften*. 2 vols. Frankfurt: Suhrkamp, 1955.

Versuche über Brecht. Frankfurt: Suhrkamp, 1966.

Bentley, Eric. *Seven Plays by Bertolt Brecht*. New York: Grove Press, 1961.

The Brecht Commentaries. New York: Grove Press and London: Methuen, 1981.

The Brecht Memoir. New York: Performing Arts Journal, 1985.

"Are Stanislavski and Brecht Commensurable?" *The Drama Review*, 9, No. 1 (Fall, 1964), pp. 69–76.

"Epic Theater is Lyric Theater." *The German Theater Today*. Ed. Leroy R. Shaw. Austin: Texas University Press, 1963.

"What is Epic Theatre?" *Accent*, 6, No. 2 (Winter 1946), pp. 110–24.

"Brecht, Poetry, Drama and the People." *The Nation*, 157 (July 31, 1943), pp. 130–1.

Berlau, Ruth, *Brechts Lai-Tu: Erinnerungen und Notate von Ruth Berlau.* Ed. Hans Bunge. Darmstadt: Luchterhand, 1985.

"Nach 25 Jahren des Schweigens," *Brecht, Women and Politics.* Eds. John Fuegi, Gisela Bahr and John Willett, vol. 12 of *The Brecht Yearbook.* Michigan: Wayne State University Press, 1985.

Berlau, Ruth and Bertolt Brecht, et al. *Theaterarbeit: 6 Aufführungen des Berliner Ensembles.* Frankfurt: Suhrkamp, 1961.

Bois, Curt. *Zu Wahr um Schön zu Sein.* Berlin: Henschel Verlag, 1980.

Brashko, S. "Die letzte Inszenierung Bertolt Brechts." *Kunst und Literatur,* 6 (1958) pp. 835–50.

Brecht, Bertolt. *Gedichte über die Liebe.* Selected by Werner Hecht. Frankfurt: Suhrkamp, 1982.

Briefe. Ed. Günter Gläser. 2 vols. Frankfurt: Suhrkamp, 1981.

Diaries 1920–1922. Trans. and ed. John Willett. London: Eyre Methuen, 1979.

Arbeitsjournal. Ed. Werner Hecht. 3 vols. Frankfurt: Suhrkamp, 1973.

Materialien zu Brechts "Leben des Galilei." Ed. Werner Hecht. Berlin: Henschelverlag, 1970. This edition differs in many essential particulars from the 1963 Suhrkamp version of materials on *Galilei.*

"Leben des Galilei" (Schauspiel): Bühnenfassung des Berliner Ensembles. Ed. Joachim Tenschert. Berlin: Henschelverlag, 1970.

"Die Mutter." Leben der Revolutionärin Pelagea Wlassowa aus Twer (Nach dem Roman Maxim Gorkis): Bühnenfassung des Berliner Ensembles. Ed. Joachim Tenschert. Berlin: Henschelverlag, 1970.

Materialien zu Brechts "Die Mutter." Ed. Werner Hecht. Frankfurt: Suhrkamp, 1969.

Die "Antigone" des Sophokles: Fassung der Churer Aufführung. Ed. Werner Hecht. Berlin: Henschelverlag, 1969.

"Der gute Mensch von Sezuan" (Parabelstück): Bühnenfassung des Berliner Ensembles. Ed. Joachim Tenschert. Berlin: Henschelverlag, 1969.

Materialien zu Brechts "Der gute Mensch von Sezuan." Ed. Werner Hecht. Frankfurt: Suhrkamp, 1968.

Materialien zu Brechts "Baal." Ed. Dieter Schmidt. Frankfurt: Suhrkamp, 1968.

"Der kaukasische Kreidekreis": Bühnenfassung des Berliner Ensembles. Ed. Joachim Tenschert. Berlin: Henschelverlag, 1968.

"Mutter Courage and ihre Kinder" (Eine Chronik aus dem Dreissigjährigen Krieg): Bühnenfassung des Berliner Ensembles. Ed. Joachim Tenschert. Berlin: Henschelverlag, 1968.

Gesammelte Werke. Ed. Elisabeth Hauptmann. 20 vols. Frankfurt: Suhrkamp, 1967.

Materialien zu Brechts "Der kaukasische Kreidekreis." Ed. Werner Hecht. Frankfurt: Suhrkamp, 1966.

Edward II: A Chronicle Play. Trans. Eric Bentley. New York: Grove Press, 1966.

Materialien zu Brechts "Mutter Courage und ihre Kinder." Ed. Werner Hecht. Frankfurt: Suhrkamp, 1964.

Schriften zum Theater. Ed. Werner Hecht. 7 vols. Frankfurt: Suhrkamp, 1964.

Brecht on Theatre. Selected and translated by John Willett. New York: Hill and Wang, 1964.

Materialien zu Brechts "Leben des Galilei." Ed. Werner Hecht. Frankfurt: Suhrkamp, 1963.

Seven Plays. Ed. Eric Bentley. New York: Grove Press, 1961.

"Tagebuchnotizen." Spectaculum III: Sieben moderne Theaterstücke. Frankfurt: Suhrkamp, 1960.

Courdgemodell 1949. Berlin: Henschelverlag, 1958.

Schriften zur Theater. Collected by Siegfried Unseld. 7 vols. Frankfurt: Suhrkamp, 1957.

Aufbau einer Rolle – Busch und Laughton. Berlin: Henschelverlag, 1956.

Mother Courage and Her Children. Trans. Eric Bentley. New York: Grove Press, 1955.

The Caucasian Chalk Circle. Trans. Eric Bentley. New York: Grove Press, 1965.

The Good Woman of Setzuan. Trans. Eric Bentley. New York: Grove Press, 1965.

The Mother. Trans. Lee Baxandall. New York: Grove Press, 1965.

Collected Plays, Volume I: 1918–1923. Ed. John Willett and Ralph Manheim. London: Methuen, 1970.

Collected Plays, Volume II. Ed. Ralph Manheim and John Willett. New York: Pantheon, 1971.

Tagebücher 1920–1922, Autobiographische Aufzeichnungen 1920–1954. Ed. Herta Ramthun. Frankfurt: Suhrkamp, 1975.

Brecht, Bertolt and Caspar Neher. *Antigonemodell 1948.* Ed. Ruth Berlau. Berlin: Bebrüder Weiss, 1949.

Brecht, Walter. *Unser Leben in Augsburg Damals.* Frankfurt: Suhrkamp, 1984.

Bronnen, Arnolt. *Tage mit Bertolt Brecht.* Munich: K. Desch, 1960.

Arnolt Bronnen gibt zu Protokoll. Hamburg: Rowohlt, 1954. Lots of revealing material on how Brecht's success was achieved in Berlin.

Büchner, Georg. *Sämtliche Werke.* n.p.: Bertelsmann, n.d.

Bunge, Hans. *Fragen Sie mehr über Brecht: Hanns Eisler im Gespräch.* Munich: Rogner and Bernhard, 1970.

"Antigone-Modell 1948 von Bertolt Brecht and Caspar Neher: zur Praxis und Theorie des epischen (dialektischen) Theaters Bertolt Brechts." Dissertation. Greifswald. 1957.

"Diary of a Production." Unpublished MSS.

Bunge, Hans, Werner Hecht and Käthe Rülicke-Weiler. *Bertolt Brecht: Leben und Werk.* Berlin: Volk und Wissen, 1963.

Clurman, Harold. *The Fervent Years: The Story of the Group Theater and the Thirties.* New York: Hill and Wang, 1957.

"The Achievement of Bertolt Brecht." *Partisan Review,* 26 (1959), pp. 424–8.

Curjel, Hans and Erwin Leiser. *Gespräch auf der Probe.* Zurich: San Souci, 1961.

Demetz, Peter (ed.) *Brecht. A Collection of Critical Essays.* Englewood Cliffs, NJ: Prentice Hall, 1962.

Dickson, Keith A. "Brecht: An Aristotelian malgré lui." *Modern Drama,* 11 (1967), pp. 111–21.

Dieckmann, Friedrich. *Karl von Appens Bühnenbilder am Berliner Ensemble.* Berlin: Henschelverlag, 1971.

Dort, Bernard. *Lecture de Brecht.* Paris: Editions du Seuil, 1960.

"Le réalisme épique de Brecht." *Les Temps Modernes,* 15 (1959–60), pp. 67–83.

Dymschitz, Alexander. *Ein unvergesslicher Frühling: Literarische Porträts und Erinnerungen.* Berlin: Dietz, 1970.

Ehrenburg, Ilya. *People and Life: 1891–1921.* Trans. Anna Bostock and Yvonne Kapp. New York: Alfred A Knopf, 1962.

Einem, Gottfried von and Siegfried Melchinger (eds.) *Caspar Neher.* Velber bei Hannover: Friedrich, 1966.

Eisler, Hanns. *Sinn und Form/Brecht Sondersheft II.* Ed. Peter Huchel. Berlin: Rütten and Loening, 1957.

Engberg, Harald. *Brecht auf Fünen.* Trans. Heinz Kulas. Wuppertal: Peter Hammer, 1974.

Erpenbeck, Fritz. *Aus dem Theaterleben.* Berlin: Aufbau, 1959.

"Episches Theater oder Dramatik?" *Theater der Zeit,* 9, No. 12 (1954), pp. 16–21.

"Verurteilung oder Mitleid?" *Theater der Zeit,* 12, No. 3 (1957), pp. 8–13.

Esslin, Martin. "Icon and Self-Portrait: Images of Brecht," *Encounter* (March 1978), pp. 30–9.

Brecht, A Choice of Evils. London: Eyre and Spottiswoode, 1959.

Fernau, Rudolf. *Üraufführung von Bert Brechts "Baal" am 8 Dezember 1923.* Berlin: Friedenau, 1971.

Fest, Joachim C. *Hitler.* Trans. Richard and Clara Winston. New York: Vintage, 1975.

Feuchtwanger, Lion. *Erfolg.* Berlin: Gustav Kiepenheuer Verlag, 1930.

Fleisser, Marieluise. "Avantgarde" and *Der Tiefseefisch* in *Gesammelte Werke,* 3 vols. Frankfurt:

Suhrkamp, 1972. Two of the most revealing texts on Brecht's treatment of friends and lovers.

"Aus der Augustenstrasse." *Süddeutsche Zeitung* (Munich), No. 129, 8 June 1951.

Frank, Rudolf. *Spielzeit meines Lebens*. Heidelberg: 1960.

"Brecht von Anfang," in *Das Ärgernis Brecht*. Eds. Willy Jäggi and Hans Oesch. Basel/ Stuttgart: Basilius Presse, 1961.

Frisch, Max. *Tagebuch 1946–1949*. Frankfurt: Suhrkamp, 1958.

Frisch, W. and K.W. Obermeier. *Brecht in Augsburg: Erinnerungen, Dokumente, Texte, Fotos*. Frankfurt: Suhrkamp, 1976.

Fuegi, John. *The Essential Brecht*. Los Angeles, Ca.: Hennessey and Ingalls, 1972.

"Meditations on Mimesis: The Case of Brecht." *Drama and Mimesis*. Ed. James Redmond. Cambridge: Cambridge University Press, 1980.

"Whodunit: Brecht's Adaptation of Molière's *Don Juan*," in *Comparative Literature Studies*, II, No. 2 (June 1974), pp. 159–72.

"The Form and the Pressure: Shakespeare's Haunting of Bertolt Brecht." *Modern Drama*, 15, No. 3 (December 1972), pp. 291–303.

"The Soviet Union and Brecht: The Exile's Choice," in *Brecht Heute/Brecht Today: Yearbook of the International Brecht Society*. Eds. John Fuegi, et al, Frankfurt: Athenäum, 1972.

"*The Caucasian Chalk Circle* in Performance." *Brecht Heute/Brecht Today: Yearbook of the International Brecht Society*, vol. 1. Ed. Eric Bentley, Reinhold Grimm, John Fuegi, et al. Frankfurt: Athenäum, 1971.

Geissler, H.W. "Das Leben Eduards II., Uraufführung in den Münchner Kammerspielen." *München–Augsburger Abendzeitung*, 80 (21 March 1924).

Gersch, Wolfgang. *Film bei Brecht*. Berlin: Henschel Verlag, 1975.

Giehse, Therese. *Ich Hab Nichts zu Sagen: Gespräche mit Monika Sperr*. Munich: Bertelsmann, 1973.

Gilman, Sander and Wolf von Eckardt. *Bertolt Brecht's Berlin*. Garden City, New York: Anchor, 1975.

Gombrich, E.H. *Meditations on a Hobby Horse and Other Essays on the Theory of Art*. London and New York: Warburg, 1971.

Gorelik, Mordecai. *New Theatres for Old*. New York: Dutton, 1962.

Grimm, Reinhold. "Von Novum Organum zum Kleinen Organon: Gedanken zur Verfremdung." *Das Ärgernis Brecht*. Ed. Willy Jäggi and Hans Oesch. Basel and Stuttgart: Basilius, 1961.

Grossvogel, David I. *Four Playwrights and a Postscript: Brecht, Ionesco, Beckett, Genet*. Ithaca, N.Y.: Cornell University Press, 1962.

Hauptmann, Elisabeth. *Julia ohne Romeo*. Berlin: Aufbau, 1977. A dreadful title for a quite useful book.

"Notizen über Brechts Arbeit 1926." *Sinn und Form/Brecht Sonderheft II*. Berlin: Rütten and Loening, 1957.

Heath, Stephen. "Lessons from Brecht." *Screen* 15, No. 2 (Summer, 1974), pp. 103–28.

Hecht, Werner and Siegfried Unseld. *Helene Weigel zu Ehren*. Frankfurt: Suhrkamp, 1970.

Hennenberg, Fritz. *Dessau-Brecht: Musikalische Arbeiten*. Berlin: Henschelverlag, 1963.

Higham, Charles. *Charles Laughton: An Intimate Biography*. New York: Doubleday and Co., 1976.

Hinck, Walter. *Die Dramaturgie des späten Brecht*. Göttingen: Vandenhoeck and Ruprecht, 1959.

Hoffman, Ludwig and Daniel Hoffman-Osterwald (eds.). *Deutsches Arbeitertheater 1918–1933*. 2 vols. Berlin: Henschelverlag, 1977.

Hoover, Marjorie. "V.E. Meyerhold: A Russian Predecessor of Avant-Garde Theater." *Comparative Literature*, 17 (1965), pp. 234–50.

Houghton, Norris. *Moscow Rehearsals: An Account of Methods of Production in the Soviet Theatre*. New York: Harcourt Brace, 1936.

Houseman, John. *Front and Center*. New York: Simon and Schuster, 1979.
Huntford Roland. "Brecht in the North." *Industria International*. Stockholm: 1963, pp. 44–5, 154, 158–60.
Hurwicz, Angelika. *Brecht Inszeniert: "Der kaukasische Kreidekreis"*. Photos by Gerda Goedhart. Velber bei Hannover: Friedrich, 1964.
Ihering, Herbert. *Bertolt Brecht und das Theater*. Berlin: Rembrandt, 1959.
Von Reinhardt bis Brecht: Vier Jahrzehnte Theater und Film. Berlin: Aufbau, 1958.
Berliner Dramaturgie. Berlin: Aufbau, 1947.
"Gorki, Pudowkin, Brecht." *Berliner Börsen-Courier*, No. 28, January 18, 1932.
Jones, Frank. "Tragedy with a purpose: Bertolt Brecht's *Antigone*." *The Drama Review*, 2, No. 1 (November 1957).
Knopf, Jan. *Brecht Handbuch: Theater*. Stuttgart: J.B. Metzler, 1980. Despite the rather promising title of this book it has almost nothing to do with the plays in actual performance.
Kopelew, Lew. "Brecht und die Russiche Theaterrevolution," in *Brecht Heute/Brecht Today: Yearbook of the International Brecht Society*, vol. 3. Ed. John Fuegi. Frankfurt: Athenäum, 1973.
Kopetzki, Eduard. "Das dramatische Werk Bertolt Brechts nach seiner Theorie vom epischen Theater." Dissertation. Vienna, 1949.
Kortner, Fritz. *Aller Tage Abend*. Munich: Kindler, 1959.
Lacis, Asja. *Revolutionaer im Beruf*. Munich: Rogner and Bernhard, 1971.
Li Hsing-tao. *Kreidekreis*. Trans. Klabund (Pseud. for Alfred Henschke). Berlin: I.M. Spaeth, 1925.
Lukàcs, G. "Grundlagen der Scheidung von Epik und Dramatik." *Aufbau*, 11, No. 11–12 (1955), pp. 87–98.
Beiträge zur Geschichte der Ästhetik. Berlin: Aufbau, 1954.
Essays über Realismus. Berlin: Aufbau, 1948.
Lyon, James F. *Bertolt Brecht in America*. Princeton, NJ: Princeton University Press, 1980.
"Der Briefwechsel zwischen Brecht und der New Yorker Theatre Union von 1935." *Brecht Jahrbuch*, 5 (1975), pp. 136–55.
Mayer, Hans. *Anmerkungen zu Brecht*. Frankfurt: Suhrkamp, 1965.
Bertolt Brecht und die Tradition. Pfüllingen, West Germany: Neske, 1961.
Meyerhold, V.E. *Meyerhold on Theatre*. Ed. and trans. Edward Braun. New York: Hill and Wang, 1969.
Mittenzwei, Werner. *Bertolt Brecht: Von der "Massnahme" zu "Leben des Galilei"*. Berlin and Weimar: Aufbau, 1965.
Münsterer, H.O. *Bert Brecht: Erinnerungen aus den Jahren 1917–22*. Zurich: Arche, 1963.
Müller, André and Gerd Semmer. *Geschichten vom Herrn B*. Frankfurt: Kindler, 1967.
Niessen, Carl. *Brecht auf der Bühne*. Cologne: Institute for Theatre Studies, University of Cologne, 1959.
Patterson, Michael. *The Revolution in German Theatre, 1900–1933*. London: Routledge and Kegan Paul, 1981.
Pike, David. *German Writers in Soviet Exile: 1933–1945*. Chapel Hill, NC: University of North Carolina Press, 1982.
Pintzka, Wolfgang. Ed. *Die Schauspielerin Helene Weigel*. Photos by Gerda Goedhart. Berlin: Henschelverlag, 1959.
Piscator, Erwin. *Das politische Theater*. Berlin: 1929. Work reissued with modifications by Felix Gasbarra by Rowohlt Verlag (Reinbek bei Hamburg), 1963. A facsimile edition of the original text, however, was issued by Henschelverlag (East Berlin), 1968.
Politzer, Heinz. "How Epic is Brecht's Epic Theater?" *Modern Language Quarterly*, 24 (June 1962), pp. 99–114.
Ramthun, Herta. *Bertholt-Brecht-Archiv: Bestandverzeichnis des literarischen Nachlasses, Band I*,

Stücke. Berlin and Weimar: Aufbau, 1969.

Reich, Bernhard. *Im Wettlauf mit der Zeit: Erinnerungen aus fünf Jahrzehnten deutscher Theatergeschichte*. Berlin: Henschelverlag, 1970.

Roy, Claude. "Des erreurs commises sur Brecht," *Nouvelle Revue Française*, 13, (Jan. 1965), pp. 114–18.

Rülicke-Weiler, Käthe. *Die Dramaturgie Brechts*. Berlin: Henschelverlag, 1966.

Sachawa, Boris. "Stärken und Schwächen des Brecht Theater." *Kunst und Literatur*, 5 (1957), pp. oo–oo.

Sanders, Ronald. *The Days Grow Short: The Life and Music of Kurt Weill*. New York: Holt, Rinehart and Winston, 1980.

Sartre, J.P. "Brecht et les Classiques." *World Theatre*, 7 (Spring 1958).

Schmidt, Dieter. *"Baal" und der junge Brecht. Eine textkritische Untersuchung zur Entwicklung des Frühwerks*. Stuttgart: Metzler, 1966.

Schöne, Albrecht. "Bertolt Brecht, Theatertheorie und dramatische Dichtung," *Euphorion*, 52, No. 3 (1958), pp. 272–92.

Schumacher, Ernst. *Drama und Geschichte, Bertolt Brechts "Leben des Galilei" und andere Stücke*. Berlin: Henschelverlag, 1965.

Die dramatischen Versuche Bertolt Brechts: 1918–1933. Berlin: Rütten and Loening, 1955. Remains one of the two or three most useful books on Brecht's pre-exile plays.

Seidel, Gerhard. *Die Funktions- und Gegenstandsbedingtheit der Edition: untersucht an poetischen Werken Bertolt Brechts*. Berlin: Akademie, 1970. A courageous if somewhat utopian attempt to describe an ideal edition of Brecht's total writings.

Serreau, Geneviève. *Bertolt Brecht: Dramaturgie*. Paris: Arche, 1955.

Spalter, Max. *Brecht's Tradition*. Baltimore: Johns Hopkins University Press, 1967.

Stark, G. and G. Weisenborn. *Die Mutter*. Published as a private *Bühnenmanuskript*. n.p., n.d. Copy of text in Bertolt Brecht Archiv (BBA) 441.

Steffin, Margarete. "Wenn er einen Engel Hätte" (unpub. mss of a play contained in BBA 531/1–56) and "Die Geisteranna" (unpub. mss of a play contained in BBA 532/1–48). As Steffin was almost as heavily involved in "Brecht's" playwriting from 1933 until her death in 1941 as Elisabeth Hauptmann was from 1924–33 and again after the return from exile, a systematic examination of the work of the various collaborators is long overdue.

Steiner, George. *The Death of Tragedy*. New York: Alfred A. Knopf, 1958.

Sternberg, Fritz. *Der Dichter und die Ratio: Erinnerungen an Bertolt Brecht*. Göttingen: Sachse and Pohl, 1963.

Suvin, Darko. "The Mirror and the Dynamo: On Brecht's Aesthetic Point of View." *The Drama Review*, 12, No. 1 (Fall 1967), pp. 56–67. A complex and very useful piece of analysis of the post-epic Brecht.

Tairoff, A. *Das entfesselte Theater*. Potsdam, 1923.

Völker, Klaus. in conjunction with Hans-Jürgen Pullem. *Brecht Kommentar zum Dramatischen Werk*. Munich: Winkler, 1983.

Brecht: A Biography. Trans. John Nowell. New York: Seabury Press, 1978.

Brecht Chronicle. Trans. Fred Wieck. New York: Seabury Press, 1975.

"Brecht und Lukàcs: Analyse einer Meinungsverschiedenheit." *Kursbuch* 7. Frankfurt: Suhrkamp, 1966.

Weber, Carl. "Brecht as Director." *The Drama Review*, 12, No. 1 (Fall 1967), pp. 101–7.

Weill, Kurt. *Die Dreigroschenoper (The Beggar's Opera. Ein Stück in einem Vorspiel und acht Bildern nach dem Englischen des John Gay, übersetzt von Elisabeth Hauptmann. Deutsche Bearbeitung von Bert Brecht*. Vienna: Universal Edition, 1928.

Weiss, Peter. *Die Ästhetik des Widerstands*. 2 vols. Frankfurt: Suhrkamp, 1978.

Weisstein, Ulrich. "From the Dramatic Novel to the Epic Theater: A Study of the Contemporary Background of Brecht's Theory and Practice." *Germanic Review*, 38, No. 3

(1963), pp. 257–71. This article is particularly useful for the light which it sheds on Piscator's theatre practice.

"The First Version of Brecht/Feuchtwanger's *Leben Eduards des Zweiten von England* and its Relation to the Standard Text." *Journal of English and Germanic Philology*, 69, No. 2 (April 1970), pp. 193–210.

Wekwerth, Manfred. "Auffinden einer ästhetischen Kategorie." *Sinn und Form/Brecht Sonderheft II*. Ed. Peter Huchel. Berlin: Rütten and Loening, 1957.

Willett, John. *Art and Politics in the Weimar Period: The New Sobriety 1917–1933*. New York: Pantheon Books, 1978.

The Theatre of Erwin Piscator: Half a Century of Politics in the Theatre. New York: Holmes and Meier, 1979.

The Theatre of Bertolt Brecht: A Study from Eight Aspects. London: Methuen, 1959.

Wirth, Andrzej. "Über die stereometrische Struktur der Brechtschen Stücke." *Sinn und Form/Brecht Sonderheft II*. Berlin: Rütten and Loening, 1957.

"Die Funktion des Songs in *Mutter Courage and ihre Kinder*." *Sinn und Form/Brecht Sonderheft II*. Berlin: Rütten and Loening, 1957.

Witt, Hubert, ed. *Brecht as They Knew Him*. Trans. John Peet. New York: International Publishers, 1974.

Wyss, Monika. *Brecht in der Kritik. Rezensionen Aller Brecht-Uraufführungen sowie Ausgewählter Deutscher und Fremdsprachiger Premieren*. Munich: Kindler, 1977.

Zech, Paul. *Vor Cressy an der Marne*. Laon: Revillon, 1918.

Zuckmayer, Carl. *Als wär's ein Stück von mir*. Frankfurt: Fischer, 1966.

Index